PARADOXES
of Culture and
Globalization

This book is dedicated with love to my wonderful and vivacious wife, Doris, in honor of our 40th wedding anniversary (June 3, 2007).

PARADOXES
of Culture and Globalization

Martin J. Gannon

California State University, San Marcos

SAGE Publications
Los Angeles • London • New Delhi • Singapore

For information:

Sage Publications, Inc.
2455 Teller Road
Thousand Oaks,
 California 91320
E-mail: order@sagepub.com

Sage Publications India Pvt. Ltd.
B 1/I 1 Mohan Cooperative
 Industrial Area
Mathura Road, New Delhi 110 044
India

Sage Publications Ltd.
1 Oliver's Yard
55 City Road
London, EC1Y 1SP
United Kingdom

Sage Publications Asia-Pacific Pte. Ltd.
33 Pekin Street #02–01
Far East Square
Singapore 048763

Printed in the United States of America

Library of Congress Cataloging-in-Publication Data

Gannon, Martin J.
Paradoxes of culture and globalization/Martin J. Gannon.
    p. cm.
Includes bibliographical references and index.
ISBN 978-1-4129-4044-3 (cloth)
ISBN 978-1-4129-4045-0 (pbk.)
    1. Culture. 2. Culture and globalization. 3. Cross-cultural studies. 4. Cross-cultural orientation. 5. Multiculturalism. 6. International business enterprises. I. Title.

HM621.G33 2008
303.48′201—dc22   2007004813

This book is printed on acid-free paper.

07   08   09   10   11   10   9   8   7   6   5   4   3   2   1

Acquisitions Editor:	Al Bruckner
Editorial Assistant:	MaryAnn Vail
Production Editor:	Diane S. Foster
Copy Editor:	Bonnie Freeman
Typesetter:	C&M Digitals (P) Ltd.
Proofreader:	Cheryl Rivard
Cover Designer:	Janet Foulger
Marketing Manager:	Nichole M. Angress

Contents

NOTE: Paradoxes are arranged by chapter in question-discussion format. Each question is designed to engage the reader and suggests the paradox to be discussed. The formal statements and treatments of the paradoxes are found within the chapters themselves.

Preface

A Third Perspective

The formal study and analysis of culture in such areas as cultural anthropology and cross-cultural psychology and management typically involve two general and distinctive perspectives, the culture-general, or *etic*, and the culture-specific, or *emic*. Originally linguists developed the terms *etic* and *emic* to classify two types of sounds: those found in all or almost all languages (etic) and those found in only one language or a small number of related languages (emic). Today the culture-general perspective is exemplified in the many studies that attempt to profile, index, and rank order a large number of national cultures in terms of a number of dimensions on which each national culture varies, such as power distance and individualism; examples include the Hofstede study of 53 national cultures (Hofstede, 2001) or the GLOBE study of 62 national cultures and national societies (House, Hanges, Javidan, Dorfman, & Gupta, 2004). In contrast, an *emic* perspective looks at each national culture in depth and simultaneously accepts and attempts to go beyond broad cultural profiling by exploring the unique and distinctive features of each culture, including its geographical position, history, religions, socialization practices, institutions such as governance procedures and laws, and managerial practices (Carroll & Gannon, 1997; Gannon, 2004; Gannon, Gupta, Audia, & Kristof-Brown, 2006).

This book introduces paradoxical reasoning as a third perspective for studying and analyzing culture, a perspective that is particularly appropriate in a rapidly globalizing world in which ethnic and national cultures are critically interacting with and influencing one another. Chapters 1 and 9 define and describe globalization in some depth; at this point, suffice it to say that *globalization* involves the increasing interactions and interdependence of governments, corporations, nonprofit organizations, and citizens of numerous nations in a number of areas, such as finance and technology. Also, Chapter 1 describes paradoxical reasoning in depth, defining a paradox, its various types, and three methods for shedding light on it. Briefly, a paradox is a statement containing inconsistent or contradictory elements that seems to be untrue but is in fact true. For instance, among long-term expatriate managers, there is a feeling of being comfortable or at home anywhere in the world but belonging nowhere (Osland, 1995). This book highlights 93 paradoxes. As the title of the book suggests, we can obtain fresh insights into globalization and the changes accompanying it through the use of cross-cultural paradoxes. In this sense, cross-cultural paradoxes are helpful and possibly essential for understanding globalization. More specifically, we employ cultural considerations to explain these changes in our globalizing world.

There are many ways of framing or structuring a book. Frequently a book begins with a proposition or a series of related propositions that the author then attempts to explain in detail and defend, as demonstrated in such thoughtful books as Jagdish Bhagwati's *In Defense of Globalization* (2004) and Thomas Friedman's *The World Is Flat* (2005). As these examples suggest, the basic proposition is often incorporated into the title of the book itself. However, such clear and distinct propositions can easily lead readers to take fixed positions either for or against them, even when the titles strongly imply agreement. For example, Bhagwati and Friedman seem to agree on globalization and its importance: Bhagwati with his spirited defense of globalization in a number of controversial areas, and Friedman with his belief that the playing field or marketplace has been leveled for nations and individuals regardless of national cultures, making it relatively easy to complete many business functions and activities in any place in the world, as the recent experience with outsourcing demonstrates. However, Bhagwati (2005) has criticized Friedman scathingly as follows:

Metaphors matter. They define how one sees reality, as when the phenomenon of skilled emigration turns into the problem of "brain drain," evoking the image of a leaky faucet that few can regard with equanimity.

The phenomenon of globalization has prompted competing metaphors. The prolific Thomas Friedman . . . writes in his latest best seller of globalization being marked by a "flat world." Writing twelve years earlier, I advanced an alternative—and less demotic—metaphor, that globalization was characterized by "kaleidoscopic comparative advantage." Let me explain why the two metaphors diverge dramatically and carry startlingly different policy implications—and why Mr. Friedman got it wrong. (p. A12)

When considering the possibility of this book more than 10 years ago, I did not want to follow the propositional format that motivates the reader to either agree or disagree with the author. My focus was on creating a large number of cross-cultural paradoxes that I hope will enhance our understanding of changes occurring because of globalization and in the process help us view globalization in a new and different light. However, as the book evolved, it became clear that indeed I was advancing a basic propositional format or a third perspective for analyzing culture that considers both etic and emic elements but goes beyond them. Specifically, rather than using metaphorical reasoning, as I had done previously to describe specific national cultures in depth (Gannon, 2004), I was putting forth the concept that paradoxical reasoning and paradoxes represent a critical key to understanding the mutual and dynamic influence of culture and a globalizing world on one another. As such, paradoxes of culture and globalization constitute a distinctive third perspective on culture. There are other specific approaches to culture, such as a social systems perspective (Mann, 2006). However, I hope to convince the reader that paradoxes of culture and globalization represent an insightful, useful, and comprehensive way of integrating a vast body of knowledge derived from many different disciplines.

Paradoxes, Education, and Training

I have employed paradoxical reasoning and other cross-cultural methods when working with numerous groups of managers and students at both the undergraduate and MBA levels and in management training programs. The participants become very involved in the discussions revolving around paradoxes, which facilitates an active educational process. Frequently they even formulate new and arresting paradoxes by themselves, in small groups, or in a general discussion of the entire group.

There are many reasons for this outcome. Paradoxes are dynamic: They represent more than a single case study or a few case studies; they go beyond static profiles of national cultures that can be obtained through the use of one standardized and large questionnaire survey completed in several nations at only one point in time or a few points in time; they are grounded in real-world situations; and the issues around which paradoxes are formulated are typically important and engaging across a wide variety of individuals and audiences. There is also the advantage that paradoxes are easy to remember and are anchored in an arresting question-discussion format.

That is, each question is designed to engage the reader actively, after which there is a thorough presentation and discussion of each paradox within the appropriate chapter.

However, it is my experience that paradoxical reasoning should be used in combination with other cross-cultural educational techniques, including case studies; videos; experiential exercises; the ranking of national cultures on various cultural dimensions obtained through surveys; and economic, political, historical, and social observations and analysis. Using paradoxes at the beginning of a training or educational session or periodically throughout it is very effective. A related effective approach is to discuss paradoxes within the framework of traditionally titled chapters, such as Chapter 6: Cross-Cultural Negotiations. In this way, the book can serve as the basic text in a course. Alternatively, it can be used as a supplementary required text in a course or enjoyed as individual reading.

By design, survey-based and etic profiles of national cultures in terms of their bipolar dimensions, such as those derived in the Hofstede study (2001) and the GLOBE Study (House et al., 2004), are static and located at one point or a few points in time (if the survey is repeated) without regard to historical context and numerous social, historical, and economic issues. Still, while such surveys occur at one or a few points in time, many basic cultural patterns are long lasting and others change rapidly. These survey-based rankings, by and large, presumably emphasize longer-lasting and slow-changing dimensions. Such studies are critical, as they provide us with a wealth of information that helps unravel the paradoxes we experience when interacting cross-culturally, either in our native countries or across national cultures. This book includes the results of numerous survey-based cross-cultural studies for this reason. However, the focus is on a higher level of analysis and generalization, such as why members of individualistic cultures behave differently from members of collectivistic or group-centered cultures on many issues.

As indicated in Chapter 1, we employ such etic or survey-based or culture-general profiles in order to structure and shed light on paradoxes. Similarly, we also use emic or culture-specific studies that provide an in-depth understanding in the framing and discussion of paradoxes. Still, while we may gain some knowledge about paradoxes, they remain paradoxes. Arguably the most important feature of our third perspective is that it provides a direct link between culture and globalization via paradoxes. In this sense, paradoxical reasoning can be considered not only a perspective but a method linking paradoxes, culture, and globalization. Hence the title of this book: *Paradoxes of Culture and Globalization*.

Exercise: Introducing the Book

An effective way to introduce this book to a class and enhance the learning experience is to take advantage of the Table of Contents when the class first meets. If some members of the class do not yet have a copy of the book, the instructor can make some copies of the Table of Contents. The instructor begins by asking, what is a paradox? Class members can talk with one another, either in pairs or in small groups, and then have a class discussion. Without defining a paradox, the instructor then asks, what is a dilemma? The same discussion format is employed, after which the instructor defines a paradox, a dilemma, the three types of paradoxes found in the book, and three ways of shedding light on paradoxes. This material is included in Chapter 1, and the instructor is encouraged to review it before the first class.

At this point, the instructor divides the class into nine groups, and each group is asked to review the paradoxes implied by the questions found in the Table of Contents for one chapter (one chapter per group, using Chapters 2–10). The instructor can ask each group to select one or two paradoxes from the Table of Contents that they find to be particularly engaging. The instructor can then ask, why did you select these particular paradoxes? Then the instructor might briefly explain each of the selected paradoxes, as described within each chapter. Alternatively, the instructor can ask each group to read its chapter and make a brief class presentation in the next session. Group members would explain why they selected their one or two paradoxes and how the paradoxes are discussed in the chapter. Group members can also add any comments they wish to make about the other paradoxes discussed in the chapter, if time permits.

I have class-tested this exercise and related material at the California State University, San Marcos; the University of Maryland at College Park; and management training sessions at Northrup-Grumman and ARINC. In addition, I have employed this first exercise in interactive seminars at Loyola Marymount University in Los Angeles and at a meeting of the San Diego Industrial-Organizational Psychological Association. Participants—students, faculty, and professionals—enjoy the interactive sessions and actively participate in the discussions. This active involvement is strengthened throughout the semester through the use of takeaways, exercises, discussion questions, and a few short case studies or critical incidents that conclude each chapter.

Exercise After Reading Each Chapter

After trainees or students read a chapter describing paradoxes, the instructor can break down the class into small groups of approximately five members each and ask each group to identify the one or two paradoxes in the chapter that tended to have the most impact on their thinking. After discussion, each group can report to the class why its members feel the way they do. Alternatively, the instructor can ask class members to discuss in pairs which paradox in the chapter changed their thinking the most. Before the discussion occurs, there should be a minute of silence for reflection and thought. After about two or three minutes of paired discussion, the instructor can call on various class members to identify the paradox or paradoxes they have chosen and explain why they chose it. Through the paired discussion preceding the larger discussion, class members take ownership of the material, thus enlivening their presentations.

A Note on Writing

In writing this book, I have de-emphasized the use of commas whenever feasible. For example, the only difference between the two sentences of "Fortunately, the comparison is apt" and "Fortunately the comparison is apt" is a comma. There is no loss of meaning through the omission of the comma and the reader is able to read and absorb the material quickly. Whenever feasible I employ the active voice rather than the passive voice to allow the reader to proceed through the material efficiently.

At times I qualify statements. For instance, "Most if not all nations adhere to this pattern." Given the complexity of the material, such qualifications are important. While this type of construction may slow the reading of the material somewhat, it is important to be precise when explaining concepts.

Finally, I have written this book for students, managers, and readers interested in culture and globalization in both the United States and other nations and have used examples, case studies, and illustrations drawn from many nations.

Acknowledgments

Work on this book began more than 10 years ago. The complexity of the topic, culture and globalization, was daunting, and coming to grips and obtaining closure on the numerous issues involved was very difficult. Fortunately a large number of reviewers facilitated the process by providing insights and very helpful suggestions. These reviewers included the following from the California State University, San Marcos: Regina Eisenbach, Gary Oddou, Raj Pillai, and David Bennett. Reviewers from the University of Maryland at College Park were Kathryn Bartol, Gilvan Souza, and

Stephen J. Carroll, Jr. Benjamin Schneider, professor emeritus at the University of Maryland at College Park, who is now with the Valtera Corporation, also served as a reviewer. Other reviewers were Clarence Mann, University of Maryland—University College; Lois Olson and Larry Rhyne, San Diego State University; Catherine Cramton, George Mason University; Michael Berry, Turku School of Economics, Finland; Christine Nielsen, University of Baltimore; June Poon, Universiti Kebangsaan Malaysia; Joyce Osland, San Jose State University; Clinton Relyea, University of Arkansas; Father Thaddeus Mkamwa, University of Limerick; Pepper de Callier, chairman of the board, Bubenik Partners, Prague; Reinhard Huenerberg, University of Kassel, Germany; Maggi Phillips, Pepperdine University; Heidi Vernon, Northeastern University; and David Weir, CERAM, and Sophia Antipolis, France. Jone Pearce, University of California, Irvine, provided helpful advice on paradoxes in the area of International Human Resource Management, and Bernardo Ferdman, Alliant International University in San Diego, directed my attention to what became Paradox 3.10. Both the Smith School of Business, University of Maryland at College Park, where work on this book began, and the College of Business Administration, California State University at San Marcos, where the book was completed, provided support and encouragement for the project. In particular, I wish to thank Howard Frank, dean at Maryland, and Dennis Guseman, dean at San Marcos.

As in the case of my previous books published by Sage, its staff performed in an exemplary fashion. I wish to thank all of them, including Al Bruckner, my longtime editor; MaryAnn Vail, his assistant; Diane S. Foster, production editor; and Bonnie Freeman, copy editor. Many authors have publicly and privately enthused about the manner in which Sage promotes a very effective partnership with its authors, and I can confirm and echo this sentiment. I have been working with Sage since 1990, and we are already at work on the fourth edition of *Understanding Global Cultures*. It has been a long, productive, and satisfying relationship for which I am very grateful.

PART I

Conceptual Foundations

Understanding the basic concepts of paradoxical reasoning and some of the major issues related to it is the focus of this part of the book. Chapter 1 begins with five illustrative paradoxes that are discussed at greater length in later chapters of the book. The chapter also provides a definition of the concept of a paradox and describes various types of paradoxes as well as the three methods used to enhance our understanding of them.

Further, globalization is defined and described at length since two of the key ideas in the book are that (1) culture and globalization can be directly linked via paradoxes and (2) paradoxical reasoning allows us to understand these cross-cultural paradoxes and why they exist in our globalizing world. Concluding sections of the chapters stress the positive features of paradoxical thinking and limitations.

Because culture is of central interest, Chapter 2 emphasizes the manner in which it is conceptualized and perceived. We begin our exploration of specific paradoxes in this chapter with a discussion of eight paradoxes in the area of conceptualization and six in the area of perception. These paradoxes constitute important building blocks for the paradoxes analyzed in Parts II and III of the book.

1

Thinking Paradoxically

We live in a world of bewildering paradoxes. As globalization has proceeded, it has created many changes that influence all or most of us, sometimes in very minor ways and at other times critically. In turn, we now confront many cross-cultural paradoxes associated directly with, and resulting from, globalization. But what is a paradox, and why are cross-cultural paradoxes helpful and frequently essential for understanding and casting light on the changes that are occurring because of globalization? These two basic questions represent the underlying rationale for this book.

Professor Maggi Phillips of Pepperdine University, who reviewed an early draft of this book, captured its fundamentals by pointing out that the following propositions could be gleaned from what I had written and the realities confronting all of us (I have edited her last point slightly):

- Paradoxes exist.
- Recognizing this reality and employing paradoxical reasoning are necessary attributes of successful functioning in the globalizing world.
- The process of globalizing highlights, develops, propels, and creates culturally-based paradoxes.
- Paradoxes are viable links between culture and globalization.
- Cross-cultural paradoxes help us understand and shed light on the changes that are occurring because of globalization.

Before defining *paradox* and the various types, let us consider some important paradoxes focusing on culture and globalization:

1. Tony Fang (1999), a native of China now teaching at the University of Stockholm, has authored an insightful book built around one central paradox,

namely, that Western negotiators regularly complain that Chinese negotiators are both very deceptive and very sincere. Frequently I have heard the same complaint when training international executives and negotiators. How can the Chinese be both very deceptive and very sincere simultaneously, and why?

2. Languages are dying at a dramatic rate, from an estimated 15,000 languages just 100 years ago to some 7,000 today. Cultural anthropologists and linguists are so alarmed by this development that they regularly hold conferences on the "death of languages." They believe, most probably correctly, that all or most languages possess unique and critical features helpful for understanding our past, present, and future. However, once lost, a language can rarely if ever be retrieved. Yet, while languages are dying, they are becoming increasingly influential. Why and how can this be?

3. Today it is generally agreed that the world is rapidly globalizing, with increasing economic, political, and cultural links within and across nations. At this point it is useful to define globalization fully before discussing our third paradox. Globalization refers to the increasing interdependence among national governments, business firms, nonprofit organizations, and individual citizens. Three primary mechanisms facilitating globalization are (1) the free movement of goods, services, talents, capital, knowledge, ideas, and communications across national boundaries; (2) the creation of new technologies such as the Internet and highly efficient airplanes that facilitate such free movement; and (3) the lowering of tariffs and other impediments to this movement (Bhagwati, 2004; Friedman, 2005; Gupta & Govindarajan, 2004). Between 1948 and 2000 the General Agreement on Tariffs and Trade (GATT) reduced tariffs from an average of 40% to less than 4% among participating nations. An outstanding example of increasing interdependence occurred in 1997–1998 when investors rapidly withdrew capital from Southeast Asian nations because of rising risk levels, nearly creating a global depression. However, the quick and interdependent actions by international financial agencies such as the World Bank and the central banks of several nations saved the day. Similarly, the World Trade Organization (WTO) was founded in 1995 as a logical extension of the GATT. The WTO now consists of 149 nations (out of the 220 in the world) and rules on numerous issues involving nations and companies, such as whether a particular nation is violating the agreed-on trade regulations governing international commerce. If a nation is found to be in violation, the WTO describes the steps it must take to avoid severe penalties.

Further, globalization as measured by trade expansion has been increasing dramatically for at least two centuries, in spite of two world wars and other impediments. Between 1820 and 1992, the following increases occurred: world population, 5-fold; income per person, 8-fold; world income, 40-fold; and world trade, 540-fold (Streeten, 2001). Since 1992 trade has more than doubled, with developing nations' trade expanding at more than twice the rate of that of industrial nations. Estimates by the World Bank and the McKinsey Company indicate that the percentage of gross world product involved in international trade will rise from the current 20–25% to a probable 80% within three decades (Mann, 2006), barring occurrences such as a widespread nuclear war.

However, at the same time that interdependence is increasing, nations are taking unilateral actions—such as the invasion of Iraq by the United States, the United States' unilateral withdrawal from the Kyoto Protocol concerning environmental degradation, and the failure of other nations to live up to their agreements on this Protocol—even when the majority of nations express great disapproval. As this discussion suggests, it is not only the United States that engages in such unilateral activities; other nations do so on a variety of issues, such as persecuting citizens of minority groups, openly flouting international law (as happened in the Balkans during the 1990s), and supporting either openly or implicitly such commercial activities as the dumping or transporting of an excessive number of low-priced goods in violation of the rules governing world trade. These examples and our discussion relate directly to our third paradox, namely, that nations are becoming increasingly powerful and powerless simultaneously in terms of the actions they can take as globalization proceeds. Why?

4. Time is a critical feature of many activities, such as negotiating across national and ethnic cultures. Time can be thought of as three separate circles, representing past, present, and future, with the size of each circle representing its assumed degree of importance. An individual can express definite preferences in terms of the relationships among the three circles and the perceived degree to which they overlap. However, time is frequently considered as only one circle. How can time be considered as both three circles and only one circle, and why? What are the implications of these differing perspectives?

5. China is the world's largest nation in terms of population, with 1.3 billion people of an estimated world population of 6.5 billion. But China is a very large and a very small economic market simultaneously. How can this be, and why?

This chapter presents some essential concepts that serve as background for understanding the links between paradoxical reasoning, culture, and globalization. We then describe the positive features of paradoxes, followed by their limitations.

Essential Concepts

Marieke de Mooij (2005) succinctly defines a paradox as a statement that seems to be untrue but is in fact true. In addition, Lewis (2000) defines a paradox as a situation involving "contradictory yet interrelated elements—elements that seem logical in isolation but absurd and irrational when appearing simultaneously" (p. 760). Similarly Quinn and Cameron (1988) point out that paradox is characterized by the "simultaneous presence of contradictory, even mutually exclusive elements" (p. 2), while Eisenhardt (2000) defines paradox as "the simultaneous existence of two inconsistent states such as that between innovation and efficiency" (p. 703). This book incorporates all these ideas into the following definition of a paradox: It is a statement consisting of inconsistent or contradictory or even mutually exclusive elements that seems to be untrue but is in fact true.

This book also highlights a particular type of paradox, the dilemma. Specifically, a *dilemma* is a situation facing a decision maker who can select only one of either two equally attractive or two equally unattractive alternatives. For example, managers can cut costs by decreasing investment in innovation, or they can promote innovation, which automatically increases costs. For additional examples of dilemmas, see Paradoxes 3.1 and 3.10. After reading each chapter, the reader may want to identify those paradoxes that are dilemmas. Class discussions can focus on the selections made by individuals or small groups.

As this discussion indicates, this book follows closely this widely shared perspective on paradox, as the examples of the thought-provoking paradoxes provided directly above confirm. Paradoxes may contain three or more contradictory or inconsistent elements, although such formulations are rare. For ease of understanding, we will focus on paradoxes of only two elements. It is the simultaneous existence of two contradictory or inconsistent elements that represents the essence of paradox.

As Osland (1995) points out, there appear to be three methods for shedding light on paradoxes and understanding them (see also Quinn & Cameron, 1988; Smith & Berg, 1987). First, an individual can accept both truths or elements in each paradox, even though they are contradictory or contrasting. Second, an individual can reframe the situation, which is the method Bertrand Russell (1913) employed to shed light on the famous Liar Paradox: All Cretans are liars; I never tell the truth. Russell argues that each of these statements is valid but in different contexts and at different levels of analysis. The third method accepts the paradox but looks for a higher unifying principle to understand it. In this book the higher unifying principle for each paradox in our globalizing world is cultural explanation, as the title of the book indicates. Still, paradoxes exist and will not go away because we have a good understanding of them. The focus is on paradoxes in a globalizing world, which can be reasonably addressed and understood through an analysis of cross-cultural considerations.

Also, the book examines the research relating to many national and ethnic cultures but formulates each of the 93 paradoxes so that no national culture is specifically mentioned (see the Table of Contents). The objective is to move the analysis of culture to a higher level, or to ask, for example, how do individualistic cultures differ from collectivistic, or group-centered, cultures?

Paradoxes are usually framed as statements. For example, a famous paradox espoused by the Bauhaus school of modern architecture is that "less is more." Advocates of this school of thought argue that the more elaborate a structure is, the less beauty there is in it. There is no reason, however, that paradoxes cannot be framed as questions, such as "Less is more?" No meaning is lost. I employ the question format in this book for several reasons, the most important of which is that it captures the imagination and the active collaboration of readers in the process of transmitting ideas from author to reader. However, the reader will note that the questions do not contain a formal statement or treatment of the paradox. Rather, the formal treatment of each paradox is found within each of the chapters. It is interesting to note that even though the paradox of "less is more" is well known, it represents an ideology or definite point of view rather than an actual reality or situation. In this book ideological paradoxes are not of interest. The focus is on using cross-cultural paradoxes to understand the changes being wrought by globalization.

There are various types of paradoxes. In this book we focus on only three major types. First, some paradoxes can be tested empirically, such as the hypothesis that there are free riders or shirkers in small groups in some cultures and very involved contributors in small groups within other cultures. I will explain such fascinating paradoxes, even when additional research seems warranted. However, proving that the paradox exists does not eliminate it. There are concrete suggestions that can be formulated to get around the paradox and soften its impact, but its reality is a fact of life. We must live with paradoxes. Second, some paradoxes cannot be tested empirically with any finality, but close observation of history and experience suggests that they are valid, such as whether globalization as we are experiencing it is significantly different from its counterparts at previous points in history or whether globalization is impossible/doomed or inevitable unless some unforeseen event such as a worldwide epidemic occurs. Our third type of paradox is the dilemma, discussed above.

I have defined *globalization* and the three primary mechanisms for facilitating it on page 4. It is noteworthy that researchers and theorists are now using the word *complexity* as a synonym for *globalization*, with all the attendant connotations of high risk, uncertainty, and unknown outcomes. For example, the *Handbook of Global Management* is subtitled *A Guide for Managing Complexity* (Lane, Maznevski, Mendenhall, & McNett, 2004). Globalization, as that book suggests, is not an easy phenomenon to understand, but paradoxical reasoning can facilitate our understanding.

Paradoxical reasoning has been much neglected and may be the least emphasized way of thinking about our rapidly globalizing world. Books have been based on a single paradox. For example, Richard Layard (2005) points out that the standard of living in developed nations has dramatically increased in the past 50 years but personal happiness has, paradoxically, declined. However, only rarely does a book move beyond one paradox and typically only in a very specific area of study, such as the treatment of nine expatriate paradoxes in Osland and Osland (2006; see Osland, 1995) or Smith and Berg's treatment of paradoxes in cross-cultural groups (1997; see Paradox 3.10). Only one book, John Naisbitt's *Global Paradox* (1994), with its major paradoxical proposition of the simultaneous increase of nationalism and globalization, has incorporated the terms *global* and *paradox* in its title. In contrast, this book describes a very large number of paradoxes and discusses them in some depth. It is my hope that we can address these paradoxes explicitly so that we can understand each one in a new and insightful manner, even to the extent of being able to offer suggestions for softening the impact of some of them. The intent of this book is to place paradoxical thinking at the forefront of the analysis and interpretation of culture and globalization.

Paradoxes and Their Positive Features

Given the complexity of both culture and globalization, it was difficult creating a structure for presenting each paradox and integrating the chapters and the 93 paradoxes. I believe that this difficulty has been overcome, as the Table of Contents indicates. Also, as a result, I invite the reader to be *actively* involved in the discussions that the question format should facilitate. The reader can easily read and critique the description that follows the paradox.

Thinking and reasoning paradoxically emphasizes a conceptual approach. There is also the possibility that because of the large number of paradoxes in this book, the reader may become emotionally committed both to examining cross-cultural issues in depth and to reasoning paradoxically. At the very least, the reader is encouraged to refine or disagree entirely with any of the paradoxes. This process may increase not only the range and power of conceptual frameworks but even the emotional commitment to undertake additional reading and action-based activities. Such activities include experiential cross-cultural exercises and residencies of 6 months or longer in another national culture.

When a reader disagrees with the formulation or resolution of a specific paradox, it should be possible to describe the reasons for such disagreement in detail. Even more positively, the reader is invited to develop an alternative explanation of the paradox. The reader can also formulate paradoxes in addition to those presented in this book. All these activities facilitate the active involvement of the reader in the learning process. You can e-mail your suggestions and thoughts to mgannon@csusm.edu. In the event that a second edition of this book is published, I will explicitly cite individuals by name if any of their ideas or paradoxes are incorporated into the body of that text.

In many instances I have also tried to facilitate active involvement by inviting the reader to respond, *before* reading the explanation following a paradox, to one of the following: a very small number of survey items, a case study or critical incident, the reader's own definition of a particular concept, or a short experiential exercise. All these activities are designed to increase both conceptual understanding and emotional commitment. There are also questions for discussion at the end of each chapter, as well as at least one exercise, and takeaways, or key points, that the reader can apply when dealing with individuals from other cultures, both within a national culture and across national cultures.

A basic premise of this book and of paradoxical reasoning is that to enhance our understanding of culture and globalization, we need to take advantage of as many ways of looking at reality as possible. As already described in the discussion of the major types of paradoxes above, some of these ways are based on theory and the rigorous testing of resulting hypotheses, while others are located in historical and current observations that are difficult if not impossible to test systematically. Sometimes it is possible to test a specific hypothesis, such as "Is globalization a myth or a fact?" However, current and historical observations suggest that the resulting test cannot be accepted with any finality, as in this particular example. I would like to avoid the possibility of overemphasizing some methods of reasoning and denigrating others or simply disregarding them. Hence I emphasize these two types of paradoxes, in addition to dilemmas, and identify when statistical testing cannot be accepted with finality.

Thinking and reasoning paradoxically about culture and globalization reflect a nuanced rather than a definitive approach. This world and its attendant issues become tones of gray rather than either black or white. Frequently it is not possible or feasible to provide definitive solutions for real-world puzzles, and paradoxes help explain why this state of affairs exists.

Further, thinking paradoxically tends to minimize distortions and stereotyping, because it focuses not on defending a statement but on attempting to resolve the paradoxes we all confront. Also, paradoxical reasoning minimizes generalizations about specific cultures that may or may not be accurate or that may have been accurate in the past but are no longer so. As indicated previously, the question-and-discussion format avoids statements singling out a cultural group in terms of features and profiles in favor of generalizing at a higher level of analysis. For example, it is possible to compare individualistic cultures, in which individuals are expected to make wise decisions benefiting themselves and those close to them, and group-oriented, collectivistic cultures, in which individuals are expected to make decisions satisfying group members and group norms.

Relatedly, this book also seeks to minimize and, when appropriate, to avoid statements derived from important empirical, survey-based studies that rank numerous nations on specific cultural dimensions such as individualism or power distance without regard for historical context and current developments (Hofstede, 2001; House, Hanges, Javidan, Dorfman, & Gupta, 2004; Inglehart, Basaanez, Diez-Medrana, Halman, & Luijkx, 2004). For example, Hofstede analyzed 53 national cultures using a standardized survey of 22 items. He statistically reduced the 22 items to five bipolar scales or dimensions, two of which are individualism-collectivism and power distance. *Individualism-collectivism* refers to the degree to which either the preferences of the individual or the values and norms of the group dominate individual decision making and choice. In an individualistic culture, people see themselves as separate and independent from the groups in which they interact, and they make decisions accordingly. Conversely, people in a collectivist culture are integrated into and dependent on the group, even for their sense of personal identity. They will sacrifice, sometimes at great cost, personal wishes and desires to satisfy the norms of the group. Hofstede then defines *power distance* as the degree to which members of a national culture accept an unequal distribution of rewards and power among its citizens. Thus it is possible to scale and rank order the 53 nations on individualism-collectivism, power distance, and other scales.

Some issues arise with any bipolar dimensions, a major one of which is that a national culture can be scaled and ranked at only one point on each dimension, making it infeasible to indicate that a specific national culture may be simultaneously individualistic and collectivistic, and simultaneously low and high on power distance, but at different points in time or in different contexts.

The focus in this book is on contradictory or contrasting paradoxical elements rather than on such statements as "Cultural Group X is different from Cultural Group Y in terms of relative scores and relative rankings on various scales or measures, including . . ."

Still, this book employs the research results from such important studies to facilitate the structuring of some of our paradoxes and to enhance the learning process. These paradoxes are framed at a different and higher level of analysis than that used in the survey-based studies. Such studies are very valuable, especially for the specialist attempting to make sense of the roiling and globalizing world in which we live.

As indicated in the Preface, disciplines such as cultural anthropology and cross-cultural psychology and management explicitly accept the distinction between *etic*, or cultural-general, analysis and *emic*, or culture-specific, analysis as two broad and overlapping perspectives for classifying cross-cultural studies. Linguists created the terms *etic* and *emic* to classify sounds into two types: those found in every language (etic) and those specific to one language or a small group of related languages (emic). The survey-based method, with its emphasis on rating and ranking national cultures along several dimensions to derive national profiles, represents an etic, or culture-general, perspective. In contrast, analyzing each national culture in depth to ascertain and highlight its unique and distinctive dimensions typifies an emic, or culture-specific, perspective. Paradoxical reasoning builds on both etic and emic perspectives but represents a third major and integrative perspective on culture. And since such reasoning indicates that cross-cultural paradoxes are helpful and frequently essential to understanding the changes brought about by globalization, it also represents a method for studying culture.

Paradoxical reasoning enlarges the manner in which individuals *frame* or *structure* their conceptual understanding of cross-cultural and global issues. As such, it is very appropriate in a globalizing world in which individuals from different cultures and nations "collide," or meet one another, with increasing frequency. While cultural differences still exist, individuals from different cultures know far more about one another than did their counterparts 100 years ago or even 25 years ago. This is particularly true for specific groups, such as businesspeople, nonprofit development specialists working around the world, and professors and students involved in international exchanges.

As a specific illustration of increased familiarity, Western visitors to China were a rarity in many Chinese cities until recent years, and many Chinese people took great interest in Western culture during the 1980s and 1990s. Until this time the vast majority of the Chinese had limited or no access to Western ways because of government policies during the Mao era, which effectively ended in 1978, when China introduced many features of modern capitalism. In the early 1990s, Rachel DeWoskin, a recent college graduate and citizen of the United States, was recruited on the streets of Beijing to become a star in the first soap opera examining the West in any fashion. As she humorously but insightfully reports in *Foreign Babes in Beijing* (2005), this soap opera became for several years the leading television show in China, with more than 50 million regular viewers. One of her key roles in the soap opera was that of the conniving Western *femme fatale* who breaks up the traditional Chinese marriage and family. Over time, Chinese television has become increasingly sophisticated about depicting Westerners and has moved away from such stereotyping.

In many ways the world in the very recent past was balkanized into very identifiable national cultures, which restricted easy movement and firsthand observation and understanding; for example, citizens of Communist nations were restricted from traveling outside them, and the ability of citizens of European nations to work in other European nations was limited until the creation of the EU. Today the opposite situation prevails in many parts of the world, and moving from one national culture to another, either temporarily or permanently, has become much easier.

Succinctly, there are numerous positive features associated with the use of paradoxes in our multicultural world, including the active involvement of readers and participants in the educational process; the dynamic nature of paradoxes, which allows us to go beyond static cultural profiles and descriptions; their grounding in real-world situations; and the formulation of paradoxes around issues that are typically important and engaging across a wide variety of individuals and audiences.

Limitations

Still, there are limitations associated with the use of paradoxes. Like other cross-cultural approaches, paradoxes are appropriate for some situations but not others; they possess both strengths and limitations. For instance, paradoxes do not provide etic, or culture-general, profiles of dimensions along which cultures can vary, as the justly popular cross-cultural survey is able to do (Hofstede, 2001; House et al., 2004; Inglehart et al., 2004). Nor do paradoxes provide an emic, or in-depth, understanding of a specific culture, as case studies and the use of metaphors in the cross-cultural arena do (see Gannon, 2004; Mendenhall & Oddou, 2000). As these examples suggest, I believe that it is critical not to be wedded to one or a few methods to the exclusion of others.

Moreover, this book accepts the inevitability of using the basic units of analysis in cross-cultural research. These units can be one or more of the following: ethnic cultures; regional and ethnic cultures within one nation; national cultures; and clusters of national cultures with similar values, languages, and religions. It is even possible to observe the dynamics of culture at the individual level of analysis. For example, a national culture may have a very strong collectivistic orientation about decision making, expressed in both its ideals and its actual practices, and the norm may be that group-based concerns generally take precedence over individual preferences. Still, some individuals within this culture may deviate from this profile and emphasize decisions that will primarily benefit them, even at the expense of others.

However, restricting the use of one or more of these units of analysis to only hypothesis-testing empirical research narrows and limits the range of possibilities under consideration and the paradoxes that can be considered. For example, the paradox that nations are becoming increasingly powerful and powerless simultaneously because of globalization most probably cannot be tested statistically, at least with any finality. This paradox, however, can be discussed and reasonably addressed through the use of historical and current examples. As noted already, this book presents two major and contrasting types of paradoxes (in addition to the dilemma). One type can be tested empirically with some degree of finality, while the other type relies on historical and current observation.

Sometimes the use of specific units of analysis and particular methodologies creates distortions in our globalizing world and limits the topics that can be considered. For example, U.S. culture has been ranked as the most individualistic among 53 nations studied by Hofstede (2001); that is, this culture tends to emphasize self-interest at the expense of group interests and cohesion. Although the Hofstede study on which this generalization is based employed data collected from 1967 through 1973, recent research—and in particular the GLOBE study of 62 national cultures—strongly supports the proposition that U.S. citizens are highly individualistic (Gelfand, Bhawuk, Nishii, & Bechtold, 2004).

Yet close observation would suggest that such citizens are frequently group oriented, as witnessed by their average involvement in three or four community or civic associations, their high rate of weekly church attendance, and their significant contributions to charity. Such contributions seem to be equal to, and probably greater than, those made by Europeans on a per capita basis once governmental support for the arts and welfare are considered. In his survey of the United States (July 16, 2005), John Parker of *The Economist* notes that charitable giving and participation in voluntary organizations have increased in the past decade. Some of this increase results

from the rise of virtual and real communities facilitated by www.meetup
.com. Users of this service indicate their interests and receive a list of specific
meetings of like-minded individuals within 15 miles of their residences.
Meetup has become the hub around which 100,000 clubs with more than
2 million members revolve. In the spring of 2005 there were 2,400 Meetup
meetings a week, up 50% from a year earlier. To complicate matters, some of
the major ethnic groups in the United States, such as Hispanic Americans,
tend to be more collectivistic and group oriented than the largest identifiable
group, white Anglo-Saxons.

In addition, there are many different types of individualism, including
"proud" individualism, aggressive individualism, egalitarian individualism,
and so forth (see Gannon, 2004). There are also many different types of collectivism, such as the relation-based kinship system of the Chinese and the
religion-dominated system in India. U.S. culture appears to exhibit more than
one type of individualism, as in the simultaneous existence of aggressive and
egalitarian individualism, at least in terms of access to opportunities (Stewart
& Bennett, 1991), as well as a high degree of collectivism among some of its
largest ethnic groups.

Further, there are many dimensions, such as individualism-collectivism
and power distance, that large cross-cultural surveys of several national cultures have identified. Rather than focusing on only national cultures and
ranking them on these dimensions to obtain cultural profiles, it is feasible
and even desirable to frame some paradoxes in terms of a single relevant
dimension relating directly to each specific paradox. For example, why are
performance and success in individualistic cultures evaluated in terms of a
multiplicative relationship between ability and motivation, while in collectivistic or group-oriented cultures, the relationship is viewed as additive (see
Chapter 3)?

Along the same line of thinking, it is noteworthy that individualism-
collectivism has been studied empirically more frequently and intensely than
the large number of other dimensions that have also been found to be relevant. In fact, formal study of this dimension began at least 100 years ago.
Power distance is the second dimension of interest to many if not most
researchers. I will emphasize these two dimensions as well as a few others
when constructing paradoxes, with the reminder that several additional valid
and reliable dimensions have been constructed to rate and rank and thereby
profile national cultures.

The remainder of the book focuses exclusively on the 93 paradoxes. Each
paradox is numbered for ease of reading and reference within the chapters.
Each paradox is followed by an explanation or essay that attempts to shed
light on it. While I would recommend reading the book sequentially because

the later paradoxes are more complex than the earlier ones and build on them, it is not necessary to do so. It seems important that the reader peruse at least Chapter 1 and preferably Chapter 2 before the other chapters because Chapters 1 and 2 lay the foundation for the remainder of the book. I have built this flexibility into the book because the reader may be interested in specific paradoxes and may want to direct attention only to them. Some important terms, however, are defined only the first time they are used in the book. The reader can find all these definitions by tracking down the terms in the Index.

This book has three major parts. Part I, Conceptual Foundations, contains two chapters that constitute the basis for understanding paradoxical reasoning, or our third perspective on culture. Chapter 1 describes paradoxical reasoning in detail, while Chapter 2 sheds light on conceptualizing and perceiving culture. Part II is Behavioral Issues, including leadership, motivation, and group behavior (Chapter 3); communicating across cultures (Chapter 4); crossing cultures (Chapter 5); and negotiating across cultures (Chapter 6). In Part III the focus is the Broader Context, such as economic development and globalization. This part includes the related topics of multiethnicity, religion, geography, and immigration (Chapter 7); economic development (Chapter 8); globalization (Chapter 9); and business strategy, the business functions, and international human resource management (Chapter 10).

Admittedly, placing specific paradoxes in one chapter rather than others is a matter not only of logic but of preference. Some paradoxes could fit into more than one chapter. By and large, however, the placement should make sense to the reader.

Finally, I welcome any comments or suggestions you may have, including your assessment and evaluation of the paradoxes and recommendations of additional paradoxes. As indicated earlier, you can e-mail these comments and suggestions to mgannon@csusm.edu

Takeaways

1. In our globalizing world paradoxes exist, and recognizing this reality and employing paradoxical reasoning help us function effectively.

2. Cross-cultural paradoxes are helpful and frequently essential for understanding the changes wrought by globalization.

3. When experiencing a perplexing and possibly uncomfortable cross-cultural situation, it is useful to structure it as a paradox and attempt to understand it. This reasoning process can help provide insight and, in the process, minimize any negative feelings.

4. It is important to note that a paradox represents an actual situation or reality. It is advisable to suspend spontaneous evaluative statements or judgments and frame this reality as a paradox to understand it through cultural considerations.

5. The definition of *paradox* is a statement of inconsistent or contradictory elements that seems untrue but is in fact true. A dilemma implies the freedom to choose one equally reasonable alternative over another equally reasonable alternative. Hence we can say that only some paradoxes are dilemmas.

Discussion Questions

1. In what way or ways does paradoxical reasoning go beyond strict scientific reasoning?

2. Do you feel that the famous statement in architecture that "less is more" is a paradox? Why or why not?

3. What are the etic and emic perspectives on culture? Why is this distinction important? Does paradoxical reasoning represent a distinctive way of analyzing culture? Why or why not?

4. What do you consider to be the three most important strengths and the three most important limitations associated with paradoxical reasoning? Why?

5. What are the three methods for shedding light on paradoxes? Which of these three methods is employed in this book? Do you feel that this method is more appropriate today than 50 years ago? Why or why not?

6. How did Bertrand Russell shed light on the famous Liar Paradox: All Cretans are liars; I never tell the truth? Is this approach emphasized in this book? Why or why not?

Exercises

1. It is typical for people to begin to think about a paradox, sometimes only superficially, when they directly experience a perplexing cross-cultural situation. Frequently, however, individuals do not go beyond this first stage. Class members should form small groups to explore and discuss personal experiences that reflect such cross-cultural perplexity, both in their home nation and outside it. Each group should appoint a secretary who can present the group's experiences to the class, along with any paradoxes its members have formulated. Small-group discussion should be limited to 15–30 minutes.

2. Formulate a paradox based on personal experiences and write a three-page paper describing it.

3. When she started teaching in an MBA program at a Taiwanese university, Professor Lois Olson of San Diego State University arrived a half hour late for dinner at the faculty cafeteria, and faculty were already leaving. She greeted all of them cordially. When the director asked Professor Olson whether she had already eaten, she replied in the negative. Quickly the director signaled that the entire faculty should return to the cafeteria, even though Professor Olson indicated that she did not mind eating alone, and a second meal was served for all.

In small groups, please discuss the following:

- Based on the material in this chapter, would you say that this incident represents a paradox? Why or why not?
- In terms of the survey-based etic (culture-general) studies discussed in the chapter, how would you explain this situation?
- Have any group members experienced similar perplexing situations?

Each group should appoint a recorder who can report the conclusions the group reached and any personal experiences to the class.

2

Conceptualizing and Perceiving Culture

W hen we are trying to understand culture and cross-cultural dynamics, nothing is more important than conceptualizing and perceiving culture correctly. Of course, all fields of study face this issue, which is exacerbated by the large number of specialized words and phrases that are initially difficult for an outsider to understand. To complicate matters, writers frequently employ acronyms. It is rare that outsiders can make sense of what is meant until they understand the jargon, specialized words, and acronyms that experts working in any field sometimes assume that everyone knows.

This issue is particularly difficult in "soft" fields such as cross-cultural studies because writers tend to use the same words and phrases but sometimes in different or slightly different ways. For specialists this presents no problem, as they are accustomed to this practice. But unlike "hard" fields, such as accounting and finance, the soft fields do not have the luxury of hard and "bottom line" numbers that provide a sense of comfort and certainty to both the outsider and the insider. Ironically, this sense of comfort and certainty about hard numbers is frequently misplaced. To cite but one example of many, we can look at Jack Welch, the former CEO and chairman of the board at General Electric and possibly the most successful CEO and business strategist in the past 50 years. He argues against investing in a new product or business if the discounted rate of return (DCRR) of 15% or more is the main criterion: "Now, I generally do not like investment criteria that are financial in nature, like DCRR, because the numbers can be jiggered so easily by changing the residual value, or any other number of assumptions, in an investment proposal" (Welch, 2005, p. 39). While cross-cultural studies tend to fall within the "soft" category, their conclusions can be very reasonable and strongly supported by surveys and field studies.

This chapter introduces you to some of the key issues related to conceptualizing and perceiving culture, and its two major sections reinforce the criticality of both conceptualization and perception. In the first section we focus on conceptualizing culture, including its various definitions and types. The second section looks at the manner in which individuals perceive culture, which they frequently do in quite different ways, and the reasons they perceive it as they do.

Conceptualizing Culture

Paradox 2.1. Why are there so many definitions of culture?

Before reading further, you are invited to provide a personal definition of culture. Is your definition clear and understandable, and does it identify critical features of the concept? Or do you feel that any definition of culture is "squishy" and limited? More pointedly, do you consider the concept of culture irrelevant? And even if you can define the concept of culture, do you feel that you can't do much about such issues as cultural change and cross-cultural differences and similarities? Why do you feel this way?

There are numerous expert definitions of the term *culture*. Paradoxically, there are wide variations, and sometimes very wide variations, in these definitions, and we begin our exploration of paradoxes by focusing on this issue. If there are wide variations, it is questionable whether the term *culture* itself is meaningful.

More than 50 years ago two well-known cultural anthropologists, Alfred Kroeber and Clyde Kluckhohn (1952), examined more than 100 definitions of culture and distilled the following definition:

> Culture consists of patterns, explicit and implicit, of and for behavior acquired and transmitted by symbols, constituting the distinctive achievements of human groups, including their embodiment in artifacts; the essential core of culture consists of traditional (i.e., historically derived and selected) ideas and especially their attached values; culture systems may, on the one hand, be considered as products of action, on the other, as conditioning elements of future action. (p. 181)

There are several fascinating and popular definitions that mirror in one way or another this distillation of definitions. Geert Hofstede (2001) defines culture as mental programming (see also Geertz, 1973). From his perspective culture is analogous to the software allowing computers to operate. It is impossible for an individual to use a computer program incompatible with this software. Similarly, if cultural values implanted by mental programming are violated in cross-cultural interactions, Hofstede posits that relationships break down. Others echo this perspective when they point out that probably the most interesting feature of culture is that it allows us to "fill in the blanks," often unconsciously, when action is required (Brislin, 2000; Triandis, 2002). It is at this time that the shared meaning system of cultural norms and values comes into play (see also Geertz, 1973).

Echoing earlier anthropologists, Edward and Mildred Hall (1990) have defined culture as communication, for without the ability to communicate within and across cultures, neither insiders nor outsiders can understand one another. The Halls liken culture to a musical score. If we can read the musical sheet or cultural sheet, we are then able to play and sing the music comfortably. A more general and popular definition was developed by Herskovits (1948), who believes that culture is or encompasses everything that is man made.

More recently, Harry Triandis (2002) has provided a short and very useful definition: "Culture is a shared meaning system found among those who speak a particular language dialect, during a specific historic period, and in a definable geographic region" (p. 16). His focus on the importance of language, a specific historical period, and a definable geographical region allows us to theorize clearly how and why specific cultures develop. For example, if one ethnic group conquers another group living in a specific geographic area and kills off or enslaves its members while forcing the remnants to speak its language and practice its religion and ways of behaving, cultural change occurs.

Theorists have also attempted to wrestle with the issue of cultural change in their various definitions. For example, members of the International Organizations Network (ION), a group of leading cross-cultural researchers who sponsored and coauthored the *Handbook of Global Management* (2004), defined culture as follows: "Culture is *a combination of interdependent, gradually changing elements—including assumptions, beliefs, values, practices, and institutions—that is distinctive to a particular society*" (Brannen et al., 2004, p. 27).

One very positive feature of this definition is the explicit recognition of cultural change as basic to the concept of culture. The authors went on to identify specific features of the concept of culture that earlier writers had stressed, namely, that it is learned and shared; that culture links individuals to groups but allows for individual variability; and that there are many different types of cultures or units of analysis, including regional, ethnic, religious, generational, industry, occupational, and corporate cultures.

The GLOBE study of 62 national cultures, discussed in Chapter 1, argues that culture at its most general level represents both practices and group values guiding behavior (House, Hanges, Javidan, Dorfman, & Gupta, 2004). As Triandis states in the Foreword to the GLOBE study, this perspective agrees with Robert Redfield's well-known definition of culture (1948) as "shared understandings made manifest in act and artifact" (p. vii), with values being equated with artifacts, or the way things should be done, and acts with practices, or what actually happens.

The GLOBE researchers, however, do not give a more specific definition of culture and argue that any definition should be specified and tailored to the goals of each research study. This is a sensible approach and explicitly recognizes the paradox that there are expert definitions and wide variations. Each definition, depending on the issues examined and the nature of the analysis, tends to enlarge our perspective on culture.

Still, this brief discussion of various definitions reveals not only wide variations but also conflicting emphases that need to be recognized, such as the respective weight given to geography, change, communication, and man-made artifacts, including values. In this book we explore some paradoxes associated with such conflicting emphases. For example, is geography still critical in light of the "death" of distance or increasing irrelevant because of modern forms of transportation and telecommunications, and do cultures change both slowly and rapidly?

At the beginning of our discussion, I asked you to provide a brief definition of culture. While the approach of the GLOBE study—that is, avoiding a specific definition other than accepting the distinction between values and practices—is sensible for a research project, I have presented several characteristics of various definitions above. It is enlightening to discover how others rate the relative importance of various characteristics, such as definite geographic location, language, and so on. Which of these characteristics are essential to your definition of culture? Are there some essential characteristics that have not been identified? You can discuss your list either with another person or in small groups before there is a class discussion on the topic. Our knowledge of culture today is relatively sophisticated, as the description of its essential features above suggests.

In short, it is both possible and feasible to define culture in general terms as encompassing values and practices. Any specific definition, especially if it involves a formal research study, should be tailored to the task at hand. Also, there are some essential features of culture, and any definition should encompass them. It is critical to provide an acceptable definition that includes specific features when appropriate, but a definition fixed in stone is inadvisable.

Paradox 2.2. Can there be a very large and a very small number of cultures?

Seasoned travelers and long-term visitors who have been exposed to many cultures tend to see a great variety of cultures or types of cultures, at least initially. Some of them eventually come to believe that the specific types can be classified or placed into a few general types of cultures.

To explore this paradox, you are invited to complete two survey items before reading further, with the proviso that you can provide only one answer per item (HI, VC, and the other abbreviations are explained below):

1. A controversy has developed in your workplace, and you need to take a position. Which is your most likely course of action?
   HI __ a. You assemble all the facts and make up your mind.
   VC __ b. You discuss it with your boss and support his or her position.
   HC __ c. You discuss it with your peers and take their views into account.
   VI __ d. You consider which position will most likely benefit you in the future.

2. Which factor is most important when hiring an employee? The applicant
   HI __ a. Is easy to get along with
   VI __ b. Has been an especially valued employee by a competitor
   HC __ c. Is a relative
   VC __ d. Is a respected member of your community

Michele Gelfand and Karen Holcombe (1998) constructed these 2 items as part of a 34-item scale measuring four general or generic types of culture or societal relations that were independently proposed by Harry Triandis (2002) and Alan Fiske (1991a & 1991b). Although there are some differences between the two frameworks, they can be treated as equivalent for our purposes, and there is a good amount of support for the four-culture, generic perspective (see Haslam, 2004; Triandis & Gelfand, 1998). Triandis essentially constructed a four-cell typology using the two dimensions of individualism-collectivism and power distance. The four cells, and the specific terms (in italics) that Fiske employs to characterize them, are as follows:

- HC, horizontal collectivism, or a low degree of power distance and a high degree of collectivism (*community-sharing cultures*)
- VC, vertical collectivism, or a high degree of both power distance and collectivism (*authority-ranking cultures*)
- HI, horizontal individualism, or a low degree of power distance and a high degree of individualism (*equality-matching cultures*)
- VI, vertical individualism, or a high degree of both power distance and individualism (*market-pricing cultures*)

Gelfand and Holcombe classified each of the choices in the two survey items above—as well as the remaining 32 items in their scale—using the designations of HC, VC, HI, and VI.

The research literature contains no representative examples of national cultures that emphasize a community-sharing orientation, although regional cultures within nations or smaller societies manifest this pattern. In theory, at least, nations following a strict implementation of Communism should stress a community-sharing orientation, but actual practices seem to deviate significantly from this pattern. For example, before the fall of Communism in the former Soviet Union, a key Marxian idea underlying the system was "To each according to his needs, from each according to his abilities." In practice, however, members of the Communist Party (about 20% of the population) received disproportionate rewards, including dachas, better food, and admission to superior medical facilities.

Reliable estimates suggest that approximately 70% of the cultures in the world are authority ranking and that this pattern is found in many parts of Africa, Latin America, and Asia. Sweden and the other Scandinavian nations are frequently cited as exemplars of the equality-matching orientation because they balance market-pricing mechanisms with an equal emphasis on a very generous welfare system. An apt example is Denmark's approach to the labor market. Denmark permits employers to downsize their workforces significantly. However, a joint program involving the employers and government emphasizes a great amount of job training, sometimes extending 3–4 years, during which the trainee receives a decent salary and fringe benefits, and after which, full-time employment is virtually guaranteed. This approach reduced Denmark's unemployment rate in the early 1990s to its current level of less than 5%. The United States supposedly represents the quintessential market-pricing orientation, as measured by its lower tax structure and greater inequality in wealth when compared to the Scandinavian nations. Retraining is primarily the responsibility of the individual employee if terminated, and 46 million Americans currently do not possess health coverage. Both Triandis and Fiske believe that all cultures can be fitted into these four generic types of cultures or meta-categories.

If the estimate that approximately 70% of all ethnic and national cultures are authority ranking is realistic, it is immediately apparent why the world faces a daunting task as it globalizes. The different orientations—for example, authority ranking versus equality matching and market pricing, and equality matching versus market pricing—are in direct conflict with each other. At times, individuals with special privileges in market-pricing and authority-ranking cultures resist change simply because of the losses in status, power, and wealth they would incur. In some cases the authority-ranking orientation has been embedded into cultures for thousands of years through the educational, religious, and legal systems used to program the mind. Changing such a centuries-old orientation can be very difficult.

Sometimes I use 10 or more items from the Gelfand-Holcombe 34-item scale in management training; some of the 34 items are appropriate only for university students. I am invariably amazed at the discomfort that some managers express in completing the survey. Many of the same managers are very comfortable with other cross-cultural training methods and with completing all types of questionnaires, including sensitive marketing surveys and psychological profiles such as those provided by the Myers-Briggs Type Indicator. Since only one response per item is possible, the Gelfand-Holcombe scale or subparts of it clearly touch on values that managers espouse. The fact that they must choose some values over others probably accounts for their sense of discomfort, especially if they have not clearly recognized or understood their own values.

Usually I explain that these scores are measures of a general, primary orientation and that a person typically has a second orientation that may compete with the primary orientation, such as market pricing (primary) and equality matching (secondary). Also, I explain that cultural values are frequently different from cultural practices, a topic to which we will turn shortly for framing our third paradox.

There appears to be, then, a small number of generic cultures into which the many different subtypes of cultures fit. However, even the four generic cultures are sometimes not distinguishable in practice, and frequently some fusion occurs, such as a mixture of market-pricing and equality-matching mechanisms. Sweden, for example, is clearly an equality-matching or egalitarian culture, but it is also home to a disproportionate number of high-performing multinational corporations and entrepreneurial firms known for the quality of their goods and services.

Paradox 2.3. Can collectivists be self-centered and selfish?

The cross-cultural etic dimension that has been of greatest interest to theorists for well over 100 years has been individualism-collectivism. Briefly, *individualism* indicates that individuals make decisions and pursue courses of action that benefit them and possibly the small number of others, such as the nuclear family, they consider important; *collectivism* refers to the fact that the individual subordinates personal desires when they conflict with the larger group or culture in which activities occur. This distinction, and even the two terms themselves, at least imply that collectivists are less self-centered and selfish than individualists.

However, nothing can be further from the truth. Both individualists and collectivists can be self-centered and selfish, as our discussion of the four generic types of culture suggests. As the Gelfand-Holcombe items highlight, it is the frame of reference that individualists and collectivists employ that indicates whether the person is self-centered and selfish. Members of an individualistic culture expect that their members will attempt to maximize their own self-interests, sometimes at the expense of group interests. In contrast, collectivists view group members as selfish and self-centered when they openly flout group norms and expectations.

A particularly difficult experience highlighting these contrasting frames of reference involved a Chinese Thai acquaintance who had received an MBA from a leading American university. She wanted to obtain a doctorate in the United States but decided to return to Thailand to marry someone she had known since childhood. My response to this announcement was "That's wonderful; congratulations." Her response startled me, as she indicated that the forthcoming marriage was about the worst thing that could happen to her; she said her fiancé was handsome but self-centered and selfish, drank too much, would run around with other women, would not help at all with any household chores, and didn't like children. Before continuing, you might want to consider what you would do about this marriage if you were in her place.

My own response focused on whether she had employed the knowledge obtained in her MBA decision-making course in making this major commitment. She replied that this knowledge was of little if any use as her mother demanded that she return to marry. If she did not do so, the mother never wanted to see her again and she would be, in her mother's vivid language, "dead." This is not an unusual response among collectivists; some ethnic and religious groups have formal funeral services for those marrying someone who is not a group member. Her mother's point of view was simply that not to return and marry as her kinship group expected would be self-centered and selfish. Fortunately the daughter had learned about contingency planning in her MBA decision-making course, and she and her mother were able to agree that the marriage would endure for at least 5 years; if the husband turned out as predicted, they would divorce. She married as promised, divorced after 5 years, and is now happily remarried. Still, the agony that she and her mother experienced for several years underscores the importance of the differing frameworks of individualism and collectivism.

Similarly, many people have difficulty understanding the motivations of terrorists and suicide bombers who take their own lives to kill others. Very frequently one hears, either explicitly or implicitly, that such terrorists must be "crazy." From an individualistic perspective, this is a logical conclusion.

However, from a collectivistic perspective, in which group values and norms dominate the decision-making process, the more logical conclusion is that such terrorists are operating out of a radically different frame of reference from that of individualists.

As discussed in Chapter 1, sometimes the methodologies researchers employ to measure such phenomena as individualism and collectivism create distortions. Hofstede, for example, classifies U.S. culture as first among 53 national cultures on his measure of individualism, but the facts suggest that U.S. citizens are both individualistic and collectivistic, and individualistic in reference to some matters but collectivistic in other matters.

In addition, as noted in Chapter 1, there are many different types of individualism, including "proud" individualism, aggressive individualism, egalitarian individualism, and so forth (see Gannon, 2004). U.S. culture appears to exhibit more than one type of individualism, such as the simultaneous existence of aggressive and egalitarian individualism, at least in terms of access to opportunities (Stewart & Bennett, 1991).

Paradox 2.4. Value paradoxes exist in all cultures. For example, how can a national culture value freedom and dependence simultaneously?

An important study of cross-cultural paradoxes has been completed by Marieke de Mooij (2005). She employs the Hofstede dimensions to analyze why specific advertisements are successful in one nation or a group of nations but not in other nations. De Mooij begins with the concept of value paradox, that is, statements that seem contradictory but are actually true. For example, the Germans cherish individual freedom but emphasize that too much freedom leads to disorder (freedom-order paradox); the Dutch and Scandinavians value individual freedom, but sometimes affiliation needs are stronger (freedom-affiliation paradox); and the French believe that individual freedom accompanies dependence on power holders (freedom-dependence paradox). This perspective allows de Mooij to develop some fresh insights into confusing issues, such as the fact that advertisements that target the group-oriented Japanese frequently employ only one celebrity, while advertisements that target individualistic Americans tend to focus on group activities at home or in a social setting. Her explanation is that value paradoxes reflect the distinction between the desired and the desirable in life. Since the Japanese are so group oriented, which is desired, they find it desirable to emphasize individuality as they see themselves as too influenced by the group. Conversely, Americans can become so individualistic, which is the desired standard, that they become isolated and lonely. Hence they find group activity desirable.

Value paradoxes are very important and constitute one of the major reasons cultures are so complex. Understanding value paradoxes in a culture enriches our understanding of it. Such contradictions in values are a fact of life in every culture, which makes understanding the relationship between cultural values and cultural practices very difficult.

Paradox 2.5. How are cultural values and cultural practices related?

As indicated in Chapter 1, the GLOBE study of 62 national or societal cultures represents a trove of research bearing on several of the paradoxes discussed in this book. One of the most interesting paradoxes is that cultural values, while sometimes positively related to cultural practices, are consistently and *negatively* associated with cultural practices. That is, the way things are (practices and the actual operations of institutions such as the law, the religious systems, and the education system) are very different from the way things should be (values), for all nine dimensions, including power distance, humane orientation, and uncertainty avoidance.

(As an aside, it can be noted that the GLOBE researchers did not directly measure actual practices occurring in each nation; their survey-based method stressed both perceived values and perceived practices. This fact does not negate the strong negative correlation between values and practices that the researchers uncovered.)

There are numerous clear examples illustrating the influence of cultural values on cultural practices. Catholic doctors and Catholic hospitals refuse to perform abortions even when they are legal because of religious and cultural beliefs. Similarly Finland, an avowedly egalitarian or equality-matching nation in terms of values, has developed the practice of relating fines to total income. The assumption goes beyond the idea that the punishment should fit the crime to include the concept that the persons paying the fines should suffer equally. Other equality-matching nations, such as Sweden and Norway, follow similar patterns. In one celebrated case, a vice president of Nokia received a fine of $103,600 for going 43 mph in a 25-mph speed zone. A speeder with much more limited resources might receive a fine of $50.

But there is also strong evidence to indicate that practices can influence values over time and that behavioral changes lead to attitudinal changes. Equal employment opportunity laws in some nations, such as the United States and India, while initially and strenuously resisted, have led to major changes in attitudes and cultural values. In India, the late K. R. Narayanan, an untouchable, or harijan, was elected to the presidency in 1997. The symbolic importance of this election was enormous, as the harijan exist at the bottom of the caste system and are not even officially part of it. While the presidency is largely a ceremonial position, Narayanan's election symbolized the changes in cultural values that India is undergoing, only some of which are proceeding rapidly. Groups that have been positively affected by equal employment opportunity laws in various nations include women, racial and ethnic minorities, and older workers.

Power distance is of particular importance when analyzing the negative correlation between values and practices. It is the degree to which a culture accepts wide differences in authority, power differences, and status privileges. Among the nine dimensions of the GLOBE study, power distance has the widest difference in the average national score for values (2.75) and practices (5.17), or a discrepancy of 2.42 on the 7-point scale, with higher scores indicating greater power distance. Thus many national cultures espouse the value of limiting power distances but in practice accept such distances in many instances. Even nations such as Finland, Sweden, and Denmark—normally considered equality-matching nations emphasizing horizontal individualism—follow this pattern.

In some ways this negative relationship between values and practices is understandable. It would seem sensible that cultural values (what should be) would tend to deviate from cultural practices (what we actually do) in some if not most instances. Still, the extent to which power distance exhibits the greatest difference between expressed cultural values and cultural practices among the nine dimensions should give pause to anyone examining our globalizing world. This particular gap suggests that it will be difficult to globalize in a manner such that "everybody benefits," as some commentators have asserted or implied (Bhagwati, 2004; Gupta & Govindarajan, 2004; see Paradox 9.10).

I have personally encountered this phenomenon demonstrating the gap between values and practices, especially with regard to the individualism-collectivism dimension, when training students and managers using the Gelfand-Holcombe scale measuring the four generic types of cultures. For a number of years I trained MBA and undergraduate students from Australia, supposedly a classic equality-matching or egalitarian nation (a low degree of power distance and a high degree of individualism). All the students completed the 34-item survey. The results consistently indicated that they were overwhelmingly expressing equality-matching values, as expected. Australia was a bleak and inhospitable land when Britain populated it with undesirables and criminals in the 18th century. To survive, these people needed to cooperate and work together, and even today the word *mate* is often used to reflect this equality-matching ideology. However, I then presented the students orally with the short case study or critical incident below, and again I invite you to think about how you would answer the final question—*yes* and *no* are the only choices—and why. Please do this exercise before you continue your reading.

> You are walking to the most important business meeting of your life. It is your responsibility to close a $100 million deal for your company, and you will receive a $3 million commission if the contract is signed. All indications are favorable, but your competitors are waiting outside the door, and if a problem or issue is raised that cannot be answered, the deal will fall through. (This is a very typical situation when several companies are offering competitive bids; see Burrough & Helyar, 1990.) In all probability everything will be fine if you are there, as you have been the key player throughout the process, which has lasted more than 4 years.
>
> The deal has special significance to you because your company pays you a low salary but promises the potential of high commissions, and this is your first opportunity, after years of hard work, to realize this possibility. You are a typical middle manager in terms of lifestyle, with a spouse and three young children, a heavy home mortgage, and overdue credit card bills.
>
> You are 5 minutes away from the meeting when your best friend in your entire life appears unexpectedly. In a very emotional fashion, he indicates that he needs your help immediately to save his business. You have known one another since childhood, and in some ways he is closer to you than your spouse. You indicate that you will help him immediately after the meeting, which may take 6 hours or more. He explains why you must help him now. His logic is sound, especially since you are very familiar with his business, business relationships, and finances. On the one hand, you can see that the loss of your $3 million performance fee will occur if you don't attend this meeting, and it will materially affect your life and family; on the other hand, you know that not helping your close friend will result in his complete bankruptcy and the loss of his friendship, which you greatly value.
>
> However, even if you miss the meeting, you are confident—although not completely confident—that you have the skills, abilities, and contacts to eventually move ahead in your financial planning and career, even if you need 3–5 years to do so. And you know without any question that your friend will help you in any way he can, as he has done frequently in the past, assuming that you help him. Only two choices are possible: Go to the meeting or help your friend immediately. What would you do?

This vignette invariably engages students and managers in intense discussions and debate because it directly touches on values and the cultural dimension of individualism-collectivism, that is, the primacy of one's own personal wants and preferences versus the primacy of group norms or friendships. When I have used this vignette without the benefit of the Gelfand-Holcombe questionnaire, the results are mixed: Some will go to the meeting, and some will help the friend. Those going to the meeting sometimes suggest that their obligations to family are greater than those to the friend, but many others simply accept the fact that a close friendship will be lost because of their assumed need and desire for the $3 million. A few managers facetiously suggest that they will tell the friend that they will go to the meeting but will split the $3 million with him, even though his business will be ruined.

What was surprising with the Australian university students is that they uniformly chose to go to the meeting, even though their cultural profile as determined by the 34-item scale was equality matching. One student in one session even opined that she could buy a lot of close friends with $3 million, but this bald expression of self-interest was greeted with unanimous disapproval and derision.

In sum, the relationship between values and practices is significantly negative, and the gap between them is generally wide, especially when it comes to power distance. Unfortunately, most studies of cross-cultural differences emphasize values only, especially if they rely on surveys to score and rank national cultures. The GLOBE researchers have enriched the field of cross-cultural studies by focusing on both values and practices.

In later chapters of this book we will return to the issue of the influence of cultural values on institutions and vice versa. Specifically, institutions such as an enlightened educational system and an equitable legal system can create the conditions for economic development. The paradox to be explored in the case of economic development is whether cultural values tend to facilitate the creation of institutions or whether institutions lead to a change in basic cultural values.

Paradox 2.6. Does culture matter?

Many factors influence the values we develop, including culture, life experiences, occupational experiences, gender, and age. At this point you may want to estimate the percentage of your values that are influenced by culture. How have you derived this estimate, and why do you feel this way?

Hofstede's seminal study (2001) of 53 national cultures demonstrated that culture accounts for 25–50% of the values that individuals express. Other values are related to such factors as gender and age. Related studies have provided somewhat lower and, in some instances, somewhat higher estimates of the impact of national cultural differences on cultural values.

Culture matters, and it matters a great deal in many instances. Lawrence Harrison and Samuel Huntington (2000) demonstrated this point of view very explicitly by titling their book *Culture Matters: How Values Shape Human Progress.*

Perhaps the most important time that culture matters is when individuals feel they are at a crisis point, their options are very limited, their support systems are inadequate, and they are even lacking what many of us would consider basic necessities. It is no surprise that individuals are attracted to militant and nationalistic religious leaders, either when they are in such a situation or when they see many others from their culture in such a situation, even if they themselves are well-off members of the culture or even very wealthy. Similarly, some research suggests that working abroad in an international company with managers from many different nations strengthens rather than weakens home-based cultural values (Laurent, 1981). Ostensibly such a phenomenon occurs because of the discomfort the managers feel in their interactions and conflicts over values and practices and their weakened support systems caused by the absence of long-term friends and family.

There are, however, many situations in which cross-cultural differences simply do not matter. When individuals are receptive to new ideas and ways of acting, there is a lower probability that culture matters. If they share many life experiences, religious beliefs, and personal values, the probability decreases markedly that ethnic and national cultures will have any major influence.

In short, culture matters greatly at times, and at other times culture is of minor or no consequence. Each of us must evaluate a given situation to ascertain whether cultural or noncultural factors are critical.

Paradox 2.7. Are demographics more important than culture?

It is useful to distinguish between demographic groups on the one hand and cultural groups formed on the basis of an association with a particular ethnic or national culture on the other. Operationally, we can profile demographic groups along one or more of several dimensions, including similarity of socioeconomic status, educational experiences, work experiences, group recreational activities, and age. Groups formed directly because of such demographic features include the Veterans of Foreign Wars, the Sierra Club, and the Kiwanis Club. In the actions they propose and take, such groups decrease markedly the importance of general cultural values found in distinct ethnic and national cultures.

You may want to consider the number and influence of demographic groups and cultural groups in your life. Simply draw a large pie chart and indicate both the various demographic and cultural groups that are important to you and their degree of importance by the size of the piece you allocate to each group. You can share your profile with others, either individually or in class, and even place it on a whiteboard or an overhead for discussion.

There are numerous demographic groups that decrease the importance of cultural groups. For instance, among nations dominated by a small number of individuals possessing an inordinate amount of control over resources and property, there is a tendency toward groupthink in terms of retaining such an elite status. There are obvious cultural differences across such nations. But members of demographic groups representing the top echelons in these nations tend to think in a similar fashion: Quite naturally, they typically want to protect their resources, property, and status regardless of vast inequalities. Other examples of demographic groups' primacy over cultural groups include doctors who volunteer their time for service with Doctors Without Borders and managers who have been educated and socialized in similar ways in major MBA programs throughout the world. Similarities in age, gender, education, life experiences, and occupational groups help to form the nucleus of such demographic groups.

As this discussion suggests, demographic groups frequently trump cultural groups in terms of both values and practices. Again, this generalization must be tempered by the realization that culture still matters and that members of demographic groups will subordinate themselves to the cultural values of their respective ethnic and national cultures if conditions warrant such behavior, such as during times of war. September 11, 2001, is well remembered in the United States, and it was associated with an immediate resurgence and strengthening of U.S. cultural values and norms. Similar reactions occurred when terrorist bombs were detonated on a Spanish train and in the London subway.

Still, in a rapidly globalizing world, the importance of demographic groups will automatically rise and increasingly trump the importance of cultural groups. We will return to this issue when we consider other paradoxes, such as the importance of the root culture and of being citizens of the world rather than of a specific nation, and the rising inequality that is correlated with globalization. Before doing so, however, it is appropriate that we conclude this section on conceptualizing culture with a paradox revolving around three research perspectives on culture.

Paradox 2.8. Should we advocate only one perspective on culture?

There are many ways of describing, analyzing, and studying culture and its variations. Historically, the field of cross-cultural studies was divided into two broad sections on the basis of the distinction between etic, or culture-general, and emic, or culture-specific, analysis, as discussed in the Preface and Chapter 1. In essence, researchers who employ the questionnaire survey as the primary method for rating and ranking many national cultures on bipolar dimensions such as power distance and individualism-collectivism are following the etic, or culture-general, tradition. The assumption is that all national cultures possess each of these dimensions to some degree.

Other researchers, however, champion a "thick" description of a culture, which emphasizes its distinctive and unique features. This approach mirrors an emic framework (Geertz, 1973). For example, Gannon (2004) provides in-depth descriptions and analysis of 28 national cultures. There is no reason why both the etic and emic approaches cannot be used simultaneously, as Gannon and others have done.

A typology of three specific approaches to the study of culture has been developed both to highlight the etic and emic frameworks and to move beyond them (Boyacigiller, Kleinberg, Phillips, & Sachmann, 2004; Sachmann & Phillips, 2004). The first approach is *cross-cultural comparison*, which is essentially an etic approach, as it stresses the rating and rankings of national cultures through the use of a survey. The second approach is *intercultural interaction*; it incorporates the concept that reality is socially constructed and that each culture has its own distinctive and unique values and practices. Hence it is critical to understand a culture in an emic, or in-depth, fashion and then focus on the interactions occurring between individuals from two or more cultures.

Perhaps the most interesting of the three approaches is the third one, the *multiple cultures perspective*. Given the importance of multiethnicity both within nations and across them and the increasing mobility across cultures in our globalizing world, it is helpful to profile the contrasting perspectives and what happens when interactions occur. To cite just one example, the 270 employees of a small German company, BrainLAB, represent 26 nationalities. Rather than being the exception, BrainLAB is similar to many global and national companies and government agencies, such as the World Bank and the International Monetary Fund. Hence researchers need to use both emic and etic methods but within the purview of multiple cultures. For instance, while both etic and emic generalizations can be made about citizens of the United States, the context must be clearly specified. A citizen who is also a *transpatriate*, or global nomad traveling constantly in search of business opportunities, is quite different from comparable citizens who never venture beyond their hometown and work in the same organization all their life. And, to complicate matters, less than 10% of the 220 national cultures in the world are monocultural, making it very desirable if not imperative to analyze ethnic, religious, and geographical groupings within each national culture.

There is, as this discussion implies, a matter of differential perceptions relative to these three approaches, at least in some instances: Observers and researchers of culture tend to emphasize an approach with which they are comfortable and knowledgeable. Also, there are other approaches in economics, sociology, psychology, and other areas that cannot easily be classified into one of the three approaches described above. Still, all three approaches highlighted above add value and insight, especially when they are employed simultaneously. The reality, however, is that the multiple cultures perspective is particularly important when we are examining business and nonbusiness activities in a globalizing world. In our multiethnic world it is much more difficult than in previous eras to work with only those who are similar to us, which necessitates that we try to understand etic and emic differences, the multiple cultures interacting with one another in a specific context both within one nation and across nations, and the overlap of values and practices among these cultures that occurs in our globalizing world.

Perceiving Culture

Although conceptualizing culture and perceiving its actual operations overlap, these two approaches represent different emphases. In this section we look at some of the actual operations of culture stemming clearly from its conceptualization.

Paradox 2.9. Do proper introductions and greetings simultaneously require kissing, bowing, and shaking hands?

Terri Morrison, Wayne Conaway, and George Borden (2nd ed., 2006; 1st ed., 1995) profiled 60 nations in a very popular book in which they employed the following format for each nation: cultural overviews, behavior styles, negotiating techniques, protocol, and business practices. The title, *Kiss, Bow, or Shake Hands*, captures some of the features of the four generic types of cultures: community sharing, authority ranking, equality matching, and market pricing.

Specifically, the authors believe that there are three types of cultures in terms of the manner in which people interact: Kissing and hugging one another represents a culture in which emotions are accorded great prominence; bowing represents an authority-ranking culture; and shaking hands represents a practice prevalent in both equality-matching and market-pricing cultures.

Japan is an exemplar of an authority-ranking nation in which bowing was the preferred mode of interaction for centuries. During the Shogun era, beginning in the 12th century and lasting to 1868, those in the lower classes were required to dress distinctively and to bow before samurai and royalty, who could kill them for the slightest infraction, including the failure to bow abjectly or not to avert their eyes to avoid direct eye contact. Although the bow and its different manifestations in other authority-ranking nations vary somewhat, the basic idea is that the subordinate bows lower than the superior; if individuals are equal in status, they bow at the same level. Some department store clerks in Japan, for example, learn to bow appropriately through training and practicing with a "bowing machine."

Today, however, the bow is being replaced by the handshake, which supposedly originated among individuals who wanted to demonstrate that they were not carrying a concealed weapon, such as a knife, in their right hand. Today the handshake connotes equality rather than superiority-inferiority, although this connotation is sometimes more fiction than fact. Even kissing and hugging as forms of greeting have become more familiar and comfortable to those not accustomed to doing so, and generally those engaged in international business and other global activities begin to operate in the fashion expected within each individual culture.

When it first came out, the Morrison book correctly focused on the *or* in its title because doing business in another country was in fact a matter of either kissing or bowing or shaking hands. Today, most people still remain most comfortable with the style of introduction and interaction germane to their own specific national and ethnic cultures. But it is reasonable to posit that there is a greater acceptance and understanding of all three forms of introduction and interaction. It is also useful to understand when and why the three basic styles are appropriate and to use the style that is most suitable for facilitating the cross-cultural interaction. Sometimes all three are very acceptable, depending on the degree of cultural sophistication of those interacting with one another. Typically, however, the visitor to another culture attempts to find the form of greeting and introduction that is traditionally most acceptable in the host culture.

Paradox 2.10. Are cultural stereotypes valid?

There is some confusion about the meaning and definition of a stereotype. At this point you may want to provide a personal definition of the term and think about whether stereotyping is accurate or inaccurate.

Minimally a stereotype represents a distorted view or mental picture of groups and their supposed characteristics, and we tend to use them to evaluate individuals from each group. Stereotypes are particularly pernicious when they are applied universally to everyone in a group and no exceptions are allowed or considered. However, all of us stereotype to some extent to handle the many seemingly overwhelming and diverse perceptions of daily life, even though we should try to avoid "no exceptions" evaluative generalizations. A stereotype can be helpful if it possesses four characteristics: descriptive rather than evaluative, the first best guess, based on data and observation, and subject to change when new information merits it (Adler, 2002). However, a generalization that admits of no exceptions automatically becomes unhelpful.

Joyce and Asbjorn Osland (Osland, 1995; Osland & Osland, 2006) have completed an empirical study of nine cross-cultural paradoxes among 35 expatriate managers. One of these paradoxes is seeing validity in the general stereotype about the local culture but also realizing that many host-country nationals do not fit the stereotype. In other words, a stereotype provides a starting point that is constantly subject to change depending on the situation and the host-country nationals with whom we interact.

In accordance with this logic, I and my associates have constructed cultural metaphors for 28 national cultures. Each metaphor represents a first best guess. Each cultural metaphor anchors our thinking in an easily remembered general stereotype (Gannon, 2004). A cultural metaphor is any major phenomenon, activity, or institution with which members of a given culture closely identify cognitively or emotionally or both, such as the Swedish *stuga* or unadorned summer home, the Chinese family altar, and American football. Again, however, such cultural metaphors represent only a starting point for trying to understand a culture and its members, many of whom deviate from the cultural portrait.

In our later discussions of communicating across cultures, we will return to the issue of stereotypes. Specifically, Bird and Osland (2006; Osland & Bird, 2000) have proposed a three-step model for such communication that includes the paradox of accepting stereotypes but moving beyond them to achieve greater understanding.

Paradox 2.11. Are the distinctions between levels of culture relevant in a globalizing world?

It is common to distinguish between different levels of culture. Generally speaking, the norms and values dominant in a culture represent the deepest level, while ways of acting and dressing dominate the most superficial level. Several years ago *Fortune* magazine analyzed the bedrooms of various male teenagers in widely different nations and found the similarities to be much greater than the differences. These similarities included posters of Michael Jordan, basketballs and running shoes, and CDs of the latest popular songs. MTV is a similar example; it has spread quickly throughout the world.

However, the reality is that many cross-cultural differences are much more important than the similarities in many instances, as they are based on the major factors influencing cultural values, including religion, geography, language, and historical development. Two of the most popular metaphors for the concept of culture are the iceberg and the tree, in large part because many of the most important features of a specific culture are hidden from view. Even MTV has had to recognize this fact, and it tailors its shows to the requirements and preferences of each national culture.

Still, as the world globalizes and individuals from different ethnic and national cultures influence and learn more about each other, it is reasonable to expect that the hidden aspects of culture will not have the same force as in previous eras. Levels of culture will still matter, but the probability has increased that the deepest levels will become more transparent, at least to some degree.

Paradox 2.12. Do insiders understand their own cultures better than outsiders do?

There are two general ways of understanding a culture: from the outsider's perspective or from the insider's. Frequently insiders tend to feel that they have much greater understanding of their own cultures than outsiders do, including such outsiders as cultural anthropologists who devote years of field study to a specific culture. Richard Shweder (2000), a cultural anthropologist, has cautioned that the insider's knowledge and understanding are frequently limited and distorted for many reasons. One major reason is that insiders can experience great difficulty detaching themselves from their root cultures when trying to understand and evaluate their own cultures. Outsiders are not so limited.

Shweder (2000) has argued that outsiders have much to offer when they study cultures in a detached manner and that all cultures possess strengths and limitations. As proof, he cites the work of Max Mueller, a German scholar and linguist who "discovered" the Sanskrit language, in which the Vedas, or sacred writings of India, were written thousands of years ago, and then translated them. It was Mueller whom Indian scholars consulted when they wanted to learn about Sanskrit and their own classical literary traditions, which they had largely discarded. Shweder (2000) even argued spiritedly against his critics during a major conference on culture by stating that inside "experts" in developing nations can depreciate the value of their own cultural traditions in their quest to mirror the cultural practices of the West. They see a higher standard of living, longer life expectancy, and related positive outcomes and immediately tend to cast aspersions on their own culture, at least according to Shweder. As a cultural relativist, Shweder sees value and limitations in all cultures and argues that no culture is intrinsically superior to others.

This is not an appropriate venue for determining whether Shweder or his critics, all of whom are from developing nations but have lived in the West for lengthy periods, are correct in assessing the relative value of knowledge attained by insiders and outsiders. Suffice it to say that both types of knowledge are relevant and that it is not appropriate to elevate one type over the other. It is, however, prudent to suggest that both types of knowledge can be meaningfully employed but in different ways and for different purposes. Being an insider provides a depth of understanding, but it can more easily create a situation in which a person is generally less objective and detached than an outsider can be. As many writers have pointed out, the major value of cross-cultural experiences is not understanding of the other culture but understanding of one's own value system and culture.

Being an insider, then, conveys significant advantages but also significant disadvantages and differential understanding. Both types of knowledge, inside and outside, while seemingly incompatible, can facilitate differential understanding and reinforce one another.

Paradox 2.13. Can global citizenship and the effects of root cultures exist simultaneously?

Sigmund Freud is widely known for positing that the first six years of life largely determine our personalities and the manner in which we interact with one another. Some authors believe that the same logic holds for our cultural propensities derived from the root culture in which our formative years are spent.

When training managers and students, I frequently ask them each to write down the amount of time they have spent outside their native, or root, cultures and the number of languages in which they are fluent. You may want to provide personal answers before proceeding. I am frequently taken aback by the number of nonnative cultures in which individuals have lived for at least 3 months. In some cases 26-year-old MBA students can identify nine cultures, with the time of residency spanning 3 months to 10 years. And many are fluent in two to six languages. There are even students and managers who argue that they have no root culture, given their rapid movement from culture to culture, even in the formative years. They are, so to speak, citizens of the world.

Some managerial practices seem to follow this pattern. There are international business executives and venture capitalists who own several residences around the world, none of which they consider home. Rather, they rotate through their residences as they pursue business opportunities in various parts of the world. Other international executives, while maintaining a permanent home, devote at least 6 months a year to traveling outside their native countries, often flying internationally 500,000 or more miles in a year. The term *transpatriate* is now employed to describe such "global nomads," who travel frequently or constantly in search of business opportunities. In contrast, the term *expatriate* denotes an individual sent by a business firm to work abroad for a relatively short time, such as 1–5 years. Today multinational corporations expect that managers will live several years outside their native cultures. Some corporations will not even hire university graduates and train them extensively for upper-level managerial positions unless the candidates have lived outside their native cultures for at least a year.

All these trends, practices, and policies suggest that the importance of the root culture has lost some of its meaning in a globalizing world. It may not be meaningful to speak of citizens of the world as both an emerging and a representative phenomenon, but it is clear that root cultures exist alongside a tendency for world citizenship to become a significant reality. In the process, we can expect that the manner in which at least some individuals perceive one another will change toward a more cosmopolitan orientation, proceeding from an ethnic focus through a national focus to a global focus.

Paradox 2.14. Can cultures change quickly?

One of the key issues in cross-cultural perception is whether cultures change slowly or quickly. You are invited to think about this issue at this point. Have you ever read about a culture and then visited it? Were your preconceptions in accordance with what you saw and experienced? How did you feel about this experience? Are you aware of examples illustrating the simultaneous presence of slow and quick cultural change? The standard answer in many well-known textbooks is that cultures change slowly, but observation suggests otherwise in many instances.

Similar to many others, I visited China several years ago—in my case, 1988—and did not return until 1999. The changes that had taken place in the interim were absolutely amazing. Although we had an official tour guide in 1988, good food was scarce and seemed to be reserved for members of the Communist Party. But the late Premier Deng unleashed the forces of capitalism in 1978 by proclaiming that "to become rich is glorious" and creating the first Enterprise Zone, which was allowed to operate in a capitalistic manner. Now, although the government is still Communist, there are several such zones, including "old" Shanghai, which was extended to an adjacent area to include the "new Shanghai," or Pudong, connected by an underground tunnel. During the 1990s supposedly 40% of all earth-moving equipment in the world was devoted to this project. Such Enterprise Zones amaze even native Chinese who have been away from the country for 5 or more years: They have difficulty recognizing their hometowns and even the streets on which they lived for years!

China brings into perspective the contrast between the visible and invisible aspects of culture. Clearly the visible aspects have changed dramatically. But how significant is the change in basic cultural values? Some argue that the change is basic: Many Chinese are seeking conveniences in life that were simply impossible to obtain prior to 1979; China is becoming a consumer-oriented society like the United States; the divorce rate has increased; and there is clearly a movement away from the collectivism of rural life to the individualism of urban existence, although at least 60% of the citizens still reside in the rural areas.

Still, the centuries-long tradition of Confucianism, with its emphasis on education and hard work, is readily apparent in the new China. Arguably the invisible values of the Chinese, particularly the concepts of Confucianism and the ideal ordered society that Confucius and his followers espoused, are propelling the visible changes.

In a similar vein, Robert Putnam (1993) offers a fascinating historical comparison of northern and southern Italy that addresses the issue of cultural change. Frederick, a German, conquered Sicily, in southern Italy, in the 12th century and became its first king. He established a fair and equitable system of governance, but after his death his successors subverted it to create a corrupt and harsh environment. There were no intermediaries between the peasants and the king, and the Mafia essentially arose as the key intermediary. Change was slow and income was unevenly distributed. Putnam demonstrates that these cultural patterns, set in motion by King Frederick's successors, persist in the south to this day.

In the north, however, guilds arose in the 14th century to educate and train workers in specific crafts. The north also introduced free and relatively clean elections at that time and successfully implemented a fair and equitable court and police system. Today citizen involvement in local activities and elections is significant in northern Italy, and it is more prosperous than Germany, in large part due to these cultural practices. The south, unfortunately, is far less successful.

In effect, cultures change, sometimes slowly and sometimes rapidly, especially in their most visible aspects. But some cultural values and practices are extremely difficult to change, and these are presumably represented by the dimensions that large-scale surveys of national cultures uncover. Still, it is possible to change the basic values of a culture through conquest, mass immigrations, business and nonbusiness activities linking cultures, and cross-cultural marriages. When long-term or short-term visitors to a culture attempt to make sense of the many and diverse stimuli surrounding them, they are confronting the paradox that cultures can change quickly *and* slowly. Therefore, it is probably preferable to be conservative and nonevaluative in generalizing from personal experiences until familiarity and a deep understanding are attained.

While this discussion ends our chapter on conceptualization and perception of culture, we will revisit these two topics as we formulate some of the paradoxes throughout the book, particularly in Part II, where the focus is on behavioral issues.

Takeaways

1. The values of a culture are frequently different from its practices. It is desirable, in order to optimize interactions, to understand how values and practices in different cultures overlap in some ways and not others.

2. Cultural issues are critically important in some situations and not others, and it is useful to approach issues and interactions from this perspective.

3. A stereotype that allows no exceptions is pernicious, but using national stereotypes as a starting point for understanding a culture can be helpful as long as they are only the first best guess, descriptive rather than evaluative, based on data and observation, subject to change when new information is provided, and exclude "no exceptions" evaluative generalizations.

4. Those inside and those outside a culture tend to perceive and understand it differentially, and both perspectives can be useful and valid.

5. Cultures can change both quickly and slowly, and it is important to recognize which cultural values and practices have changed, which have not changed, and why.

Discussion Questions

1. How do individualism and collectivism relate to frames of reference and selfishness?

2. There are several definitions of culture in this chapter. Which specific definition do you prefer? Why? What do you consider to be the three most essential features of any definition of culture? Why?

3. Why do the GLOBE researchers distinguish between values and practices? Describe one situation you have personally encountered that highlights this distinction.

4. Describe and critically analyze the four generic types of cultures. Please draw a four-cell table, the x dimension of which is individualism-collectivism and the y dimension of which is power distance (low and high) and place each of the four types within the appropriate cells. List representative examples of nations that fall within each of these four cells, and explain why you have selected these nations.

5. What are demographic groups and cultural groups? How do they differ? Please give specific examples.

6. Please cite and explain one factor not described in the chapter that nullifies the importance of culture.

Exercise

Several colleagues and I have tested the validity of emic descriptions of national cultures in six nations, two at a time, using both survey items and paragraphs (see Gannon, Gupta, Audia, & Kristof-Brown, 2006). Below are two paragraphs from this research study that contrast U.S. culture and Indian culture. University students from the United States and India indicated, on a scale of 0 to 10, the degree to which each paragraph represented the United States and then, separately, India. In small groups please discuss these paragraphs. Each small group should appoint a recorder to report back to the class. Please address the following questions:

- What features would you add and delete from the paragraph for each culture, and why?
- Is globalization influencing these descriptions? Why or why not?
- Some Indians informally refer to the nation's three income classes (lower, middle, and upper) in terms of walking, owning a bike, and owning an automobile. India has a population of more than 1 billion, and estimates suggest that 250 million are in the middle class. How would you describe these three

income classes in the United States? What does your comparative description tell you about these two nations?

- Does the caste system in India relate to its three income classes in a globalizing world? Why or why not? This centuries-old system involves four distinct classes in addition to those not part of it, the harijan, formerly called the untouchables because they performed work considered dirty and unsanitary. The four classes are Brahmans, or religiously focused individuals; administrators and businesspeople; producers, such as craftspeople and farmers; and others, such as unskilled workers.

The instructions and paragraphs follow. All survey items and descriptive paragraphs for the six nations can be found in Gannon (2001), *Working Across Cultures*, which is now available at www.csusm.edu/mgannon. You may be interested in discussing additional paragraphs and survey items with others individually or in class.

Please indicate, by filling in any single number between 0 and 10, the degree to which you feel each statement or description represents the United States. Then, alongside this rating, please indicate the degree to which you feel each item represents India. Use 0 for "do not agree at all," 10 for "totally agree," or any number in between.

_____Most people in my culture would agree that this nation's culture revolves around religion and family/kinship groupings. The major themes in the culture are predetermination of life (destiny), cyclicality of life activities stressing origination, existence, chaos, and destruction, and then reorganization. All deeds and acts are seen as having consequences that can extend beyond earthly existence. Duties associated with kinship groupings are clearly defined. There is a strong in-group orientation based on kinship groups that emphasizes the hierarchical relationships within the group based on age and gender. Between kinship groups, there is a clearly demarcated hierarchy that subsumes other bases for differentiating people, such as race, language, and geographical origin.

_____Most people in my country would agree that there is intense competition, constant geographic movement, and continual striving to improve one's position in life in this culture. There is a high degree of individual specialization, a pervading sense of urgency, and rapid acceptance of new technology in this society. The individual is the most important unit within society; people have a strong concern for protecting their rights as individuals and are ready to defy authority if they feel wronged by decisions that may affect them. There is a belief that the individual is capable of anything he or she wants to accomplish if he/she sets his/her mind to it. As a result, people are mobile, energetic, and motivated to achieve specific goals. People generally pursue their own personal interests but will cooperate with each other to achieve specific goals. Personal success or failure is generally attributed to the efforts of the individual, and there is celebration of winners.

PART II

Behavioral Issues

In Part II, we build on and move beyond the foundational concepts of conceptualizing and perceiving culture delineated in Part I and focus specifically on behavioral issues. Such issues are particularly important for globalizing activities because individuals from strikingly different ethnic and national cultures are interacting with one another with growing frequency and intensity. Frequently they possess only a limited understanding of people outside of their own cultures. It is common to hear that business deals and similar activities in the global arena have not worked out because of a "difference in culture," although the specifics as to why this is so are many times not provided.

We begin our analysis by examining three related topics in Chapter 3: leadership, motivation, and group behavior. As indicated in Chapter 1, cultural anthropologists and others have stressed the criticality of communicating across cultures, and some experts have defined culture as communication. We address the topic of communication in Chapter 4, followed by a discussion of the issues a person faces when crossing cultures (Chapter 5). The final topic of discussion is negotiating across cultures (Chapter 6), which assumes that a person has at least some cross-cultural knowledge about all the topics treated in the previous chapters.

3

Leadership, Motivation, and Group Behavior Across Cultures

There is probably no other topic generating more interest in business and nonbusiness organizations than that of leadership. More books and articles are published on this topic than on any other management topic, not only in the United States but in nations as diverse as Poland, China, and India. There are also countless educational and training programs devoted to the topic of leadership. And there are endless discussions of the factors that differentiate entrepreneurs starting their own businesses and executives rising to top-level positions in large, multinational corporations. All this frenzied activity is understandable given the obvious importance of the topic to leaders, potential leaders, and organizations of all types.

We begin this chapter by focusing on leadership across cultures. Next, we turn our attention to the related topic of motivation across cultures. Specifically, what motivates managers and employees in different cultures, and how is this topic related to leadership? In the final section of the chapter we consider group behavior and the manner in which the dynamics of leadership and motivation play out within this cross-cultural context.

Leadership

Paradox 3.1. Framing leadership: Is the essence of leadership being stuck on the horns of a dilemma?

Before reading the analysis of Paradox 3.1, you may want to assess your own theories and definitions of leadership. Briefly, how would you describe successful leaders in terms of specific characteristics, and what differentiates them from unsuccessful leaders? Defining a metaphor as the use of one phenomenon to describe another, what is your metaphor for leadership? Many if not all of us theorize about leadership in one form or another either consciously or unconsciously, and it doesn't matter if you borrow your metaphor and theory from others or develop it yourself. But knowing your own metaphor and theory establishes a helpful baseline. You may also want to reflect on your personal views about the dynamics and models of leadership within different cultures and clusters of national cultures, in terms of both metaphors and theories.

A seemingly incalculable number of research studies of leadership have tested hypotheses derived from specific theories. Simultaneously a voluminous literature that is post hoc and circuitous in nature has developed. Leaders are frequently assumed to be effective if they occupy positions of power, even when performance is substandard.

Chester Barnard's classic book, *The Functions of the Executive* (1968), originally published in 1938, serves as an excellent initial framework for describing and defining leadership in management. Until the end of World War II, the focus was on a firm's *tangible* resources, such as plant and equipment, as they represented an effective way of creating barriers to entry against competitors in the manufacturing-based American economy. At the time, total labor costs were the largest component of total costs. Hence it was logical for managers, writers, and researchers to focus on workers and to develop methods of motivating them to become more productive. Today the more *intangible* aspects of firms—customer perceptions of service quality, brand image, tacit knowledge based on organizational learning, and organizational culture—are frequently much more important than labor costs as they provide formidable barriers to entry against potential competitors. John Kendrick (as cited in Hitt, Ireland, & Hoskisson, 2003, p. 81), an economist, has demonstrated that the ratio of intangible to tangible resources in 1929 was 30–70; by 1990 the ratio was almost the reverse. Far ahead of other writers, Barnard in 1938 swung the focus away from the worker level and toward management in ways that are still reverberating in the management field.

Influenced by his long business experience, including the presidency of Bell Telephone of New Jersey, Barnard began by defining the three essential elements of an organization: systems of communication between individuals and groups, motivation (willingness to serve), and common purpose integrating the efforts of individuals and groups. He then described the three fundamental tasks of the executive or manager: to develop systems of communication linking individuals and groups throughout the organization; to motivate subordinates; and to define the common purpose, or what the organization is attempting to accomplish. In short, the executive is the critical factor in an organization, since the three key tasks of the executive mirror exactly the three essential elements of the organization.

Barnard's book, which is a long and somewhat disjointed narrative, proved to be popular with management specialists but not the general public. He is credited with many interesting ideas that are still influential beyond those discussed above. One of the most important concepts, the *zone of indifference*, which has been aptly renamed the *zone of acceptance*, arises in the area of motivation, the second of the manager's fundamental tasks. To Barnard, the manager's task is to motivate subordinates so that they expand their zones of acceptance of the strategy, vision, and goals that the leader is promoting. Motivational theory has built on this framework in many useful ways since Barnard's time.

For example, a body of research focuses on good *Organizational Citizenship Behavior* (to borrow the title of a book by Organ, Podsakoff, & MacKenzie, 2006), that is, the degree to which members of an organization are motivated to go beyond the "letter of the law" to follow the strategy, vision, and goals of an effective executive leader. Such organizational citizens might work all night to finish a project, come to work in a blizzard, and engage in similar activities that are far beyond their official job duties, in large part because of the motivational impact that a particular executive has. One such leader among many is Herb Kelleher, a founder and former CEO who imbued seemingly everyone at Southwest Airlines to work in such a fashion.

Barnard recognized that the specific activities of executives change as they move from position to position and, more particularly, as they are promoted. Organizational levels at which managers operate and the proportion of time they devote to planning are positively correlated, while face-to-face communication with subordinates declines simultaneously. Still, regardless of the organizational level, the manager must complete Barnard's three essential tasks.

Given the manager's complex roles, it is little wonder that dilemmas in fulfilling them occur. The term *dilemma* is of Greek origin and denotes two compelling, logical, and competing premises. In an influential article, Thomas Stewart (1996) summarized the results of a large, interview-based research project in Canada, which found that leaders must address the following nine dilemmas:

1. Revenue growth versus cost containment

2. A short-term versus a long-term focus on plans and results

3. Creativity versus organizational discipline, that is, allowing individuals to deal creatively with issues versus demanding that they complete specific and defined activities

4. The needs of people, including adequate time away from work, versus the demands of productivity

5. Specific capabilities of subordinates versus their leadership potential

6. Independence versus dependence of organizational members and departments (independence achieved at the expense of others, through such activities as withholding information and not sharing resources, would be unacceptable)

7. Bureaucracy busting versus creating economies of scale, which leads to a large, complex bureaucracy

8. Trust versus the demand for change

9. Broad-based projects versus only high-visibility projects

The Canadian researchers argued that managers must emphasize two essential roles to be effective: *polarity management*, or balancing the two premises in each dilemma smoothly, and *ambiguity management*, as managers live in a world of uncertainty and ambiguity.

Stewart recommends that for each dilemma, a manager should construct a simple, two-dimensional chart with a 45° angle, which will allow the manager to see the current situation in terms of what is above the line and what

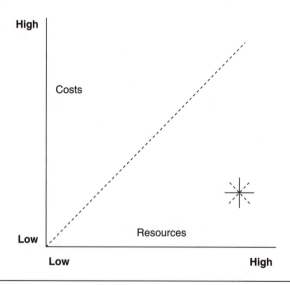

Figure 3.1   Managing the Dilemma of Balancing Cost Containment and Revenue Growth (10-point scale for emphasis on cost containment and resources devoted to revenue growth)

NOTE: As the emphasis on revenue growth increases, cost containment declines in importance. An optimal balance is achieved only along the 45° dotted line.

is below it. Each dimension goes from low (1) to high (10) on a standard 10-point scale (see Figure 3.1). In this way the manager has a general guideline for deciding whether one side of the dilemma should be emphasized rather than the other at a given time. To help the leader manage such polarities, Pfeffer and Sutton (2005) have developed a set of guidelines in six key areas, including strategy, leadership, individual versus group incentive systems, organizational change, balance of work-nonwork activities of organizational members, and specific financial incentives for particular purposes.

However, our review of the definitions of paradox (for example, Eisenhardt's specific definition: "the simultaneous existence of two inconsistent states such as that between innovation and efficiency"; 2000, p. 703) indicates that these polarities facing managers are in actuality that particularly important type of paradox, the dilemma. Similarly, Williams's *The Paradox of Power* (2002) revolves around the concept that a leader, in order to execute effective leadership, must give leadership away, or delegate authority to capable subordinates. The term *dilemma* connotes two equally compelling and competing premises, and the manager must choose one of two equally attractive or unattractive premises at any given moment. This perspective finds apt expression in the aphorism "caught on the horns of a dilemma." That is, managers must manage polarities and integrate the two elements of each dilemma.

For example, Jeffrey Immelt, the current CEO of General Electric (GE), who succeeded Jack Welch in that role a few years ago, is currently stressing innovation, which was downgraded in importance during the Welch years in favor of efficiency and total revenue growth to maximize the stock market valuation of the company. Immelt's actions, and those of any manager, represent the reason managerial leadership is so complex. As expected by the GE board of directors, Immelt's long-term focus on innovation did not lead to an immediate significant increase in GE's stock market price. Many investors are much more interested in positive short-term financial results than in the predicted favorable results associated with long-term investments in innovation. Thus the trade-off of selecting one premise over another tends to be a constant struggle.

When cross-cultural considerations enter the picture, leadership becomes even more complex. What is acceptable in one nation may be socially and even legally unacceptable in another nation, and the manager may be forced to adapt differential solutions to dilemmas in different nations. We do not yet possess a useful profile of the dilemmas that managers in various ethnic and national cultures face, but the role of the leader typically becomes more complex as the extent of global activities facing a particular firm widens.

Relatedly, research on what makes an expatriate manager successful indicates that such factors as flexibility and openness to new experiences are critical. For a recent review by the GLOBE researchers, see Javidan, Dorfman,

Sully de Luque, and House (2006). Their data support the concept of *cultural universals*, or practices that effective leaders employ throughout the world, such as being honest, decisive, and motivational. But they also present evidence for the existence of *cultural specifics*, that is, that some leadership practices, such as emphasizing subordinate participation in decision making and being team oriented, work well in some cultures but not in others. Our treatment of the four types of generic cultures is consistent with the perspective of cultural specifics; what works well in an authority-ranking culture will tend to be ineffective in market-pricing and equality-matching cultures. The GLOBE researchers also indicate that some leadership practices are universally perceived as reprehensible, including being autocratic or irritable. See Table 3.1.

Table 3.1   Cultural Views of Leadership Effectiveness (Partial List)

Universal Facilitators of Leadership Effectiveness
- Being trustworthy, just, and honest (integrity)
- Having foresight and planning ahead
- Being positive, dynamic, motivating, and building confidence
- Being communicative, informed, a coordinator, and a team builder

Universal Impediments to Leadership Effectiveness
- Being a loner and asocial
- Being noncooperative and irritable
- Being autocratic

Culturally Contingent Endorsement of Specifics That Work in Some Cultures but Not in Others
- Being individualistic
- Being status conscious
- Being a risk taker

See House, Hanges, Javidan, Dorfman, & Gupta, 2004; Javidan, Dorfman, Sully de Luque, & House, 2006.

Nevertheless, as Stewart has argued, polarity management and ambiguity management may be the essence of leadership. In this sense the essence of management is being hoisted or stuck on the horns of a dilemma. Still, a manager is typically mired in day-to-day activities in which such choices are difficult to identify. As Mintzberg demonstrated in 1973, the nature of managerial work is that managers work long hours on a bewilderingly large number of activities at an unremitting pace. They must react to problems as they arise, and their work is brief in the sense that they do not have much time to devote to any one activity. The CEOs in Mintzberg's study engaged in activities extending from less than 2 minutes to approximately 2 hours. Performing the mundane tasks of leadership daily and implementing plans successfully are critical and just as important as selecting one strategy rather than another or selecting one premise rather than another. Charon and Colvin (1999) convincingly demonstrated that the major reason CEOs fail is that they fail to implement a strategy thoroughly and successfully. Such failures include delaying the termination of a key subordinate while this individual harms the firm significantly, not being actively involved in the implementation phases of a strategy, and exercising ineffective leadership that undermines the confidence of organizational members.

In sum, it is important to select the correct premise of any dilemma, but it is equally important to implement it thoroughly. In this sense effective and thorough implementation is always required, even when the manager selects the correct premise.

Paradox 3.2. Who is more effective, the instrumental-visionary-transformational leader or the headman?

Sports have become increasingly prominent in our world, and today sports programs are broadcast throughout the entire week and television channels are devoted specifically to promoting them. One reason often cited is that competition in sports mirrors the intense competition found in many nations, including the United States. You can reflect on what makes a successful leader on a sports team and a successful coach. Are the same characteristics that are preconditions for leadership on a sports team or for success as a coach identical to those predicting success as a manager?

The focus in this section is on the relationship between the four types of generic cultures and the appropriate pattern of leadership in each of them. You can obtain some general idea about your own leadership preferences by completing two items from the Gelfand-Holcombe (1998) survey directly below. After indicating your preferences, you may want to review briefly the description of the four generic types of culture (see Paradox 2.2) and the two Gelfand-Holcombe items discussed in that section. The answers to the two items below are provided at the end of this chapter.

- Suppose you had to use one word to describe yourself. Which one would you use?
  ___ a. Unique
  ___ b. Competitive

___ c. Cooperative
___ d. Dutiful

- A famous photographer has offered you a very reasonable price for having a picture taken. Which picture would you choose? You with
  ___ a. Your three best friends
  ___ b. A very important person (a person who is bound to get into the history books)
  ___ c. No one else
  ___ d. Many members of the community, whom you are helping; it shows that you are sacrificing yourself for them

Most of our discussion will compare leadership within authority-ranking and market-pricing cultures, the two generic types of cultures found most often throughout the world. We will also discuss briefly the GLOBE study of leadership in 62 nations, with particular attention to equality-matching, or egalitarian, national cultures.

In the developed and market-pricing nations, the focus is on visionary and transformational leadership capable of moving an organization to a new plateau of success (Collins, 2001; Collins & Porras, 1994). *Transformational leadership* represents the degree to which the leader is able to effect a change not only in the firm's culture but also in profitability. *Visionary leadership* is the degree to which the leader provides a vision of the future to which organizational members subscribe so that the transformation can occur.

Jack Welch achieved enormous success as CEO of General Electric and was a transformational and visionary leader. Overall valuation of the company increased more than 400 times during his tenure. Echoing Chester Barnard, Welch argued that it is the leader's obligation to be transformational, regardless of the number of subordinates or the organizational level at which he or she operates (Welch, 2005). To that end, starting in 1985 he and his team developed a radical strategy focused on creating a borderless or global organization, emphasizing quality of production while minimizing costs and reducing the cycle time of production, and selling off strategic business units if they could not be No. 1 or No. 2 in their respective industries worldwide.

Welch was also the major supporter of the 20/70/10 managerial performance evaluation system, with those identified in the upper 20% in terms of performance receiving disproportionate rewards, 70% receiving adequate rewards to stimulate them to try to move into the 20% category, and 10% receiving few if any rewards. The disproportionate distribution of rewards is a cardinal feature of a market-pricing culture, whether it is an organizational culture, an ethnic culture, or a national culture. General Electric counsels members of the lowest-performing group to leave the company if their performance does not improve quickly and significantly.

As this discussion of Welch's approach implies, the visionary and transformational type of leadership must be accompanied by *instrumental leadership*, with individuals being rewarded if they achieve the goals set by the leader or leaders. This is particularly true in a market-pricing culture. Visionary and transformational leadership without adequate instrumental rewards may work in the short run in a market-pricing culture, but after a short time at least some desired rewards must be forthcoming.

Welch and many others feel that effective visionary and transformational leaders come in all shapes and varieties (Collins, 2001; Collins & Porras, 1994). Alfred Sloan, the legendary CEO of General Motors who is largely credited with its extraordinary success from 1920 until 1960, was known as "Silent Al." He spoke sparingly at group meetings but normally followed up with memos outlining action items. Lee Iacocca led the product team at Ford for the path-breaking Mustang and later performed spectacularly as CEO of the moribund Chrysler when it faced bankruptcy in 1980, but his personality was quite different. Iacocca is an extroverted, hard-playing, and visibly energetic presence. He is frequently cited as a classic exemplar of *charismatic leadership*, with its focus on a larger-than-life individual capable of galvanizing and motivating subordinates through his assumed special abilities. The assumption of difficult-to-measure special abilities (*charisma*) that separates the leader from followers is the critical feature of charismatic leadership. Both Sloan and Iacocca represent visionary and transformational leadership, but Sloan was not charismatic.

Most important, visionary and transformational leadership is primarily one-way and restricted to behavior at work, with the leader developing both the vision and the transformational strategy and the followers implementing it. At the highest organizational level there may well be a high degree of subordinate involvement in the discussions of the strategic plan. Still, it is the CEO, with input from the board of directors, who decides what vision and strategy shall dominate. And, as CEOs know and at times have stated publicly, implementing the transformational plan successfully tends to require a Herculean effort. It is normally much more difficult to implement a strategic plan than to create a vision and a transformational strategy. Still, the game involving both the transformational strategy and its implementation plan is relatively simple: If subordinates do not achieve their specific and measurable goals, they are not rewarded and are usually asked to leave if more-positive results are not quickly forthcoming.

Today it is popular to talk about leadership within the context of sharing power with subordinates, although the reality may be much different in that practices do deviate from values. Even in this instance, in market-pricing cultures instrumental rewards and punishments accompany not only visionary and transformational leadership but also *shared leadership*.

There is, however, a competing type of leadership in authority-ranking cultures found in such areas as Asia, Latin America, the Middle East, and Africa and termed "the headman concept of leadership" (Westwood & Chan, 1995). In the case of *headman leadership*, a *two-way psychological* relationship based on mutual obligations exists between leader and follower and *extends beyond work to include cultural and community factors*. The leader may receive disproportionate rewards, but he also has an obligation to look out for his employees at all costs, just as the head of a family looks out for other family members and the village head is responsible for everyone in the village. In return, subordinates are expected to be committed fully to the organization's vision, strategy, and implementation plan.

For instance, Japanese automotive firms operating in the United States tend to retrain their workers and pay them their regular salaries for 6 months or more when an economic downturn occurs; American automotive firms have moved to downsize their workforces much more quickly under similar circumstances. In Japan and other authority-ranking nations governed by a sense of shame, some owners and managers will devote a year or more to ensuring that downsized employees are placed in positions elsewhere. By contrast, some Western firms provide outplacement counseling but are not as actively and directly engaged in placing downsized workers and managers.

Annually in Japan, approximately 1,000 suicides are reported among corporate executives and entrepreneurs, and many more are unreported. Many of these suicides occur because the owners and upper-level managers feel a sense of *shame* if they fail their employees in any way, and particularly in guaranteeing employment. S. Sugawara (1998) recorded a particularly incisive example of this phenomenon revolving around Nobuo Shibata, a 48-year-old president of a small sheet metal company, and his brother. These executives took their own lives and left a plaintive note apologizing to all their employees for the slump in business.

You can obtain a copy of a recent international film, *The Secret Life of the Japanese*, which mirrors such realities in modern Japan. This film vividly portrays the wrenching changes occurring in Japanese corporations as they de-emphasize the authority-ranking model. This de-emphasis encourages and even mandates the increased use of informal ways of communicating and interacting at work, faster decision making, and quicker implementation. The new model, essentially a reflection of a market-pricing culture, also moves away from *guaranteed lifetime employment* and toward *employability* through continual educational and training programs and skill-enhancing job rotations. If a company downsizes its workforce, presumably workers and managers will be able to obtain work elsewhere because of their enhanced skills and abilities.

Downsizings in Japanese companies are now more common than in previous eras. Some of the impoverished unemployed have constructed tent cities in parks because of the situation, something unimaginable prior to 1990. In one isolated rural area, so many individuals cut off from their families and society have committed suicide that the spot is now popularly known as Suicide Mountain. Japan has moved from an authority-ranking model toward a market-pricing model largely because of the impact of globalization and a deep economic recession lasting nearly two decades.

It is very unusual for a Western CEO to commit suicide because he has failed in his obligations to his employees and subordinate managers. *Personal responsibility* is much more important than shame in market-pricing cultures, and their legal systems reinforce this emphasis. The focus is on instrumental-visionary-transformational leadership that is primarily one-way in nature and restricted to the workplace. As might be expected, some companies deviate from this norm. Costco pays its workers an average salary of approximately $40,000 per year, in comparison with $8,000 for Wal-Mart; has a no-layoff policy; and willingly accepts labor unions and works with them effectively. Other companies that are exceptional in this regard are GEICO Insurance Company, a subsidiary of Berkshire-Hathaway, and Southwest Airlines. But this small group of companies constitutes an exception rather than the rule. And other U.S. companies guaranteeing lifetime employment just 30 years ago, including IBM and Hewlett-Packard, now emphasize employability.

Guaranteed employment and employability bring into perspective the two sharply differing leadership orientations found in market-pricing and authority-ranking cultures.

A reasonable justification can be made for the practice of employability in market-pricing national cultures. For instance, American-based corporations now devote more resources and money to education and training than do all the university and college business schools in the United States in combination. Numerous companies sponsor "corporate universities" offering excellent courses tailored to specific corporate needs and required for internal promotions. Also, the United States has for decades been creating jobs far more rapidly than many other nations have, due in part to the geographical mobility of its workers and the emphasis on employability.

It is also possible to justify the practice of guaranteed employment and related practices that are more prevalent in authority-ranking national cultures than in market-pricing cultures. The relationship between top management and other organizational members is tightly entwined and tends to reflect the two-way psychological relationship based on mutual obligations. Sharply in contrast to General Motors, Toyota is an outstanding example of this close fit. Comparing General Motors and Toyota will allow us to spotlight and contrast how leadership is actualized in market-pricing and authority-ranking cultures.

During the 1980s, under the leadership of CEO Roger Smith, General Motors decided that the major problem it faced was the uneasy relationship with its workers and labor unions (Finkelstein, 2003). In short, the workers and their labor unions were the problem, and technology was the solution. Smith advocated building technology-intensive factories requiring far fewer workers than the labor-intensive factories common in the industry at the time. This strategy was so popular that *Fortune* magazine once recognized Smith as its CEO of the Year during the 1980s. Unfortunately, the new factories experienced great difficulty, at least in part because of employee opposition and the one-way manner in which Smith attempted to implement the strategy.

Toyota, on the other hand, decided that the technology was the cause of difficulty for the workers and not vice versa. Its executives and workers rearranged the assembly line so that the worker had easy access to the necessary tools and resources and a feeling of empowerment. In the Toyota System individual workers can shut down the assembly line if they see a major problem, workers are guaranteed lifetime employment, and quality circles of workers meet regularly to address issues and problems they face on the assembly line.

General Motors was following the instrumental-visionary-transformational model of leadership befitting a market-pricing culture in which the relationship between the leader and subordinates is one-way and limited to work. Toyota, conversely, was using the headman model of the classic authority-ranking culture. Ironically, General Motors and Toyota established a joint venture in Fremont, California, in a troubled General Motors factory in the late 1980s. General Motors wanted to learn about the Toyota System and chose the Fremont factory because it had an extremely low level of productivity and extremely high levels of employee dissatisfaction, absenteeism, and labor union hostility. Without changing the technology, management implemented both the Toyota production system and the Toyota philosophy in this factory in a spectacularly successful manner, making it one of the most successful in the General Motors system. Unfortunately, Smith and General Motors disregarded the results and failed to capitalize on this success. Today Toyota has become the largest automotive company in the world, replacing General Motors.

Of related interest, countless Western executives have traveled to Toyota City in Japan to study the Toyota System, which consists of two parts: its philosophical assumptions and the actual production system. These executives easily comprehend how the production system works and have borrowed heavily from it in their own company operations. They have also attempted to introduce some of the philosophical assumptions in their own organizations, such as including "Respect for People" in corporate vision statements. Thus far Western executives have implemented the Toyota Production System far more successfully than the philosophical assumptions. Jeffrey Liker (2004), a longtime observer of the worldwide automotive industry, believes that no Western company has effectively copied and implemented Toyota's philosophy, which he views as much more important than the Toyota Production System. Given that Western firms tend to emphasize market-pricing organizational cultures rather than authority-ranking organizational cultures, Liker's conclusion seems warranted.

Some Japanese companies have moved away from the authority-ranking model espoused by Toyota. Nissan, for example, was facing the possibility of bankruptcy in the 1990s. Its CEO, Carlos Ghosn, a native of Brazil, spearheaded a dramatic turnaround of the company. Some of his actions involved downsizing the workforce and relocating factories to new areas in Japan and outside the nation in order to minimize costs. In most instances, workers were given the choice of either relocating to the new factories within Japan or accepting a generous buyout offer. Nissan also reduced the number of suppliers of parts, many of whom had been working with the company for decades, to save billions of dollars. The general public in Japan saw these actions as necessary for the company's survival and hailed Ghosn as a corporate hero.

Unfortunately, there are limitations and consequences associated with both the market-pricing and the authority-ranking models as actualized in the practices of guaranteed employment and employability, as our discussion suggests. Guaranteed employment can allow employees and managers to work below their potential if they so choose. There is also a tendency to have more workers than is necessary for operating efficiently. One negative consequence of employability occurs in a downsizing, especially for workers and managers older than 40. Many of them struggle to obtain work elsewhere commensurate with their abilities and work experience. In some cases they must accept an undesirable position; in many cases, especially those older than 50, they cannot obtain any position. Skilled workers and managers also begin to view their relationship with the firm in purely instrumental terms, are more likely to be less committed, and are more prone to leave for perceived better opportunities, taking with them valuable knowledge and contacts.

At this time it is infeasible to recommend employability as superior to guaranteed employment or vice versa. It is also infeasible to recommend an ideal system integrating aspects of both the authority-ranking and market-pricing models, although Ghosn's approach at Nissan represents a successful mixture of the two approaches. Whether his successful model can be employed by other firms is questionable given different industry and environmental conditions.

Still, in a highly competitive global environment, even the best-intentioned corporations using the market-pricing model often fail to meet their obligations, even to shareholders. A case in point is IBM Corporation from the late 1970s to 1992, even though *Fortune* magazine identified IBM as the most outstanding company in the world for 3 years in the 1980s. IBM also championed guaranteed lifetime employment during this period and was explicitly recognized in *In Search of Excellence* (Peters & Waterman, 1982), one of the best-selling books of all time, as one of the 24 outstanding American companies. But by 1992 the possibility of bankruptcy or being purchased by another company was realistic and threatening, largely because the capacity power of IBM's critical mainframe computers was challenged by the dramatic increase in computing efficiency of desktop computers.

When Louis Gerstner became the CEO of IBM in 1993, he created a vision around the concept of IBM's being the best company in the world offering high-tech computer-related services but one that no longer guaranteed employment. Gerstner correctly reasoned that a farsighted strategy focusing on high-end services and a de-emphasis of mainframe computing would generate increased profits, compensation, self-confidence, and commitment in the workforce. His vision and strategy were clearly successful.

There are, then, sharply contrasting leadership orientations in authority-ranking and market-pricing cultures. In some instances, as in the case of Nissan, they seem to enrich one another. Another striking illustration of enrichment involves Puter Sampoerna, who was educated in the United States and is president of the Sampoerna Company in Indonesia, the most profitable maker of Indonesian clove-based cigarettes. He employs all the modern financial, accounting, marketing, and production techniques learned at business school in the United States. But he also structures the factory in terms of the Indonesian villages in which workers were born. Each subdivision of the factory elects a headman or elder, who is responsible for hiring and disciplining workers in the "village" and handling any other matter of importance. Puter Sampoerna and other top executives do not even come onto the factory floor. They do, however, meet regularly with the headmen or elders (Blustein, 1994).

Beyond the cross-cultural comparison of authority-ranking and market-pricing leadership patterns, the empirical research linking leadership to culture in the GLOBE study of 62 nations confirmed that some *universal* leadership factors are endorsed across all 62 national cultures:

The portrait of a leader who is universally viewed as effective is clear: The person should possess the highest levels of integrity and engage in Charismatic/ Value-Based behaviors while building effective teams. (Dorfman, Hanges, & Brodbeck, 2004, p. 678)

Such a leadership pattern represents an ideal, whether the generic culture is authority ranking, market pricing, community sharing, or equality matching. However, as our discussion of Paradox 2.3 indicated, actual practices frequently are far different from the ideal. It is important to note that the GLOBE study's definition of charismatic leadership is equivalent to this chapter's notion of instrumental-visionary-transformational leadership rather than to the narrow concept of charismatic leadership as defined by special abilities, or charisma, separating the leader from followers.

Briefly, the salient points of difference between the generic cultures of market pricing and authority ranking are a one-way versus a two-way psychological relationship between leader and subordinates; restriction of this relationship to the workplace versus extending it to include integration into the family, kinship group, and larger community; and radically different underlying models, one being instrumental only and the other structuring the corporation as a family.

In the GLOBE study, the researchers reduced the 62 national cultures to 10 clusters, within each of which nations expressed similar cultural values. However, there were still significant differences in values within each cluster. The researchers found that their 10 clusters and 62 national cultures differentially endorsed some distinctive leadership factors and de-emphasized others. Of particular relevance to our discussion is the Nordic-European cluster, which includes Denmark, Finland, and Sweden, generally considered to be nations epitomizing the ideal of the equality-matching culture. That is, these nations emphasize both a high degree of individualism and a low degree of power distance as manifested in an unusual combination of highly successful corporations, entrepreneurial firms, a generous welfare system, and a legal system relating monetary fines for violations to a person's income level. The GLOBE researchers indicate that this cluster strongly endorses the charismatic/value-based, team-based, and participative leadership dimensions. Such results are consistent with the major emphases in this generic type of culture.

However, the equality-matching model is found primarily in a small number of nations with small populations, particularly Scandinavian nations, which historically have had limited multiethnicity. Today these nations are experiencing increasing multiethnic tensions, a topic considered in Chapter 7. It is questionable whether the equality-matching model is appropriate in nations with large populations, and it is even questionable whether the Scandinavian nations will maintain their traditional egalitarian focus in a globalizing world where multiethnic tensions are increasing. Also, as indicated earlier, Hofstede's research was not able to identify any nation employing community sharing, although it did not include the Communist nations such as Cuba and Russia, which officially endorse community sharing but in practice operate quite differently. Unless there is a resurgence of Communism or a new variation thereof throughout the world, which seems to be happening in some Latin American nations in which socialistic populism is gaining strength, it appears reasonable to conclude that globalization will play out in a world in which the authority-ranking and market-pricing models will contend with one another in many instances or integrate with one another in some fashion, as our discussion of Nissan suggests.

Paradox 3.3. When should a leader allow subordinates to participate in decision making?

One of the most popular topics in the area of work motivation is the degree of subordinate involvement in decision making. Participation makes eminent sense when time is not an issue, the subordinates possess knowledge that the leader does not, and participation will increase the probability of the acceptance of the leader's program. Research has consistently confirmed such findings.

However, much of the research was completed in the United States. Brockner et al. (2001) obtained survey data in several nations in a series of related studies. They demonstrated that commitment to the organization and participation were much more positively linked when respondents endorsed low power distance than when they supported high power distance. Such careful studies suggest that a leader or manager should probably consider the degree of power distance in a culture before either maximizing or minimizing the participation. These ideas are also consistent with our previous paradox emphasizing the difference between the instrumental-visionary-transformational leader and the headman concept of leader. When individuals expect that there will be a high degree of power distance in a culture, a manager who stresses the use of participation is directly challenging some core cultural values. Power distance, in short, should be taken into consideration when one is deciding whether to emphasize subordinate participation in decision making, and actions should be consistent with the extent to which it exists in a given culture.

Paradox 3.4. Can an effective leader be someone who publicly humiliates subordinates?

You are invited to indicate whether you would enjoy working for a superior who engaged in any or all the following: publicly humiliated and closely supervised workers, regularly pointed out supposed errors, and suggested strongly how each step of the work process should be completed.

In individualistic cultures, such a pattern of leadership would be considered not only ineffective but distasteful. Individualists would tend to favor a leader who would employ positive reinforcement, provide negative feedback in private, and allow the subordinates to work independently without close supervision. Carly Fiorina, the deposed CEO of Hewett-Packard, was roundly criticized for publicly firing three senior executives when the company's sales did not meet the expectations that she was largely responsible for creating, at least in part because of the public humiliation she heaped on them (Loomis, 2005).

Surprisingly, at least in some collectivistic cultures, subordinates sometimes view public humiliation in front of peers and coworkers very positively. For example, subordinates in Japan will tend to react more positively to a manager who chastises them harshly than will their U.S. counterparts because the manager's behavior is seen as a sign of genuine care and consideration (Bond, Wan, Leung, & Giacalone, 1985). Similarly, Adler (2002) described an overbearing Filipino working in the Royal Bank of Canada who closely supervised Canadian subordinates and treated them severely. When a superior of the Filipino discussed the matter with him, the superior learned that many Filipinos view such a managerial style as reflective of deep concern for subordinates. Also, Gausden (2003) analyzed feedback among Albanians, who tend to be collectivistic. She confirmed that the Albanians she studied viewed strictly positive feedback as having no value.

While such empirical results concerning authority-ranking cultures have been uniformly reported in the research literature, seasoned observers have pointed out that some collectivistic cultures would regard negative chastisement in public as humiliating to subordinates. For example, in macho collectivistic cultures in Africa and Latin America, such behavior by a leader would be viewed as a personal attack and an affront. And if economic development is related to the rise of individualism, we can expect to see a more negative reaction to such leadership behaviors (see Paradox 3.4).

As Gary Oddou and Raj Pillai have pointed out (personal communication), the predictors of effective leadership, such as empathy, the ability to work with others, and flexibility, may be identical across cultures. However, their *surface* features, or the manner in which the leader implements these predictors, vary enormously by culture. This is consistent with the distinction between cultural universals and cultural specifics. For example, the GLOBE study concluded that individualized consideration, which is a component of transformational leadership, was manifested as concern for the employee and the person's extended family in China and Mexico; the same concern would constitute an invasion of privacy in the United States. On the other hand, behavior such as complimenting a female job applicant or peer on her appearance is illegal in the United States but not in other nations. Hence it is probably wise for visitors to withhold judgments and evaluations when crossing and communicating with other cultures until they are able to understand the entire situation clearly.

Motivation

Regardless of whether the relationship between the leader and subordinates is one-way or two-way, leadership involves motivation. More specifically, how do leaders in different cultures motivate their subordinates?

> **Paradox 3.5. Is the relationship between motivation and ability additive or multiplicative in the prediction of individual success and performance?**

One of the most fascinating paradoxes in the cross-cultural arena revolves around the issue of performance and success among individuals in both their organizations and their careers. At this point I invite you to assess the relationship between ability and motivation (sometimes thought of as effort) as either multiplicative or additive in terms of explaining the performance and success of individuals. This may seem like a trivial request, but as we will see, it is pivotal in the area of motivating across cultures.

In market-pricing generic cultures, Paradox 3.5 nestles in perhaps the most general theory of motivation: the expectancy theory. Simply stated, its basic postulate is that individuals must *perceive* that

- They have the proper resources, skills, and abilities to be successful.
- If they make a given effort (motivation), they will be successful and will be rewarded.
- The rewards are ones they desire.

Collectivistic cultures, particularly authority-ranking cultures, tend to assume that the relationship between ability and motivation, or effort, is additive. Conversely, individualistic cultures, particularly market-pricing cultures, tend to assume that the relationship between ability and motivation is multiplicative (Triandis, 2002). It is difficult to overestimate the salience of this distinction. For example, on a standard 10-point scale, receiving a 6 for both ability and motivation would give a score of only 12 for an additive relationship but 36 for a multiplicative relationship. In other words, individualistic, market-pricing cultures generally expect far more from their managers and workers than do collectivistic, authority-ranking cultures, at least in terms of putting forth maximum effort, thereby achieving a higher score for the relationship between ability and motivation. This, in turn, increases the total score or level of performance expected.

There are many programs and systems directly related to this emphasis on a multiplicative relationship between ability and motivation in individualistic market-pricing national cultures. In the United States, for instance, there is a strong belief that equality of opportunity but not equality of outcomes should prevail (Stewart & Bennett, 1991). Also, such well-known programs as "pay for performance" and "management by objectives" originated in the United States. They clearly suggest that individuals should be compensated for their levels of performance and that motivation or effort can dramatically influence performance.

Most probably, the contrasting cross-cultural leadership frameworks employed in our discussion of this paradox significantly influence whether there is a multiplicative or additive relationship between ability and motivation, or effort. As indicated previously, the authority-ranking culture sees the organization as a family in which the relationship between superior and subordinates is psychological and two-way in nature. In such cultures there is even a tendency to avoid rating and ranking managers and employees who must work with one another for 30 or more years. Statements of "average performance" or "above-average performance," at least in part because they save face for the superior and subordinates, are common. By contrast, individualistic cultures, particularly those emphasizing market pricing, are well known for regularly and systematically rating and ranking organizational members and being far less concerned with saving face. For instance, the emphasis at GE on a 20/70/10 performance evaluation system has been copied by many other organizations in the United States and elsewhere. As discussed previously, 20% of the managers receive disproportionate rewards, 70% adequate rewards, and 10% few if any rewards. However, an excessive emphasis on the 20/70/10 system is controversial, in both theory and practice, and organizational members have sued their companies in some instances.

As in the case of leadership, numerous empirical studies have tested various theories of motivation and hypotheses derived from them. However, when culture is included in the framework, the relationship between ability and motivation is assumed to be significantly different.

Paradox 3.6. Can an individually based need hierarchy exist in a collectivistic culture?

It is useful to contrast two general types of motivational theories. The first focuses on the *process* of the motivational system used. Expectancy theory, discussed above, represents one of the major types of theories in this category. The second type emphasizes *internal states* such as the assumed needs and the concepts motivating individuals to behave in a particular fashion.

Abraham Maslow (1970) proposed one of the best-known needs theories. He essentially posited that an individual must satisfy needs sequentially, starting with the lowest level, physiological needs. The individual then proceeds to satisfy sequentially the remaining four levels: safety and security needs; love and belongingness needs, or social needs; esteem and self-esteem needs; and self-actualization needs, or realizing one's full potential. In several management sessions in which I have been involved over the years, the trainer asks the executives to identify the theory that they have found most helpful in their organizations and careers. Maslow's needs hierarchy ranks at or near the top of the list.

Many excellent studies have focused on this theory, and one well-accepted conclusion is that Maslow's five levels can be reduced to two levels. That is, individuals must satisfy their physiological and safety needs before they can consider satisfying the remaining, higher-order needs. Hence the hierarchy consists of only two levels. The assumption of sequencing extends to only these two levels and not to the original five levels proposed by Maslow.

As our discussion of leadership theory has indicated, however, market-pricing cultures tend to focus on the following: individual responsibility, a one-way relationship extending from leaders to the subordinates they are attempting to motivate, and an emphasis on high expectations as demonstrated in the multiplicative assumption between motivation (effort) and ability. Authority-ranking cultures emphasize a family model that is two-way between the leader and subordinates in terms of obligations and responsibilities, and an additive relationship between motivation (effort) and ability.

Such differences are important when considering the cross-cultural dimension of individualism-collectivism. In the studies scoring and ranking national cultures on this dimension, many Western nations, such as the United States, Germany, Sweden, and France, tend to rank higher on individualism than on collectivism. The opposite situation exists for many non-Western nations, whose citizens stress collectivism.

Generally speaking, collectivism emphasizes the primacy of social needs and obligations. Individuals will tend to make decisions acceptable to the larger community and kinship groups in which they reside, even when they must sacrifice their own desires and needs. They tend to see themselves as dependent on and embedded in such groups. Individualism is the exact opposite: Individuals make decisions maximizing their own self-interests, and they view themselves as distinct entities apart from the groups in which they interact. These patterns imply that motivation in authority-ranking cultures is different from motivation in market-pricing cultures, and at least some research supports this interpretation. Iyengar (1998; see also Iyengar & Lepper, 1999) found that children of European-American backgrounds were more motivated when they had a choice and showed less motivation when the choice was made for them by either authority figures or peers. Asian-American children, however, were more motivated when trusted authority figures or peers made decisions on their behalf. Similarly Yu and Yang (1994) showed that achievement motivation in authority-ranking cultures accords primacy to group needs, even when the individual must suffer. In addition, Yu (1996) developed separate measures of individually oriented and socially oriented achievement and found them to be largely independent of one another among Chinese respondents. Those who possess a high degree of socially oriented achievement tend to look to others in the group to define goals.

Admittedly, motivation is a murky area, but our analysis suggests that its primary sources in collectivistic, authority-ranking cultures are social, while in individualistic, market-pricing cultures, such sources are person specific and ego centered. There are, of course, commonalities in motivation across cultures. For example, people generally want to be treated equitably and receive adequate rewards, but notions about equity and adequate rewards differ radically between market-pricing and authority-ranking cultures. Still, the remaining paradoxes in this chapter reinforce and support this interpretation of differential motivation in market-pricing and authority-ranking cultures.

Paradox 3.7. Do effective executives attribute success to themselves or to others?

While leadership and motivation are closely related, it is difficult to understand them without reference to *attribution theory*. This theory essentially explores the manner in which people integrate the various perceptions and stimuli they experience, after which they make generalizations or attributions about personal responsibilities, happenings, and environmental phenomena.

Of particular interest are the *fundamental attribution error* and its derivative, the *self-serving bias*. This error is generally understood to involve attributing success or failure to one or two of three possible causes: oneself; others, including subordinates, superiors, and peers; and the environment or situation. When a person in an individualistic, market-pricing culture is successful, there is a self-serving bias, or a tendency to attribute the success to the individual's own efforts and to de-emphasize the efforts of others and the impact of the environment or situation. For example, a newly appointed CEO may take the major credit for a company's success, even when it is the result of the painstaking work of many organizational members and the strategic decisions of the previous CEO or when global demand for a company's products unexpectedly rises. Conversely, when the person is unsuccessful, there is a self-serving tendency to blame the environment or others in the situation or both.

These results are not surprising, given our previous discussion of the relationship of ability and motivation, or effort, as either multiplicative or additive. Almost all the studies focusing on the fundamental attribution error have involved individuals from individualistic, market-pricing cultures. When someone succeeds in such a culture, it is assumed that the relationship between ability and motivation, or effort, is multiplicative, with effort dramatically altering the results. However, when culture is introduced into the equation, the results change dramatically.

Specifically, collectivistic, authority-ranking cultures also exhibit a fundamental attribution error but not a self-serving bias. In such cultures, when individuals succeed, they attribute their success largely to the work of others, such as subordinates, mentors, peers, and superiors. When they fail, however, they accept the responsibility and blame and argue that neither others nor the environment is a causative factor (Steers & Sanchez-Runde, 2002). In point of fact, the individuals may not be responsible for the failure and may have been a major causative factor for the success, but they incorrectly credit causative factors that seemingly do not serve their personal interests.

Korea stands as an exemplar of this type of perceptual framework. This nation, with its focus on a collectivistic, authority-ranking society, has deep Confucian roots. A study comparing Americans and Koreans found a self-serving bias in the American sample but not in the Korean sample (Nam, 1991). Behavior found in many Korean firms confirms the underlying model of the corporation as a family and the non-self-serving attribution error that appears to emerge because of it. For instance, in 2001 the Daewoo Motor Company was facing bankruptcy, and Lee Jon Dae, its chairman, had to authorize a downsizing of 7,000 employees. His subsequent extraordinary actions seemed to indicate that he was responsible for the unfortunate condition of the company. This was not accurate, as its founder was largely responsible and had fled the country with company funds (and is now in a Korean prison). Mr. Dae's actions included enlisting politicians in a public endorsement of buying Daewoo cars; asking each politician to buy a Daewoo car; sending a personal letter to his counterparts at 26,000 companies, begging each of them to hire at least one of his downsized employees; and abjectly bowing to a downsized employee at a job fair the company organized and profusely apologizing to him for having to lay him off. The employee was surprised at such total acceptance of responsibility and consoled Mr. Dae with the statement that the downsizing was not his fault. Such CEO behavior is virtually unthinkable in the United States.

Gelfand et al. (2002) compared the collectivistic Japanese culture and the individualistic U.S. culture empirically in terms of their relative egotistic perceptions of fairness in negotiations within Japan and the United States. Their result strongly supported the self-serving bias found in the United States (taking credit for success but blaming others or the environment or both for failure) but much less so in Japan. Given our discussion of individualistic and collectivistic cultures, these results are expected. But the statistical support for them indicates that the self-serving bias is stronger than expected.

There are, then, clear linkages between leadership, motivation, and perceptions across cultures. Such differences help explain actual behaviors, as highlighted in our final section.

Group Behavior

Many fascinating research studies focus on small-group behavior. For example, some groups include "token minorities," whose status is questionable until the percentage of minorities increases to 20%. Automatically, it seems, such individuals are no longer perceived as tokens. Similarly, groups frequently tend to follow the *linear four-step pattern* of (1) *forming*, or deciding who will be a member of the group, getting to know one another, and defining precisely what the group is going to do; (2) *storming*, or debating and fighting over specific priorities and tasks; (3) *norming*, or creating standards and mutual expectations that group members should follow in discussions and in completing tasks; and (4) *performing*. In this section we discuss three key paradoxes focusing on the relationship between culture and group behavior.

> **Paradox 3.8. Do groups contain free riders, or are all members equally responsible contributors?**

At least since the time of Aristotle, writers have commented on the *free rider effect* found in groups. In small groups, this effect is evident. That is, if there is no way of assigning individual responsibility, one or more members of the small team will not do their equitable share of the work, thus forcing other members of the group to pick up the slack. It is for this reason that peer-group ratings frequently accompany group projects, both in industry and in other settings, such as colleges and universities.

Also, as the size of the group increases and assigning individual responsibility becomes increasingly difficult, the free rider effect seems to strengthen. For example, many members of labor unions willingly contribute monthly dues but rarely attend union meetings, and many more people watch public television than contribute money to support it (Olson, 1971).

When culture is introduced into the equation, the free rider effect found in individualistic, market-pricing cultures is reversed. That is, in collectivistic, authority-ranking cultures, individuals work harder in groups than they do if they work alone (Steers & Sanchez-Runde, 2002). Karau and Williams (1993) completed a meta-analysis of 147 social loafing effects from studies completed in the United States and 15 effects obtained in collectivistic Pacific Island nations. They confirmed that on complex tasks, the results reported by Steers and Sanchez-Runde held, as expected. This pattern is consistent with our perspective on collectivism, which makes it difficult for the individual to be considered a separate entity apart from the group. Understanding the role of individualistic and collectivistic cultures, and whether individuals within each of these two cultures possess values consistent with the values of their cultures, helps us to see why the free rider effect is influenced by culture. Such consistency predicts whether the outcome will be free riding or the active acceptance of group goals (Earley, 1993).

Paradox 3.9. In general and in small groups, do the personalities of individuals primarily reflect the influence of culture?

There are, however, individual personalities that deviate from the values of a specific culture. It is possible to discern individualistic personalities within collectivistic cultures and collectivistic personalities within individualistic cultures. You may want to obtain a very rough estimate of the individualism-collectivism dimension of your own personality by listing 20 items, adjectives, and brief descriptions in response to the phrase "I am . . ." before reading the next paragraph.

At this individual level of analysis, collectivists tend to emphasize group-oriented items, such as being a member of a family, church, or social club. Individualists, on the other hand, tend to stress person-centered items such as being achievement oriented, personally responsible, and personable. There is no magic number to be derived from the "20 items" exercise, but it does provide a rough measure of a person's tendency to favor either collectivism or individualism.

When personalities interact within either individualistic or collectivistic small groups, the results generally support the criticality of culture. A collectivistic personality strives harder in a collectivistic than in an individualistic small group, and an individualistic personality is less cooperative in an individualistic small group than in a collectivistic small group (Chatman & Barsade, 1995). It appears that individualists will adapt to collectivistic norms if they want to be accepted by the group, while collectivists begin to adopt a more individualistic orientation while in individualistic groups.

De Mooij (2005) points out that East Asians, who tend to be collectivistic, believe in the continuous shaping of personality traits by situational influences. They do not make a sharp distinction between the individual and the situation. Indeed, collectivistic cultures throughout the world tend to follow this pattern. Conversely, a Western personality assumes a norm of consistency and acting in character rather than being shaped by the situation and acting differently in different situations (see also Smith, Bond, & Kagitcibasi, 2006, Chapter 6). Such a viewpoint is consistent with the values of individualistic cultures. Similarly, Allik and McCrae (2004) have demonstrated that geographic clusters of nations exhibit sharply different personality profiles.

Paradox 3.10. Should multicultural small groups be managed differently from single-culture groups?

Kenwyn Smith and David Berg (1987) have developed some counterintuitive concepts about the functioning and management of multicultural small groups. In a single-culture small group, the emphasis is understandably on the similarities of group members, the open recognition of which allows the group members to establish common norms quickly and to work together very efficiently. Smith and Berg point out that such similarities are frequently nonexistent in multicultural small groups, where differences predominate.

As a result, these researchers have developed a three-phase process to enhance the functioning of multicultural small groups. In the first phase, learning how to learn together, they ask group members to describe situations in which they learned something of value. An answer might describe an open sharing of information in an atmosphere encouraging and rewarding learning, for example. They then ask group members to describe situations in which learning was inhibited, which might elicit situations when time was consumed pandering to inflated egos and a climate of blame prevailed. The second phase, discovering members' unique cultural contributions, can be addressed in many ways, such as asking group members to describe the major events in their home cultures during the past decade. Typically the descriptions vary widely, leading members to acknowledge that their knowledge of other cultures is limited. During the third phase, exploring group polarities, Smith and Berg (1987) ask each member to list 8–10 sacred, or major, rules for the way small groups should function in the member's home culture. Next, each member sits with a member from another culture to discuss their respective sacred rules, after which there is a group discussion.

As in the case of the nine dilemmas of leadership described in Paradox 3.1, this three-phase process appears to result in a description of dilemmas that small groups face, such as an emphasis on collectivism or individualism; autocratic versus participative decision making; spontaneous versus orchestrated decisions decided before the meeting, with the meeting serving only to legitimate them; task orientation versus process orientation; and quality versus quantity of actions taken. Smith and Berg (1987) argued that the group, by openly acknowledging these polarities, is now positioned to take actions that incorporate each element of each polarity.

Whether complete success in the functioning of each small multicultural group is attained is beside the point. Rather, the movement is away from a linear and nonparadoxical way of thinking to a nonlinear way of thinking that accepts paradoxes openly. Just this open acknowledgment of polarities and the need to integrate each element of the paradox should facilitate the group's dynamics, at least in many instances. Still, the paradoxes that Smith and Berg (1987) identified are of a special type, namely, dilemmas. It may simply not be possible to integrate both elements of each polarity, even when there is open acknowledgment of their existence.

This paradox, as well as the others described in this chapter, confirms that perception, leadership, motivation, and actual behavior differ significantly across cultures, particularly when we compare collectivistic, authority-ranking cultures and individualistic, market-pricing cultures. In the next three chapters we explore what happens when cultures collide or interact.

Takeaways

1. Leadership is a dilemma, and an individual should recognize this fact before accepting any leadership position that might be uncomfortable without such understanding. From this perspective, leaders perform two key roles: polarity management, or balancing both sides of a dilemma smoothly, and ambiguity management.

2. There are some cultural universals that characterize effective leaders across cultures, but there are also some cultural specifics of leadership behavior that

work well in some cultures but not others. There are also some leadership practices, such as lying and being ruthless, that are universally seen as reprehensible.

3. Charismatic leadership as described in this chapter is not a necessary prerequisite for effective visionary and transformational leadership.

4. While the four generic types of cultures are clearly separable from one another, it is possible to integrate at least some of them in actual situations, as in the case of Carlos Ghosn at Nissan.

5. There are strengths and weaknesses associated with each of the four types of cultures, and emphasizing one type to the complete exclusion of the other three types can be problematic in many instances.

6. Assumptions about motivation vary by culture, especially in regard to whether the critical relationship between motivation and ability is additive or multiplicative.

7. The dimension of individualism-collectivism without reference to any other dimensions is very useful for understanding many cross-cultural issues in such areas as leadership, motivation, and group behavior.

8. Individualistic cultures display a greater tendency toward free riding in small groups than collectivistic cultures do.

Discussion Questions

1. Did Chester Barnard argue that workers were of minor significance compared to managers or leaders? If yes, why? If no, why not?

2. How does charismatic leadership differ from transactional and visionary leadership? Identify a transformational leader who was not charismatic; explain why.

3. How does the size of a nation's population and its multiethnicity seem to influence its equality-matching, egalitarian focus?

4. What is the fundamental attribution error? How does it relate to the self-serving bias in individualistic and collectivistic cultures?

5. How does group size relate to the free rider effect? Please explain. Critically compare this effect in individualistic and collectivistic cultures.

6. This chapter employs the dimension of individualism-collectivism not only when talking about groups but even when talking about individuals. Does this suggest that individualism-collectivism is not only a cultural or group concept but also a personality concept? Why or why not?

7. Compare and contrast the advantages and disadvantages of guaranteed employment and employability from a cross-cultural perspective.

8. How does individualism-collectivism relate to Maslow's needs hierarchy?

Exercises

1. Class members should each identify an organization about which they are knowledgeable and draw nine charts to explore Thomas Stewart's framework for nine leadership dilemmas. The charts can be shared with another class member or the entire class. Also, this exercise can form the basis of a written assignment focusing on why the charts have been constructed in specific ways, the general profile that emerges of both leadership and the organization, and the conclusions or recommendations to management that can be derived.

2. In this chapter several exercises were suggested, including the identification of personal metaphors for leadership and the "20 items" relating to individualism and collectivism. Each small group in the subdivided class can discuss these two exercises and the differential responses they generated, and report back to the entire class what they have learned.

3. You are a first-line supervisor in a production company. As you are observing the factory floor, you notice that one employee is working with his safety guard up. Such a practice speeds up the work and makes it easier for the worker to complete the tasks. However, having the safety guard up is a serious violation and has resulted in several accidents. As he sees you, he immediately puts the safety guard down. How would you expect the first-line supervisor, as a leader, to respond in the four types of generic cultures (community sharing, authority ranking, equality matching, and market pricing) to handle this situation? Would the leader immediately confront the worker and punish him with a 3-day layoff, as required? Would the leader take the worker aside and talk to him about the dangers but still give the layoff? Would the leader take the worker aside and discuss the matter with him, holding off on any action until he hears what the worker says? Would the leader chastise the worker in front of other workers and use him as an example? What else could the leader of each selected generic culture do that would be consistent with the values of the culture?

   The instructor may choose to focus a general class discussion on this topic or to form small groups and let each of them appoint a recorder to report back to the entire class, followed by discussion.

Answers to the Two-Item Survey

For the Gelfand-Holcombe two-item survey in the chapter (pp. 53–54), the corresponding answers for the first item are c, community sharing; d, authority ranking; a, equality matching; and b, market pricing. For the second item, the answers are: a, community sharing; d, authority ranking; c, equality matching; and b, market pricing.

4

Communicating Across Cultures

There are very few if any topics in the cross-cultural arena that are as relevant and critical as cross-cultural communication. Without clear and effective communication it is difficult if not impossible to emphasize cooperative relations that eventually result in mutually satisfactory goals and results. As indicated in Chapter 2, Edward Hall followed the lead of earlier cultural anthropologists by describing culture as communication, and he compared cross-cultural communication to reading the notes on a sheet of music (Hall, 1959; see also Hall & Hall, 1990). If a person understands how to read a sheet of music, it is easy to relate to others who have the same knowledge. But without such knowledge a person is at a decided if not critical disadvantage.

There is a close relationship between a culture's language and music. Aniruddh Patel and his colleagues at the Linguistics Institute of La Jolla have demonstrated that people internalize acoustic patterns and express them in the pitches and rhythms of their music (see Brown, 2006). We tend to recognize immediately Debussy's *Afternoon of a Faun* as distinctly French, Copeland's *Appalachian Spring* as American, and Elgar's *Pomp and Circumstance* as English. Language can even shape the way our brain functions. Researchers in Italy and Britain compared university students in those two nations and discovered that Italians read faster, probably because the combinations of letters in their native language tend to be associated with the same sounds. This is not the situation for English speakers. The researchers also discovered that Italian and English students use different parts of their brains when reading. These findings reinforce the work of Hall and other cultural anthropologists who have argued that cultural factors influence the development of language, even to the extent that culture is equated with communication (see Stein, 1999).

Communication, however, involves much more than the spoken language. Generally speaking, only about 7% of the total impact of a message on a receiver is based on the words used, 38% on the manner in which a person speaks the words (i.e., tone of voice, inflection, loudness, etc.), and 55% on nonverbal activities. Anderson (2000) classifies *nonverbal* activities into the following eight categories, or *codes*, that must be deciphered correctly for communication to succeed:

1. Time (*chromenics*), such as saving time by keeping to schedule or giving time by extending a meeting to handle a person's issues, even at the expense of delaying the next scheduled meeting by an hour or more.

2. The use of space (*proxemics*), such as keeping office doors closed so that visitors must knock before being granted admission, as happens frequently in Germany and northern Europe, and talking comfortably with another person whose face is only a few inches away, a behavior found in Arab nations.

3. Eye movements (*oculesics*); for example, the Chinese and Japanese habit of expressing anger only in their eyes, and when a non-Chinese or non-Japanese person finally recognizes that there is a problem, it is many times too late, as the pot has boiled over and become an outburst (Gannon, 2004).

4. Body motions (*kinesics*), including shrugs and blushes, such as giving the A-OK gesture by holding the thumb and index finger in a circle, something that is highly positive in the United States but a terrible insult in Iran and vulgar in Brazil.

5. Touching (*haptics*); for example, Asian cultures usually emphasize nontouching behavior, while Latin American cultures tend to exult in touching.

6. Physical appearance; for example, many subcultures in Latin America and Asia stress the need for a proper physical appearance, including proper dress, while other cultures, such as many found in the United States, put less stock in this element, and Buddhists and Hindus tend to associate physical deformity with karma, or the consequence of a person's actions in a previous life.

7. Speaking (*vocalics*); for example, while the Cantonese and Mandarin languages are identical in written form, Mandarin is very formal orally, while Cantonese tends to include many more slang words and is spoken more loudly than Mandarin, even to the extent that two people expressing love to one another can sound to outsiders as if they are quarreling (Pierson, 2006).

8. Smelling (*olfactics*); for example, citizens of Arab cultures frequently interact comfortably face-to-face and can even smell the other person's breath, while white, Anglo-Saxon culture takes a dim view of such activity.

As you can undoubtedly observe, knowing how to behave in these eight areas while communicating cross-culturally is a daunting task. Even when all participants in the cross-cultural communication process speak the same language, the probability of making a major error is very high because of the complexity these eight areas create.

In this chapter we focus first on language and some of the paradoxes that exist in this area. Next, we examine some of the paradoxes that exist in the eight areas identified above, using Edward Hall's work as a springboard for identifying and resolving these paradoxes. We then turn our attention to symbolism and its importance in cross-cultural communication. Finally, we look at mediated communication, or cross-cultural communication that is not face-to-face, which is becoming increasingly important due to the widespread acceptance of modern technologies such as cell phones and the Internet.

Language

Paradox 4.1. How can knowing the language of another culture be a disadvantage?

Participants in management training sessions frequently raise this question, and you are invited to provide your personal answer at this point.

There is really no clear answer to this paradox, which is typically phrased as the following question: Which is more important, knowing the language of another culture or knowing the norms, values, and behaviors that are expected by its members and abiding by them? The question emphasizes an "either-or" answer, but the *or* can reasonably be changed to *and* in accordance with the rules of paradoxical reasoning. Clearly, knowing the language well is a necessary but not sufficient condition for understanding a culture in depth, but not necessarily for effective cross-cultural communication. For example, Glen Fisher (1988) describes a U.S. mission to a Latin American country that was nearly ruined by an insensitive but high-ranking official who spoke fluent Spanish. Fortunately a low-ranking member of the group, who did not speak Spanish, saved the day by being an enthusiastic learner interested in the culture's history, food, current situation, language, and so on.

Also, if a person is fluent in the culture's language, its natives tend to assume that the person genuinely understands the culture. They expect that such a person will abide by its norms, which are frequently difficult for an outsider to recognize. Thus, not knowing the language can be a decided advantage in some instances. For example, sometimes the native speakers in a culture, when using the visitor's language, unknowingly reveal information that enhances the visitor's bargaining power.

To make matters even more complicated, executives may visit a culture for only a short duration, such as a week or two, to transact business, and some executives are constantly on the road. Learning the new language is time-consuming, and busy executives tend to have very little time to devote to the matter. An extreme example involved the owner and CEO of a midsize furniture company in North Carolina that was losing significant business to competitors from other nations such as Thailand and Indonesia. This executive, who had never been outside the United States until he was 50 years old, visited 55 nations in 5 pressure-filled years in an attempt to increase business significantly and to save his firm. To expect such an executive to learn all the languages in these 55 nations is unrealistic, and even to expect him to be fluent in one new language is questionable. While his case is extreme, short-term, multicountry visits focused solely on business are quite common.

Even for short-term visits, the executive can at least learn some words for greeting, asking for directions, and so on. Not to learn such words can offend the culture's natives. And knowing a few hundred words so that the executive feels confident when walking the streets of a strange city, ordering dinner, asking for directions, and taking taxis can help relieve a great deal of stress.

Is there an answer to this paradox? Yes, but only in the very limited sense that the answer depends on the situation, similar to the solution to the Liar Paradox (see page 6). There is no higher-level cross-cultural explanation that can serve to integrate the two opposing elements in this paradox: knowing the language and understanding the culture. In some circumstances, such as being able to talk to local citizens when someone has suffered a heart attack, being fluent in the language is more important than understanding the culture. In other circumstances the opposite situation prevails. Still, proponents of the primacy of language over cultural understanding tend to be vociferous in defending this position, and vice versa. But the fact remains that it is now possible to do business in all or most parts of the world, at least on a short-term basis, without being fluent in the culture's language. English is accepted as the language of business, and terms such as *Chinglish* and *Spanglish* suggest that the citizens in the culture being visited are willing to try to converse in novel ways. Also, the executive can use an interpreter, and the interpreter can help out not only with the language but even with understanding the culture's nuances.

It is, however, critical to understand a culture's values, practices, norms, history, current situation, and so forth. This is fairly easy to accomplish today, especially compared to learning a language from scratch, through reading, watching cross-cultural videos, and talking to others before undertaking a trip to another culture.

Nevertheless, if an executive is going to return to the culture periodically or will stay beyond a month, it is advisable to study the language in depth. Without fluency in the culture's language, all communication must be in English or interpreted. It is quite possible that the executive in such a situation will feel limited and even isolated from native counterparts. Isolation of this sort is problematic not only for business activities but also for a person's feelings of self-confidence.

For longer stays, not knowing the language can be not only awkward but even injurious. One U.S. company, for example, established a joint venture in China that was underwritten entirely by three native Chinese businesspeople. The U.S. company, which had a great product and reputation, sent to head up the joint venture a high-ranking executive who was not fluent in the Chinese language. However, the three Chinese businesspeople appointed their own manager, who was supposedly going to report to the American. Instead, the Chinese manager fired all the staff reporting to the American, isolated him in a distant plant of the joint venture, and demanded that all managers and staff report directly to him rather than to the American executive. In response, the American executive hired an interpreter, who was at his side every day while he battled with his adversary, who finally lost his job and left the company, but only after several months of tension and conflict. The American executive did begin to study the Chinese language. However, even when he became more fluent, he always had an interpreter at his side, using two interpreters each day so that one of them was always present and energetic.

A company would be wise to hire competent interpreters to accompany executives, translate contracts and other business documents, help out on advertising, and so forth. Table 4.1 contains some examples of actual advertising slogans that proved to be extremely problematic. Because of such problems, there are at least 10,000 companies throughout the world that specialize in translations. Still, the problems in this area continue. For instance, in the area of contracts, Northrop-Grumman had to pay an additional $2 million because its interpreter used the term *fence* rather than the proper term *electric fence*.

If feasible, it is also important to make the interpreter responsible for imparting cultural knowledge and facilitating relationships. Recently I was teaching an Executive MBA course in China, and the interpreter provided background information on the class and identified some issues I should avoid. She also translated all questions and comments of the trainees completely, which strengthened cross-cultural communication and interaction with the trainees. This very helpful approach did not occur when I used another interpreter in a similar class. For example, her class behavior was to engage in interchanges with the trainees for several minutes and then to provide me with a few seconds of feedback as to what was said, even when I advised her that this behavior was unacceptable. One Northrop-Grumman executive team, which was negotiating with a Korean firm about a possible contract, terminated its relationship with an interpreter when he engaged in a lengthy and heated exchange with the Korean executive team but then told

Table 4.1   Mangled Translations: Real Advertising Slogans

- Kentucky Fried Chicken in China: The "Finger Lickin' Good" slogan translates as "Eat your fingers off."
- Pepsi in Taiwan: The translation of the slogan "The Pepsi Generation" came out as "Pepsi will bring your ancestors back from the dead."
- Salem cigarettes in Japan: The slogan "Salem—Feeling Free" translates as "When smoking Salem, you feel so refreshed that your mind seems to be free and empty."
- Ford in Brazil: When the Pinto flopped, the company found out that the slogan translated as "Tiny male genitals."
- Chevy in Mexico: Sales of the Nova may have been affected by its literal Spanish translation, "No Go."
- Purdue Chicken in Mexico: Frank Purdue's tagline or slogan, "It takes a tough man to make a tender chicken," may have worked well in the United States, but it shocked people in Mexico because the literal translation can also mean, "It takes a hard man to make a chicken aroused."
- One airline advertised, after translation, "We take your bags and send them in all directions."
- A major hotel advertised that in case of fire, guests should do their utmost to alarm the hotel porter.

the Northrop-Grumman team that the matter had been resolved and provided no additional information, even when asked directly. The team felt much more comfortable and was more effective communicating in English directly with the Korean team than communicating through the interpreter, although it still employed an interpreter for rendering the contract and related business documents into English.

Addressing the polarities of the paradox by emphasizing both language fluency and cultural knowledge is ideal, as they tend to overlap significantly. Still, as the examples indicate, it is not always feasible to become fluent in a new language, in which case it is incumbent on the executive to learn cultural specifics and at least some words and phrases. Becoming fluent and obtaining cultural knowledge are equally reasonable premises, and so this paradox represents a dilemma (see Chapter 3, Paradox 3.1).

Paradox 4.2. How can languages be rapidly dying while becoming more influential?

As described in the opening paragraphs of Chapter 1, languages are dying at an alarming rate, from an estimated 15,000 languages 100 years ago to

7,000 today. At the same time, languages are becoming more influential. How can this be?

While languages are dying, the major language groups—English, Chinese, Spanish, and so on—are strengthening, partly because of the growth of the global population. And while English is the language of business, it is possible but not probable that Chinese may replace it. Mandarin Chinese is used by more than 1 billion people as their primary language, while English is in a distant second place. However, English is used in 115 nations as either the primary or the secondary language, particularly in business and university educational programs, while only 5 nations use Mandarin Chinese similarly.

A common criticism among citizens of other countries is that U.S. citizens don't seem to be very interested in learning secondary languages, and the criticism is frequently accurate. While our discussion of Paradox 4.2 emphasized the problematic issues that fluency in a secondary language entails, the benefits far outweigh the costs. The major language groups, counting both primary and secondary users, rank as follows: Mandarin Chinese, English, Spanish, Russian, French, Hindi/Urdu, Arabic, Portuguese, Bengali, Japanese, and German. For those contemplating any long-term activities in nations using these languages, it seems prudent to prepare by learning at least one of them, for all the reasons discussed under Paradox 4.1.

Paradox 4.3. Critical words and phrases: How can there be immediate recognition by members of the culture and radically different interpretations?

At this point you are invited to think of distinctive words and phrases in your primary language that are difficult if not impossible to express in another language. It is typically insightful when you offer your various selections in a class setting.

All cultures employ such words and phrases. For example, the Thai phrase *mai pen rai* is virtually untranslatable, as it has slightly different meanings in different situations. Thais are very familiar with this phrase and use it frequently. Its essential meaning reflects the belief that humans have little if any control over nature, technology, and many other forces. Carol Hollinger (2000), an American high school teacher in Thailand, fell in love with Thai culture, particularly this aspect of it, and even titled her popular book *Mai Pen Rai Means Never Mind*. This phrase does not signify the acceptance of a fatalistic view of life, sometimes found among conservative Muslims or Christians. Rather, it is the acceptance of things as they are and the willingness to make life as pleasant as possible regardless of life's circumstances.

Michael Agar, a cultural anthropologist, has authored a delightful book, *Language Shock* (1994), focused specifically on such distinctive and rich words and phrases. While teaching at the Language Institute in Austria, he informed his colleagues over lunch that he was planning to study a rich Austrian word or phrase and was thinking of focusing on the word *Schmäh*. As he indicates,

> Everyone at the lunch said it was a good idea. I asked if they knew what Schmäh meant and they all looked at me like I'd asked if the sun rose in the morning. Of course they did. But then, as we discussed it, all kinds of disagreements followed. Schmäh was Viennese. No it wasn't, it was Austrian, or universal. It was something men did. No it wasn't. It was more characteristic of the lower classes. No it wasn't. It was telling jokes, picking up a woman in a bar, manipulating a situation, what politicians did, a way of life. No it wasn't. Yes it was.

His students then interviewed a large sample of Austrians and found even more bewildering and numerous interpretations; Agar skillfully describes these various interpretations for several pages. The general consensus was that all Austrians know immediately what the meaning of Schmäh is, that it expresses a unique Austrian worldview, and that the situation largely determines its interpretation. Still, each Austrian seems to have a favorite definition that transcends any individual situation.

Visitors frequently fail to understand the meanings associated with a culture's rich words and phrases and their critical importance. An egregious example of such failure occurred on a *60 Minutes* segment, "Tango Finlandia," which focused on the shyness of Finnish men. This segment has been repeated on American television at least seven times since 1993. Morley Safer, a well-known interviewer from CBS's *60 Minutes*, visited Finland and attended a dance for adults in which there was a seemingly clear separation of the men and women, even to the point that some of the men had to be encouraged to dance. Safer commented on the shyness of Finnish men and the negative impact it has had on the nation's falling birthrate. For Safer and many people in the United States, 75% of whom are classified as extrovertic in terms of the Myers-Briggs Type Indicator Inventory, shyness is a negative concept. (Strictly speaking, Jungian psychologists use the term *extrovertic* for personalities whose source of energy is interaction with others; the other end of the continuum is introversion, and the source of energy for introverts is being alone; interactions tend to deplete energy.) However, Finnish respondents in various studies tend to think of shyness and introversion in a very positive way: reflective, in tune with nature and its quietness, mature, responsible, hard working, and so forth. Hence there was a classic misunderstanding between the visitors from the United States and the Finns, who unsuccessfully tried to explain the positive features of shyness (Berry, Carbaugh,

& Nurmikari-Berry, 2004). The *60 Minutes* segment, which described the Finns satirically because of their supposedly excessive shyness, was actually a broad-based and distorted stereotype that did little if anything to improve cross-cultural communication and understanding.

Perhaps the cultural metaphor most appropriate for Finland is the native sauna, which is attached to many homes. Many business firms have their own company sauna, and after using it and taking a very cold shower, the executives relax at the end of the day by drinking beer and conversing animatedly. Out come the cell phones, and they begin to call clients to finalize deals! The supposedly introvertic and shy Finns are anything but that in the sauna!

All languages seem to possess comparable rich words and phrases that are critical for understanding particular cultures and, as a general rule, follow the same situational pattern of meaning and interpretation. When communicating across cultures, it is useful to identify such words and phrases and use them appropriately as communication and relating to others become easier to achieve, even when language skills are limited.

Paradox 4.4. Are proverbs effective descriptors of a culture?

At this point you are invited to identify one or two proverbs that give insight into your root culture. These proverbs can be discussed in class or serve as the basis of a short written assignment.

Many of us avoid using proverbs, as they tend to be simplistic. More important, most if not all proverbs have an antithesis, such as "Absence makes the heart grow fonder" and "Out of sight, out of mind." However, Weber and Hsee (1998) showed that survey respondents from China are significantly less risk averse than those in the United States in financial decisions but more risk averse in social decisions or situations. Weber, Hsee, and Sokolowska (1998) then completed a study in which participants from China, Germany, and the United States rated the risk-taking advice imparted in Chinese and American proverbs. The results confirmed the earlier findings and also indicated that the interpretation of proverbs made explicit certain "long-standing cultural differences in social cohesion and cooperation" (p. 183) contributing to the explanation of these differences in risky behavior. Thus proverbs seem to be effective descriptors of a culture, but there is nearly always an antithesis to the thesis, which neutralizes their impact.

Finally, you are invited to discuss whether the proverbs listed below accurately reflect American culture and, if so, what they suggest:

- Life is just a bowl of cherries.
- It's lonely at the top.

- Early to bed, early to rise, makes a man healthy, wealthy, and wise.
- One step at a time.
- Where there's a will, there's a way.
- It's never too late.

Context and Beyond

The writings and frameworks that the late Edward Hall developed for understanding communication across cultures represent one of the most influential, if not the most influential, perspectives in this area. He lived in the Southwest during his early years and interacted with a variety of fascinating people, including Native Americans, homesteaders, and cowboys. These early experiences influenced his view of many phenomena, such as time and space. For example, he described the same trip taken in three contrasting modes: walking, riding a horse, and traveling by car. Time became compressed as the trip moved from walking all day to riding a horse for a few hours and then to traveling by car for 30 minutes, and his view and perception of the landscape changed dramatically as the time required for the trip markedly decreased. While there are familiar and objective measures of time and space, Hall (1966) pointed out that there are also subjective or cultural measures, exemplified by this experience of time compression.

Over the years Hall constructed a useful and insightful framework for understanding communication that begins with the concept of *personal space* (Hall, 1966). People dislike being forced to be either too close to or too far apart from other people, and this preference is culture specific. For instance, white, Anglo-Saxon Americans have an intimate zone extending from the surface of the skin to 18 inches, into which only a few individuals are allowed. In a second zone, from 18 inches to 4 feet, comfortable interactions reflecting friendship and closeness take place. The third zone extends from 4 feet to 12 feet, and most impersonal business takes place in this area. Finally, there is a public zone of 12 feet and beyond, in which individuals recognize one another and say hello but do not engage in comfortable interactions.

Germans follow this pattern, but not the pattern of open-door offices. Rather, they view their offices as an extension of their personalities. They expect a person to knock and be invited to enter before doing so, and to respect the four zones described above. Hall describes an extreme situation in which visiting American salespeople upset a German manager by constantly moving the visitor's chair closer to the manager to establish physical contact and to gain a feeling of intimacy and psychological advantage. This German manager bolted the visitor's chair to the floor to ensure that his personal space would not be invaded. Hall also noted that there seems to be no concept of personal space in the Middle East, which explains why people from this area of the world are comfortable interacting with their faces almost touching.

In addition, Hall makes a distinction between *monochronic* and *polychronic* time. Writers tend to define these two terms as doing one thing at a time and multitasking, respectively. However, Hall includes much more in the definitions and comparisons (Table 4.2), and he arrays cultures on a continuum from monochronic to polychronic. Generally speaking, individualistic cultures tend to be monochronic, while collectivistic cultures gravitate toward the polychronic end of the continuum. Hall then introduced the concept of context, or the culturally influenced situation, by arguing that there is a continuum of cross-cultural communication extending from low context to high context. A *low-context communication* is one that is explicit and expressed orally or in writing or both. For example, a manager may send written instructions to subordinates and summarize them at a group meeting. Individualistic cultures such as those found among white, Anglo-Saxon Americans and Germans tend to be low context. Conversely, a *high-context communication* is one in which members are thoroughly socialized to understand the message without the necessity of written or direct oral communication, and communication is implicit. These tend to be collectivistic cultures. Citizens of such cultures become uncomfortable saying "no" to a direct request, and they employ all sorts of euphemisms, such as "that might be difficult" or "we can consider your request at a later time," to avoid giving insult. Even slight body gestures, such as in some Buddhist nations, which follow the cultural dictate that emotions and body movements should be minimized as one pursues "the Middle Way," may be a very implicit way of saying no, and a visitor may need to observe closely for several months to learn to recognize the message. Japan, a high-context culture, has incorporated such subtlety even into the length of pauses in speech, as expressed in the aphorism "Silence is communication." The Japanese have become so socialized to each other's attitudes that the length of an individual's pause in communication at a group meeting conveys the message, such as a disagreement with a position of the other group or outright rejection.

Most important, Hall points out that the amount of information conveyed and understood in both low-context and high-context cultures can be equal. It is the techniques and methods employed to convey the information that distinguish these two types of cultures, which he also arrays along a continuum extending from low context to high context. Of course, someone dealing with a particular culture must know whether the culture is monochronic or polychronic and the specific communication techniques its members employ. Hall makes no evaluative assumption about whether one form of

Table 4.2   Monochronic Versus Polychronic Time

Monochronic	Polychronic
Employees do one thing at a time.	Employees do many things simultaneously (multitasking).
Employees make time commitments (set deadlines).	Time commitments are flexible and have low priority.
Employees are committed to the job.	Employees are committed to people and relationships.
Employees concentrate on the job.	Employees are easily distracted.
Employees emphasize promptness.	Employees base promptness on relationships.
Employees are accustomed to short-term relationships.	Employees tend to form deep and lifelong relationships.
Employees are low context and need *explicit* information.	Employees are high context and so socialized that they already possess *implicit information*.
Employees adhere to plans.	Employees change plans often.

communication is superior to the other form, which allows him to emphasize techniques and methods. Admittedly, low-context communicators experience more difficulty handling periods of silence than do high-context communicators. They tend to "fill in the blanks" of silence with words that may not relate to the topic at hand and may make high-context communicators uncomfortable. Still, Hall maintains that both low-context and high-context communication can be either effective or ineffective, depending on the situation and the communication process favored by the culture in which the cross-cultural interaction occurs.

Paradox 4.5. Can a culture be simultaneously monochronic and polychronic?

Generalizing about a specific culture in terms of Hall's framework is helpful but should be accompanied by caveats. For instance, Hall treats U.S. culture as monochronic, but managerial work within it tends to be polychronic. The well-known portrait of such work by Henry Mintzberg (1973) described it as long hours of unremitting work consisting of activities that are fragmented, varied, and brief. John Kotter (1982) provides in-depth descriptions of managerial work that reinforce this profile. For example, one manager performed a dizzying array of activities within one 2-minute period. And, at least in part because of the sharp increase in global competition and the decrease in product life cycles, firms are calling on managers and employees to perform many more activities, in response to which they engage much more in multitasking or polychronic behavior.

However, as Table 4.2 indicates, Hall infused the dimension of monochronic and polychronic time with many more meanings than just the simple concept of doing one thing at a time versus multitasking. It is the more expanded perspective of this dimension that is important. Also, it is possible to generalize about cultures that emphasize monochronic or polychronic time, with the understanding that globalization is making the characterization less appropriate in many instances. For example, Japanese firms operating in Thailand recognize that the group-focused and polychronic Thais translate the Thai word for *work* as *party* (*ngan*) and, as a consequence, believe that work should be enjoyable. Sensibly, the Japanese managers punctuate the workday with short breaks going beyond just a coffee break so that the Thais can interact in their groups. Still, European and American firms operating in Thailand sometimes pay their workers at a higher rate than the Japanese firms do, and they have no difficulty attracting Thai workers who are willing to trade time off during the day for higher salaries.

Paradox 4.6. Can a culture be simultaneously low context and high context?

Since Hall arranges cultures on a continuum going from low-context to high-context communication, he seems to suggest that a low-context culture cannot be high context. However, his descriptions of cultures argue against this proposition. For example, he describes the high-context way that the Japanese communicate with one another but the low-context way they communicate with Westerners. Tony Fang (2006) points out that the karaoke bar is a Japanese innovation and that it is popular in other Asian nations such as Korea and Malaysia, presumably because it allows for the expression of low-context behavior and serves as an emotional outlet for such rules-focused and high-context cultures. Even when businesspeople from a high-context culture entertain their counterparts from a low-context culture in a karaoke bar, they tend to move away from high-context behavior toward low-context behavior.

We can, then, accept Hall's basic formulations about low-context and high-context communications and cultures, but with caveats. While it is possible to describe the dominant profile of a culture as either low context or high context, we must realize that cultures can be both low context and high context but in different situations and contexts.

Symbolism

We have already touched on the issue of symbolic meaning in cross-cultural communication. But the topic's importance merits additional treatment. As Anderson's classification (2000) of nonverbal activities highlighted at the beginning of this chapter suggests, the complexity in this area is high. Just before visiting a new culture, it is useful to review its "dos and taboos" (Axtell, 1990), and books and Web sites are readily available to facilitate the process. Knowing, for example, that showing the bottom of one's shoes in Asia and the Mideast tends to be insulting helps a visitor avoid this behavior. Similarly African American and African cultures tend to avoid direct eye contact, while other cultures, such as white, Anglo-Saxon culture, tend to emphasize it. It is not unusual for white Anglo-Saxons to be uncomfortable when greeting a person who avoids eye contact and has a weak handshake, as they interpret these behaviors only from their vantage point.

Numbers and related phenomena are also important in many cultures as symbolic expressions. For example, the Chinese avoid using the number 4 because its pronunciation is similar to the word for death. In the Chinese language the pronunciation of the word for clock also sounds like the word for death, and so it is advisable to avoid giving a clock as a gift. Colors and flowers are also important. For example, an American businesswoman was experiencing difficulty obtaining business in China for her company until she began wearing red dresses, and red is a sign of good fortune and luck in China, encouraging the Chinese to interact with someone wearing anything with this color. All cultures possess phenomena that are symbolic in meaning, and knowing the symbolism is very helpful.

> **Paradox 4.7. How can the same phenomenon represent different symbolic meanings?**

A key issue is the manner in which the same phenomenon possesses different symbolic meanings in different cultures. For example, the Spanish bullfight is a ritual of death in a culture also known for contagious vitality. Some of us intensely dislike the Spanish bullfight because of the blood and gore and the killing of the bull. But, as some Spaniards like to tell those from other cultures, to understand Spanish culture it is critical to comprehend the nuances of bullfighting. It is not a sport but a ritual celebrating death, and the purpose of the ritual is to remind people that they should live a full and vitally engaging life.

However, as one discovers when visiting Portugal, not all bullfighting has the same symbolic meaning as the Spanish version. In Portugal, the padded bull is not killed. More than a hundred years ago the king outlawed the killing of the bull because of the frequency of deaths among the matadors. Rather, a small team of men must stop the bull in its tracks. Frequently one seemingly foolhardy member of the team will try to accomplish this task on his own, and the bull will unceremoniously flip him high into the air. Although injuries are obviously frequent, both for the seemingly foolhardy individuals and the team, typically no one—either man or bull—is killed. Symbolically, the bullfight is a community manifestation of bravery that serves to unite the audience and the team. Hence the same phenomenon can have different or similar symbolic meanings, depending on the specifics of the cultural situation.

Paradox 4.8. How can the same phenomenon represent changing symbolic meanings?

The only difference between Paradoxes 4.7 and 4.8 is one word (*different* versus *changing* symbolic meanings). As the world globalizes and interactions across cultures become more frequent, they influence one another, and as a result, symbolic meanings tend to change.

For example, all cultures tend to enjoy smiling at different times, but some extrovertic cultures, such as U.S. culture, do so with more frequency and vigor than others. However, the Chinese, the Japanese, and other cultural groups tend to associate smiling with a lack of self-control and tranquility (Smith & Bond, 1998). Sometimes the Chinese and Japanese tend to stereotype Americans as friendly, cooperative, and aggressive but somewhat simplistic in both outlook and deep cross-cultural understanding. For example, they tend to assume that Americans can talk knowledgeably *only* about sports and business. Over the years several international surveys of many Asian and non-Asian nations have found Americans portrayed in this fashion.

But, at least partially as a consequence of globalization and the increasing interactions occurring because of it, symbolic meanings are changing. In 1969 my wife, Doris, and I visited France for the first time and were struck by the rudeness of some French people, especially in Paris. We also noticed that even when French people were helpful, they did not smile, and later we learned that the French supposedly prefer to establish a deeper relationship than do Americans, although this is debatable. The French manifest such deep and close friendship by smiling frequently but do so much less frequently with strangers.

However, on a visit to France in the late 1990s, we stayed at the Hotel Novatel, where the staff and waiters surprised us by smiling and extending themselves to make visitors feel comfortable. On our return to the United

States, we read a newspaper article describing this change in demeanor and relating it to globalization. A senior executive from this hotel visited California and observed the helpful and smiling behavior in the hotels, after which he introduced a program at the Novatel designed to incorporate these behaviors in the hotel's staff and waiters.

Such examples are multiplying in our globalizing world, and it is no exaggeration to say that the world is flat in this sense of the word (Friedman, 2005). The same phenomenon is subject to different symbolic interpretations, but it is also subject to rapidly changing symbolic interpretations.

Technology and Mediated Communication

Mediated communication such as e-mail, the cell phone, and the Internet is rapidly becoming a major force in cross-cultural communication. In some respects these communication vehicles favor low-context communication because messages are explicit. The preponderance of e-mails both domestically and across cultures tends toward informality, briefness, and the use of linguistic shortcuts, such as salutations beginning with "Hi" rather than "Dear Mr. XXX" and abbreviations such as "Xmas" for "Christmas."

However, major business contracts have been lost simply because citizens and especially older generations in high-context and authority-ranking cultures expect formal communications in their e-mails. In one instance a multibillion-dollar contract was lost when an American engineer, to save time, began an e-mail to a senior executive in a Malaysian firm informally and without using "Dear Mr. XXXX."

To complicate matters, the ability of college graduates in the United States to express themselves effectively in writing is declining. Several private surveys underwritten by business firms confirm that more than 50% of the e-mails sent to clients contain serious errors in spelling and grammar and do not answer questions correctly. A recent adult literacy assessment by the National Assessment of Educational Statistics indicated that only 31% of college graduates could understand a simple table relating blood pressure and physical activity and could read a complex book and extrapolate from it (Romano, 2005). In a world becoming increasingly dependent on the Internet to transact business and other activities, this trend is very problematic.

Cell phones also favor low-context communication, especially since callers can compress time by multitasking when using them, even while walking or driving a car. The use of cell phones is becoming widespread around the globe. As a result, it is plausible that their widespread use will result in a decreasing emphasis on high-context communication and an increased focus on compressed time. It is difficult to engage in high-context communication while walking and conversing on a cell phone. The only available cues are voice, choice of words, and inflection. As a result, the formality characteristic of high-context communication deteriorates and is replaced by low-context communication emphasizing informality, briefness, and multitasking.

Paradox 4.9. Can face-to-face and mediated communication be functionally equivalent, either individually or in small groups?

Face-to-face communications are obviously important and have been the predominant focus of the communications research literature for years. However, as suggested above, mediated communication such as that provided by cell phones, e-mails, and the Internet has risen in importance, and many if not all business firms have moved or are moving to the Internet.

There are both advantages and disadvantages of communicating over the Internet, especially when negotiating or finalizing a business deal. Cellich and Jain (2004) describe some major advantages, including the elimination of time zones and distances, a reduced role of status, minimized gender bias, an increased feeling of personal power among those not skilled at face-to-face interactions, and an expanded audience or customer base. However, they balance this description with some disadvantages of the Internet, including a greater ease of becoming antagonistic and assuming a "take it or leave it" stance when not working face-to-face, greater emphasis on price as the only issue of concern, failure to consult others, obsession with winning at all costs after several rounds of communication, and decreased trust levels. While these disadvantages can be overcome, they frequently are not addressed. Thus while face-to-face communication and mediated communication via the Internet can be functionally equivalent, they frequently are not and can operate in strikingly different ways.

As the world has globalized, the role of global work teams whose members rarely if ever see one another has also become a subject of intense interest. Such teams communicate primarily by phone, e-mails, the Internet, and webcams that allow them to see all team members simultaneously. Jarvenpaa, Knoll, and Leidner (1998; see also Jarvanpaa & Leidner, 1999) have demonstrated that such teams operate as effectively as face-to-face teams provided that their members get to know one another through some initial face-to-face meetings, which creates a situation of "quick trust." However, Cramton's research (2001) on geographically dispersed teams indicates that establishing "quick trust" in geographically distributed teams is very problematic. She identifies five types of problems:

1. Failure to communicate and retain *contextual information*, for example, eye contact and head nods that provide cues as to what the speaker in a face-to-face communication means; information about one another's ethnic and national cultures and more-specific issues such as differing holiday schedules and time differences across time zones, which sometimes results in telephone calls at 3 a.m. to team members who are less than happy to receive them; and information about the problem-solving and decision-making styles characteristic of the ethnic cultures in different locations

2. *Unevenly distributed* information, with some members of the team in one or more locations possessing much more data and background information than members elsewhere

3. Difficulty in understanding and communicating the *salience and importance of information* obtained in one location to members operating outside it

4. Differences in *speed of access* to information in different locations due to differences in the sophistication of the technology available

5. Misinterpreting *silence or failure to respond*, which could signify one of the following at different times: I agree. I strongly disagree. I am indifferent. I am out of town. I am having technical problems. I don't know how to address sensitive issues. I am busy with other things. I did not notice your question. I did not realize that you wanted a response. (Cramton, 2001, p. 359)

Cramton and Hinds (2004) have provided a summary and update of the research literature on geographically distributed teams that builds on Lau and Murnighan's insight (1998) about *fault lines* in groups, which are analogous to fault lines in the earth's crust, predictive of earthquakes. Most of the prior research on groups has emphasized a group's total diversity as a major predictor, if not the major predictor, of group conflict and performance. The more diverse a group becomes, the more probable that conflict will increase and performance or effectiveness will decrease. However, Lau and Murnighan suggest that total diversity is much less important than fault lines. For example, a group consisting of equal numbers of engineers and designers and equal numbers of men and women would possess stronger fault lines if there were equal numbers of engineers and designers of each gender. More specifically, Cramton and Hinds posit that the most likely outcomes of groups with proportionately more cross-cultural and geographically dispersed fault lines will be higher levels of conflict and lower levels of performance. Even more recently, research by Polzer, Crisp, Jarvenpaa, and Kim (2006) has indicated that when fault lines increase, there is heightened conflict and reduced trust.

The most likely outcome of extreme cross-cultural differences and geographic dispersion among groups is *ethnocentrism*, or the assumption that
one's own group is the center of everything and that all other groups are scaled
downwards and unfavorably relative to it. However, ethnocentrism is not the
only outcome, as cross-cultural learning can also occur if there is willingness
and motivation to engage across cultural and geographic differences, to stress
mutual positive distinctiveness, and to share information. As Cramton and
Hinds (2004) state,

> According to the literature concerning the contact hypothesis, mere contact
> between an ingroup and outgroup is not sufficient to reduce ethnocentrism.
> Contact must occur under appropriate conditions. Decades of research have
> produced consensus on these conditions: cooperative interdependence toward
> achievement of a common goal; equal status between the groups; and social or
> institutional support for positive intergroup contact. (p. 247)

Such findings hold, whether the group is face-to-face or geographically
dispersed. In this sense the two types of groups are functionally equivalent.
However, they are quite different from one another in that the complexity
and the range of problematic issues that arise in face-to-face teams pale in
comparison with the turmoil that can erupt in geographically dispersed
teams. Still, cross-cultural differences and geographic dispersion are facts of
life in a globalizing world, and it is critical that both researchers and practitioners give greater attention to these important topics.

Paradox 4.10. Is the Internet integrating the world or creating wide differences?

It is apparent that the use of the Internet has increased dramatically and globally. As a result, it seems logical to argue that the Internet is integrating national
cultures. Thomas Friedman (2005) takes this argument to the extreme in his
world-is-flat formulation, signifying that national governments, business firms,
and individual citizens can communicate with one another directly and easily.
As such, the Internet has helped integrate our global world.

Still, a close reading of the research literature suggests that the Internet is
associated with at least as much differentiation as integration (Wallace,
1999). Individuals with specific needs and preferences tend to communicate
over the Internet. Outside of this narrow or differentiated focus, they have
little if any interest in other groups around the globe. Such specialized groupings can be problematic for the spread of globalization, and they include terrorist groups, those involved in illegal immigration and slavery, and criminal

groups in different nations who can cooperate with one another more easily because of the Internet. The jury is still out on whether integration will swamp differentiation in influence, and it may not be possible to obtain a final answer. It seems that the Internet is both integrating and differentiating cultures simultaneously.

Paradox 4.11. Is colonization or communitarianism winning in the battle for the Internet?

Scientists created the Internet to take advantage of large bodies of data easily and quickly and to communicate more rapidly with one another than was previously possible. Right from its inception, controversy has surrounded the Internet, and the controversy is usually expressed in terms of *colonization* and *communitarianism*. Business firms, quite logically, became interested in the Internet when they began to perceive that money could be made by using it as a vehicle for transacting business matters. They seek to establish their domination or colonization of the Internet by protecting their software programs through the use of patents, creating protected trademarks and advertising taglines that others cannot use, offering a distinctive but generally not a unique service that others would be able to imitate if such protections did not exist, and charging significant fees for such services.

However, as the origin of the Internet suggests, there are many communitarians who would like to minimize the use of such protections and expand the user base by charging minimal service fees, if any at all. The site www .craigslist.com is an outstanding example of such communitarian impulses, and it contains free advertising and information on a variety of topics, such as rentals available in specific areas. Its funding comes from an entrepreneur who is dedicated to the communitarian ideology. Similarly, a number of software developers, such as Linus Torvalds, who spurred the development of the Linux software system through the use of volunteer programmers, are intent on producing programs available to all at a very low and reasonable cost, which runs counter to the idea of colonization.

More recently, the Internet's power has been threatened by the development of comparable rivals. German engineers are in the process of building such a rival, while a Dutch firm has built one to make money. The Chinese now use three suffixes in Chinese characters to substitute for .com and similar venues, which makes their Web sites and e-mail addresses inaccessible to outsiders. Even the 22-nation Arab League has initiated work on a similar system using Arabic suffixes. Thus they have taken the colonization issue to a new level, even to the extent of avoiding the use of the Internet. Part of this movement has occurred in response to the dominance of American firms on the Internet, while some of it is due to the anti-Americanism that has plagued the United States since the invasion of Iraq in 2001 (Rhoads, 2006).

Paradox 4.12. Why is the information superhighway a poor metaphor for describing modern communication systems such as the Internet?

Perhaps the most well-known metaphor for the Internet and other modern communication systems is the information superhighway. This metaphor directly engages the imagination, as it suggests a superefficient and lightning-fast system along which millions of individual pieces of information flow effortlessly. For this reason we speak disparagingly of traditional forms of communication, such as by calling traditional hard-copy mail *snail mail* when comparing it with e-mail. The superhighway metaphor incorporates all the key features of modern communication systems, including the devices employed, the transport of information, the software, the content, and even the governance.

However, while this metaphor is readily accepted in the United States because of the preponderance of superhighways on the landscape, Georgiadou, Puri, and Sahay (2006) found it to be less appealing in Canada, which has far fewer superhighways than the United States does. Also, these authors point out that the metaphor implies extremely high returns on investments; that is, the cost-benefit analysis overwhelmingly favors benefits, which may or may not occur. As an alternative, they introduced the rainbow metaphor as a way of communicating the influence of modern communication systems such as the Internet. The rainbow metaphor also is less threatening than the superhighway metaphor, in which some feel efficiency drives out the human element.

After success using the metaphor of the rainbow in Canada, the authors employed it very successfully in India, where the highway system is substandard. Cars travel, on average, about 30 miles per hour, and all sorts of animals—dogs, cats, elephants, monkeys, cows, and more—regularly slow traffic. To pass another car, a driver must honk the horn, which leads to a cacophony of unpleasant sounds. Indians have difficulty relating to the concept of a superefficient superhighway, and even the term can confuse them, given their experiences. In comparison, all Indians are familiar with the rainbow and view this metaphor very positively, which makes it easy for them to understand and accept modern communication systems presented in this manner.

A metaphor is valuable only to the extent that citizens of a particular nation understand it. Having only one metaphor, such as the information superhighway, can undermine projects, particularly in developing nations, where the experiences of citizens do not include such a highway. Employing a nonthreatening and easily understood metaphor such as the rainbow generates not only acceptance but enthusiasm. Thus, paradoxically, the well-known metaphor of the information superhighway, even when it encompasses all the elements of modern communication systems, is deficient in achieving initial acceptance by the citizens of developing nations.

Takeaways

1. Knowing whether a culture is low context or high context is important for understanding its communication patterns. Still, natives of low-context cultures can use high-context communication in specific situations. Similarly natives of high-context cultures can use low-context communication in specific situations.

2. Neither low-context communication nor high-context communication is superior to the other. Each is effective if employed in appropriate situations.

3. Given that only about 7% of the total impact of a message is based on the words used, and that there are at least eight nonverbal codes, such as time and eye movements, it is generally preferable to withhold judgment in cross-cultural communications until one understands the other culture's communication styles fully or is at least able to base judgments on several types of data, such as one or more of the eight nonverbal codes.

4. Being fluent in the language and understanding the nuances of a new culture are both important, but it generally takes much more time to become fluent than to understand a culture's history, norms, customs, and so forth. At a minimum, a short-term visitor should attempt to learn some basic words and phrases that will simultaneously help put the culture's members at ease and minimize any anxiety the visitor may experience.

5. Every culture possesses some critical words and phrases (such as the Thai phrase *mai pen rai*) that are difficult if not impossible to translate, and understanding the various meanings of such words and phrases helps facilitate the communication process.

6. Knowing a culture's proverbs provides both insight into and understanding of the culture's values and practices.

7. Understanding a culture's symbols and symbolisms facilitates communication across cultures, but sometimes the same phenomenon, such as the bullfight, can evoke both different and changing symbolic meanings.

8. Mediated communication through such vehicles as cell phones and the Internet can facilitate cross-cultural communication, but it can also be a source of difficulty if employed incorrectly.

9. Particularly in developing nations, but also in developed nations, it appears that the rainbow metaphor rather than the metaphor of a superhighway is the best way of communicating the elements and characteristics of modern communication systems such as the Internet.

Discussion Questions

1. How does the definition of culture as communication relate to music?

2. How can a low-context culture be high context, and vice versa?

3. Identify a proverb from your root culture that seems to generate an opposing proverb, for example, "Absence makes the heart grow fonder" and "Out of sight, out of mind."

4. Identify a phenomenon from your root culture that has a different symbolic meaning in another culture. Please describe why.

5. Identify a phenomenon in your root culture that has a changing symbolic meaning. Please describe why.

6. Mediated communication through cell phones, the Internet, or other devices can be beneficial and problematic. Why and how? Please be specific and provide examples from your own experience if possible.

7. When is understanding a culture more important than learning its language, and vice versa?

Exercise (Critical Incident)

In 2001, I was a member of a task force sent to China by the Smith School of Business of the University of Maryland to meet with various Chinese business schools. We were interested in establishing a joint EMBA Program in China and were accompanied by a broker who facilitated the daily business meetings. Every night for a week our broker invited us and the professors at the school visited that day to a sumptuous dinner. One member of our party, however, preferred to eat only at McDonald's. After much coaxing, he agreed to join us on the third day, provided that only vegetables would be served. The broker was very happy to honor this request and indicated that he knew of an excellent restaurant specializing only in vegetables.

The dinner on that third night was, as usual, sumptuous. It did, however, include different types of meat and fish, as well as a variety of vegetables. Near the end of the banquet, one member of our party sitting next to the broker thanked him profusely for the wonderful dinner and then added as an innocent afterthought, "But I thought we were going to have only vegetables." Immediately the broker called the head waiter over to the table and ordered a second banquet consisting only of vegetables, in spite of our spirited objections that all of us were very happy with the dinner and could not eat anything else. Nevertheless, the broker persisted and a second banquet was served. All in our party felt obliged to eat dinner for a second time and did so, even at the cost of personal discomfort.

NOTE: Please reread Exercise 3 in Chapter 1, which describes a similar but independent situation involving Professor Lois Olson of San Diego State University. What are the similarities and differences between Exercise 3 in Chapter 1 and the current exercise? Are there any symbolic meanings attached to any of the actions in these two exercises? Why or why not? If yes, what are the symbolic meanings? Please discuss in small groups and report back to the class.

5

Crossing Cultures

E ffective cross-cultural communication is of obvious importance for successful interactions, both within a culture and across cultures (see Chapter 4). It is, however, only one element that visitors, especially those on assignments of 3 or more months, must consider when crossing cultures. Even visitors who are in the host culture for less than 3 months can benefit significantly from knowledge about crossing cultures. Such knowledge greatly improves the probability of a successful experience, particularly when business must be transacted in a limited time, such as a few days or a week.

In crossing cultures there is, first, the issue of culture shock, which affects some visitors much more than others. *Culture shock* is the natural response that an individual manifests when attempting to react to and control the many new stimuli, perceptions, and feelings a visitor experiences. In extreme form, such shock is similar to what a stressed-out soldier in front-line combat undergoes. There may be so many new and unfamiliar stimuli, experiences, and feelings that the visitor becomes shell-shocked, even to the point of rarely venturing out of a "safe" apartment for a year or more before returning to the home culture. Fortunately, this occurs only rarely.

Frequently the spouse accompanying the expatriate, or expat, manager suffers more from culture shock than does the manager, who is immediately engaged in the culture through full-time work. Some spouses give up attractive positions in their home cultures to accompany the expat and cannot find comparable work, or any at all, in the host culture; other spouses devote so much time to the expat and their children, who are also actively involved in the host culture through school, that they begin to feel isolated. It is important to take the needs of spouses and children into consideration, as the expat can easily experience more difficulty at home than at work if other family members are unhappy. In turn, performance at work may suffer.

However, most of us become relatively well adjusted to the host culture after approximately 6 months. We tend to follow a U-shaped pattern in responding to culture shock: During the initial period we experience an elevated and positive mood, which becomes negative and declines after a few weeks, reaching a low point between the fourth and fifth month and then gradually rising and leveling off after 6 months, but at a lower point than at the start of the visit (Gullahorn & Gullahorn, 1963). In some instances a person may undergo a second bout of culture shock, especially if the individual avoids contact with the host culture.

The focus in this chapter is on four issues directly related to culture shock. In the first two sections we examine the paradoxes associated with culture-based ethical systems, although arguably this term is an oxymoron: Cultural experiences and judgments tend to lead to the creation of ethical systems. Even when we are fluent in the language, surprises tend to occur because of conflict between the ethical systems of the visitor's home culture and host culture. Next, we examine the specific paradoxes that a long-term visitor or expat manager confronts. Then we look at both a three-stage model and a four-stage model for understanding the host culture. In the final section we look at the issue of reverse culture shock that visitors, particularly expat managers, experience when returning to the home culture.

Culture-Based Ethics: Relativism and Universalism

Paradox 5.1. Are ethical norms and standards universal or relative to the situation?

The word *ethics* stems from the Greek *ethos*, which relates specifically to the character and sentiment of the community. *Ethical behavior* refers to the degree to which individuals conform to these norms and standards. Any group can develop, either implicitly or explicitly, a statement or list of its norms and standards, and its members will tend to label behavior as either ethical or unethical in terms of them. Ethics can be in conflict with the legal system, as the sentiment of the community may be at variance with it.

Ethics may even differ from what most of us would view as acceptable and moral behavior. Jared Diamond (1997) describes a natural experiment involving the Maori and Morriori, close ethnic cousins who had been geographically separated for centuries. The Morriori were peaceful hunter-gatherers living in the Chatham Islands, 500 miles east of New Zealand. The Maori were farmers living on the densely populated North Island of New Zealand. On

November 19, 1835, the Maori arrived on the Chatham Islands armed to the teeth and demanded that the peace-loving and consensus-seeking Moriori become their slaves. Ironically, the Moriori outnumbered the Maori two to one and could have won any fight with the Maori, but their peace-loving and consensus-seeking ethics called for an offer of friendship, peace, and a division of resources. Before they could deliver the offer, however, the Maoris attacked and handily manhandled the surprised and disorganized Moriori. Resistance met with extreme brutality, including the deaths of hundreds of Moriori, cannibalism, enslavement of the remnants, and the random and whimsical killing of the slaves over the next few years. Clearly the ethical systems as well as the moral systems of the Moriori and the Maori were sharply different.

One of the well-known paradoxes that many visitors experience is that between universal and relative or particularistic ethical standards. Especially in individualistic cultures, there is a tendency toward widespread acceptance of *universal ethical standards* that apply to all, although there are exceptions. Most of us would oppose murder, cannibalism, deliberate corporate theft, and so forth. Collectivistic cultures tend to emphasize *relative standards*: What is ethical in one situation may be unethical in another situation, but again there can be exceptions.

Trompenaars and Hampden-Turner (1998) present a striking illustration of this difference between universal and relative standards. They asked more than 15,000 managers in 31 nations to respond to the following critical incident: You are riding in an automobile driven by a close friend, and your friend hits a pedestrian. The maximum allowed speed was 20 mph, and your friend was driving at 35 mph. Other than you, there are no witnesses. Your friend's lawyer says that if you testify under oath that the car was traveling at 20 mph, your friend may avoid serious consequences. First, does your friend have (a) a definite right, (b) some right, or (c) no right to expect you to protect him? Second, what would you do: (d) testify as requested or (e) refuse to testify as requested? Before reading further, you are invited to provide personal answers.

Trompenaars and Hampden-Turner posited that if a manager answered b plus e or c plus e, the manager was considered to possess a universal ethic. The overall results are striking, as illustrated by the following percentages for those nations with the most extreme scores at each end of the continuum of 31 nations: Venezuela, 32; Nepal, 36; South Korea, 37; Russia, 44; China, 47; Switzerland, 97; United States, 93; Canada and Ireland, 92; and Sweden and Australia, 91. The collectivistic and individualistic cultures clearly diverge from one another in terms of their responses.

One reasonable explanation for such divergence is that citizens in some collectivistic nations do not trust the honesty and objectivity of their institutions, including the legal system. In this instance individuals place their trust in well-established relationships, family networks, and kinship groups, as occurred in southern Italy at the time the Mafia originated (see Paradox 2.14). Southern Italy is more collectivistic than the north and accords situational ethical considerations higher priority than universal ones, in large part because the institutions, including the legal system, have a long-standing reputation for corruption. The Mafia became a broker for, and protector of, the average citizen who was attempting to work within the institutional frameworks of the legal system, educational system, and so on.

As globalization proceeds, the movement toward individualism and universal standards seems to be intensifying, although there is a countermovement, as events in such nations as Russia and Colombia suggest. It is very difficult to transact global business in an environment in which situational standards dominate: One party may terminate a contract unilaterally without being penalized, there is widespread acceptance of outrageous bribes, both citizens and visitors openly disregard patents and copyrights, and counterfeit products are sold openly. Mexico, in fact, had to develop a new legal system parallel to its traditional legal system to meet the demands of foreign investors who insisted on universal standards.

A few years ago I visited the area in Beijing around the American embassy where merchants would blatantly disregard patents and copyrights, selling pirated and counterfeit products such as computers and musical instruments at very low cost. My host repeated a refrain that I had heard many times when visiting developing nations: The United States is a very prosperous country, and we are a poor country trying to become better off; such matters as counterfeit goods are of little consequence to the United States. However, developed nations, including the United States, voice the opposite sentiment. Because of intense pressure from the World Trade Organization, the Chinese government closed down this area. We can expect many similar actions in the future among national governments seeking to be a part of the globalized trading system.

There is also a related movement among business ethicists toward universal standards that apply globally. Donaldson (1989) argued that all cultures should respect 10 fundamental rights, including the rights to ownership of property and to a fair trial and freedom from torture. Donaldson also created a method called an *ethical algorithm* to facilitate ethical decision making among firms doing business globally, particularly when what is allowed in the host nation is outlawed in the home nation. This algorithm consists of two rules, the first of which is that if the difference is based *solely* on economic conditions, the practice is permissible *only if* the members of the home national culture, under similar economic circumstances, would regard the practice as legal and permissible. Some host cultures are developing nations with such a great need for food that they condone the use of risky and dangerous pesticides outlawed in the home culture, and under such circumstances

Donaldson would approve of a global firm selling these pesticides outside the United States. Donaldson's second rule is that if the conflict between the laws of the home culture and the host culture is not based on economic differences, a practice will be permissible *only if* it (a) is required to conduct business successfully in the host culture and (b) does not violate a fundamental international right.

Donaldson and Dunfee (1994, 1999) have expanded on these ideas in their *integrative social contracts theory*, which revolves around the concept of *hypernorms*. These are fundamental universal principles that become higher-order norms by which lower-order norms are judged. Hypernorms include fundamental human rights or basic prescriptions common to most major religions. Donaldson and Dunfee encourage managers to think in terms of hypernorms when making a business decision, even if the decision-making process needs to be extended.

However, a culture's history, in terms of its trials and tribulations, its geographical location, and its resources, appears to influence whether universal or relative standards prevail (Carroll & Gannon, 1997). China serves as an excellent example of a nation that developed relative ethical standards because of these factors (Fang, 1999). In this nation's 5,000-year history, invaders have been such a major and constant threat that the famous Great Wall of China was erected to keep them at bay. Periodically China also experienced civil war, including two in the 20th century. As a result of the most recent civil war, Mao Tse-tung put the nation through a wrenching and startling period (1949–1976) unique in history, during which he concocted wild schemes that resulted in the deaths of millions of Chinese.

One such scheme was the widespread seizure of woks from the peasants, who had relied on this one valuable household item for centuries to cook food. Mao strove to move China from an agricultural base to a technological base, and so the centuries-old woks were melted down to provide raw material for pitiable "steel mills" that unfortunately did not work. Without the woks the peasants were unable to cook their meager rations, and many died as a result (Lou, 2005). Similarly Mao wanted to get rid of all sparrows, which he regarded as unhealthy. On an appointed day everyone in the nation clanged pots and pans to keep the birds disoriented and flying until they dropped to their deaths. This effort was very successful. Unfortunately, the sparrows served a major function of eating bugs, which, uncontrolled, created an outbreak of widespread and deadly diseases.

Mao even attacked the core of the Chinese culture by separating family members geographically into different communes, encouraging children to spy on their parents, and publicly humiliating selected parents, teachers, professors, and professionals. Also, he believed that "to learn to swim, one only needs to jump in the water" and, analogously, anyone could be a professional such as a doctor or lawyer with minimal amounts of training. In one celebrated instance a professional woman was jailed, during which time she developed a very serious stomach ulcer, but an 18-year-old "doctor" diagnosed it as a heart problem requiring an operation; she lived in prison for several years with the untreated ulcer rather than submit to such an unnecessary and dangerous operation (Cheng, 1982). Given such a tumultuous history, it is understandable why the Chinese developed relative norms and came to rely on family members and kinship groups—a phenomenon captured by the Chinese term *guanxi*—rather than on the legal system.

There is, then, an ongoing tension between cultures espousing universal ethical standards and those espousing relative ones. This tension is not likely to go away in the foreseeable future, but the trend seems to be toward globalized business activities in which individualism and the rule of universal principles predominate. For instance, major Chinese companies that want to operate multinationally in numerous nations are now abiding not only by the dictates of the World Trade Organization but also by each and every contract they sign, thus minimizing the impact of *guanxi*. There are, however, exceptions to this trend; for instance, the Russian government has seized private firms, and the culture is struggling with rampant corruption, disease, pollution, poor health facilities, and a decrease in life expectancy. As globalization strengthens, we can expect that the spread of universal norms will increase, although slowly and arduously, and that there will most probably be exceptions such as Russia.

Generic Cultures and Ethics

In this section we return to the four generic types of cultures developed independently by Harry Triandis and Alan Fiske (see pages 22–23): community sharing, authority ranking, equality matching (egalitarian), and market pricing. There are some minor differences between these formulations, but for our purposes they can be treated as equivalent, and there is ample documentation supporting the typology (see Haslam, 2004; Triandis & Gelfand, 1998).

> ### Paradox 5.2. Are there universal ethics across generic cultures, or do ethics vary by generic culture?

As in previous chapters, we invite you to select one of the four choices for the two items below, which Gelfand and Holcombe (1998) included in their instrument measuring these four generic types:

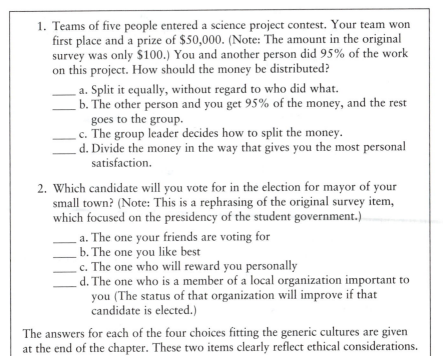

1. Teams of five people entered a science project contest. Your team won first place and a prize of $50,000. (Note: The amount in the original survey was only $100.) You and another person did 95% of the work on this project. How should the money be distributed?

_____ a. Split it equally, without regard to who did what.
_____ b. The other person and you get 95% of the money, and the rest goes to the group.
_____ c. The group leader decides how to split the money.
_____ d. Divide the money in the way that gives you the most personal satisfaction.

2. Which candidate will you vote for in the election for mayor of your small town? (Note: This is a rephrasing of the original survey item, which focused on the presidency of the student government.)

_____ a. The one your friends are voting for
_____ b. The one you like best
_____ c. The one who will reward you personally
_____ d. The one who is a member of a local organization important to you (The status of that organization will improve if that candidate is elected.)

The answers for each of the four choices fitting the generic cultures are given at the end of the chapter. These two items clearly reflect ethical considerations.

Fiske (1991a; see also Fiske, 1991b), in particular, effectively relates the four generic cultures to the four types of statistical scales: nominal, ordinal, interval, and ratio. His argument is that individuals have difficulty making decisions because the demands of daily life require them constantly to evaluate situations and reach conclusions, frequently very quickly. Individuals use these four scales as rough approximations for determining how to interact with others. Thus community sharing represents *nominal scaling*, as names are given *only* to entities, such as African Americans and white, Anglo-Saxon Americans. Under such conditions there is one set of norms for in-group members and another set for out-group members. In-group members may openly share resources, leave their doors unlocked, welcome in-group visitors even when they have not given advance notice, and so forth. However, they may well condone unfair treatment of the out-group members, including charging them more for products, restricting them to dangerous parts of any geographical area, treating them as second-class citizens, and even forcing them into slavery, as happened with the Moriori and the Maori.

In an authority-ranking culture, individual A may be more important than B, and B is more important than C, but there is no common unit of measurement, for example, a unit of 1 between successive points on the scale. The scale is *ordinal* in nature. Hence we cannot say that A is twice as important as C. But it is clear that those in higher-status positions are treated deferentially and receive a disproportionate share of the community's resources and rewards. Nations such as Japan and Korea fit into this generic category.

In equality-matching or egalitarian situations, the culture has a common unit of measurement, but its members do not make value judgments about individual worth. There are too many dimensions along which people can be measured, and there is no true zero point allowing one dimension to be compared directly to another. In this sense the scaling is *interval*, as happens in the Scandinavian nations. Finally, in market pricing, there is a common unit of measurement and a true zero point (zero money), which allows members of the culture to transform all dimensions and compare them monetarily. In this case the scaling is *ratio*. The principle of pay for performance, especially the rank ordering of managers and employees, represents such scaling and logic, as our discussion of GE indicates (see Chapter 3).

Fiske provides an insightful example of these four types of culture in his discussion of a small town's decision about the purchase of an expensive fire truck. The issue becomes, who should receive the new fire protection? The choices are the following: (a) Only those in the community receive equal protection, and out-group members remain unprotected; (b) all members of the in-group (those who contributed to the purchase) receive protection, but the leaders and other high-status people receive more attention and monitoring of their homes, and out-group members are excluded; (c) everyone in the city and those living close to it should be protected; and (d) only those who contributed to the truck's purchase should be protected. You may want to stop at this point to make a personal choice.

Here are the answers: (a) community sharing, (b) authority ranking, (c) equality matching, and (d) market pricing. This example is not far-fetched. In the United States there have been several recorded instances of fire trucks that did not respond, sometimes because a home was just outside the fire department's district and sometimes because the owners of the homes had not contributed monetarily to the fire department's upkeep.

The visitor to a host culture frequently can ascertain whether it tends toward one of these four generic types. There are variations within each type; for example, some authority-ranking cultures may become more individualistic as globalization proceeds, and some adhere more closely to democracy or at least the electoral process than others do. However, such cultural changes are much slower than economic changes.

The perceptive reader has probably noticed that there is tension between Paradoxes 5.1 and 5.2. Since ethical systems are culturally based, and since there are four generic cultures, any ethical system would need to fit into one of them. There is, however, a trend to go beyond the nation-state, incorporated in the concept of a world or global culture and allegiance of citizens to it, in which case there would be no such phenomenon as generic cultures. Euro-Watch regularly conducts surveys in Europe that indicate a growing and close identification among citizens of some European nations with the European Union. As the European Union grows in strength and maturity, the intensity of this identification will probably grow (see Chapter 10). Eventually what is happening in the European Union may generalize beyond it into a movement toward a world or global culture.

As this and the previous section demonstrate, ethics are culture based and cannot be imposed on a community, although it is possible to impose a perceived unfair law at variance with community sentiment. Knowing a culture's generic type can facilitate and enhance our understanding of its ethical system. In turn, we increase our probability of successfully traversing a host culture by avoiding areas where there will be open conflict between the ethical systems of the host and home cultures.

Expatriate Paradoxes

There is a well-developed literature on expat managers that analyzes their experiences in several ways, such as the types of training and education they should receive for their sojourn in the host nation, the personal characteristics predictive of success in the host culture, such as being flexible and open to new experiences, and the problems they face when reentering the home culture (see Bird & Osland, 2006; Mendenhall, Kuhlman, Stahl, & Osland, 2002). More specifically, Joyce and Asbjorn Osland (2006; see also Osland, 1995) have completed an intensive and interview-based empirical analysis identifying nine paradoxes that expat managers face. The Oslands have also identified four independent areas or dimensions into which their nine paradoxes fall: cultural intelligence, mediation, self-identity, and cautious optimism. This chapter's discussion of the nine paradoxes, which I have shortened and paraphrased, follows the lines of this classification.

It is noteworthy that the Oslands (2006) correlated several measures of involvement in the host culture both at work and in interactions with others outside work and demonstrated that as involvement increased, so did the expats' awareness of paradoxes. Increasing awareness of paradoxes, then, can be viewed as a very positive rather than a negative development. Awareness of each of the nine paradoxes among the expats ranged from 46% to 77%.

Paradox 5.3. Is the general stereotype of the host culture valid?

The Oslands begin with a discussion of cultural intelligence, or the social acuity necessary to decode behavior in the host culture and respond flexibly. Although they oppose universal stereotypes that allow for no exceptions, they show that expats see as valid the general stereotype of the host culture but also realize that many host-culture nationals do not fit the stereotype. There are numerous exceptions, and the more involved in the host culture one is, the easier it is to identify them. Similarly, as globalization brings us closer together, these exceptions will increase in number. The largest percentage of the expats, 77.1%, were aware of this paradox.

Paradox 5.4. How can the expat manager be simultaneously powerful and powerless?

Expatriate managers are typically very powerful, as they have the force of the home office behind them. They are in a position of authority and are expected to accomplish goals using it. However, they soon discover that they need to operate within the framework of the host culture in many instances. Since the locals have cultural knowledge and contacts, the expats are dependent on them, which is a form of powerlessness. If the host culture emphasizes participative decision making that slows down processes and activities, the expat must adjust to the situation in order to accomplish long-term goals. One U.S. expat manager working in Britain failed to honor the slower process. He belatedly and at great cost discovered that the statement of a top British manager about being 99% in support of a proposed major organizational change actually represented a message of extreme disapproval to all at a companywide meeting. In the Oslands' study 68.6% of the expats described this paradox as important in their lives, both at and outside work.

Paradox 5.5. How can the expat manager be simultaneously free of home-country norms and restrained by host-country norms?

Mediation is the area or category into which three of the paradoxes (5, 6, and 7) fall. It represents the mediation that the expat must emphasize when trying to resolve issues involving the home office and the local subsidiary and the markets in which it operates, as well as the differing perspectives of the home and host cultures.

One of the most exhilarating experiences is the freedom from home-country norms that require the expat to behave in a very predictable manner in the United States. In fact, the home office frequently requires only periodic reports of progress and achievements, as superiors have great difficulty monitoring an expat closely. Simultaneously expats tend to enjoy the freedom to respond to new situations differently from the way they would in the United States. There are permanent expats who grow to love this style of life outside the United States so much that they deliberately try to avoid a reassignment to the home office, sometimes marry a host-country national, and settle in the host nation for several years if not permanently.

Simultaneously, however, the expat must conform to the norms and expectations of the host culture for full acceptance, both at home and at work. In authority-ranking cultures the expat is expected to act as the distant superior, demanding special treatment but sensitive to the needs of all.

Joyce Osland (1995) described an amusing situation in this area of mediation encountered in various forms by many visitors. Both Asbjorn and she were in the Peace Corps working in Colombia, during which time her position involved traveling periodically in the organization's jeep. Although she would reserve the use of the jeep days in advance, the driver on the appointed day would inform her that "someone else" had been granted its use, and apparently that meant everyone in the organization other than this lowly Peace Corps volunteer. When Asbjorn left the Peace Corps and became the local director of a development agency, the largest employer in town, the issue disappeared. Suddenly he was "*Don* Asbjorn, *el patron*" and she was "*Doña* Joyce," even though she continued working for the Peace Corps. She went from "fighting for a chauffeur to fighting off obsequious chauffeurs who were more than willing to make other employees wait if the boss's wife needed a car" (p. 105).

However, Joyce was expected to behave in terms of the cultural dictates of authority-ranking cultures, and she admits—as many who have experienced this phenomenon do also—that there was a specific psychological enjoyment and prestige in doing so. One expat claimed that he was unable to readjust to the U.S. environment on reentry simply because he had grown accustomed to others' handling his daily routine, including preparing meals, taking care of all household tasks, and being available at all hours of the day and night. Nearly 63% of the expats touched on this paradox in their interviews.

Paradox 5.6. How can the expat manager simultaneously accept the ideal cultural values of the home culture and realize that they do not exist in the home culture or exist only in attenuated form?

The second mediation paradox represents the tension between the ideal and actual values of the home culture. The United States prides itself on supporting a level playing field in all realms, including hiring, treatment of customers, and employee promotion. However, even in the United States, there are numerous situations in which such ideals do not equate with actual practices.

Still, when abroad, the expat is representative of the ideal that is portrayed in American films, television, and books and articles. Moreover, the expat realizes that this is the general stereotype of the United States. As such, the expat attempts to act out the home-country values as much as possible, although there are clearly tensions between many of these values and those in the host culture. Expats feel pressure to act as good ambassadors of their country and to demonstrate the home-country values, even though they realize those values are not always followed at home. For example, in an authority-ranking culture, nepotism and favoritism based on various criteria not related to actual performance dominate actions in organizations to a far greater extent than they do in the United States. When expats want to hire someone competent rather than someone with connections, they may experience great difficulty. They realize their performance at home is being judged in terms of goal accomplishment; they also realize nepotism occurs in some situations in the United States. Also, they need to satisfy others in the subsidiary who expect the expats to play favorites and hire the candidate with prestigious connections. In the Osland survey (2006), 54.3% of the expats identified this paradox in their work and life abroad.

Paradox 5.7. How can the expat manager resolve the conflict between contradictory demands of the home office and the host-culture subsidiary?

The final mediation paradox focuses on the tension created by the contradictory demands of the home office on the one hand and the host-culture nationals and situation on the other. For example, the expat's headquarters superior in the home culture may demand that the work be completed in a way that tramples on the values and expectations of host-culture nationals. Acting in such a manner creates tension for the expat, who is trying to act out the ideals of fairness of the home culture but still meet the wishes of his home-culture superior. This paradox frequently revolves around the time allotted for the completion of goals. The home office in the United States, following the cultural norm of specific sequencing of activities and the times allotted to each, tends to demand the completion of goals in a short and constricted time frame. However, this is frequently not feasible and in many cases not possible, given the resources available in the subsidiary, the laws and regulations of the host culture, and the cultural bias toward a longer time frame than that preferred by the home office.

Sometimes the expat will closely follow the dictates of the home office and demand the completion of specific tasks and goals, only to realize subsequently that the resulting work is substandard because of differing cultural expectations about which tasks are most important. Moreover, the expat may realize that it is not feasible to make such demands if long-term goals are to be achieved. Of the expats surveyed, 51.4% identified this paradox as problematic in their work.

Paradox 5.8. How can the expat manager simultaneously give up some home-country values and strengthen other home-country values?

The next two paradoxes fall into the category of self-identity, or the willingness of the expats to open themselves to new experiences and the risk of being changed in the process.

It is a truism that visitors to a host culture learn as much about the home-country values as they do about the host-country values, and many times much more. Admittedly, the visitor gains a tremendous amount of knowledge about the host culture in a short time simply out of necessity if not interest. However, just as important, expats develop great insight into home-country values and the unconscious or semiconscious manner in which they have accepted those values until the exposure to the host culture.

As a result of this dynamic, it is not unusual for the expat to give up some home-country values. A few expats take this dynamic to the extreme, giving up all home-country values and practices. They convert to the host-culture's religion, immerse themselves completely in the host culture, and wear the distinctive clothing of the host culture. However, the normal pattern is for expats to give up some noncore values of the home culture while strengthening core values to gain acceptance or to be effective. For instance, they may become less extroverted and informal while coming to believe even more fervently in the emphasis on a level playing field in the hiring and promotion of subordinates. Laurent (2002) touches on this paradox when he shows that expats tend to become more identified with the home culture after being sent abroad than prior to departure. Among the expats surveyed, 60% talked about this paradox in their interviews.

Paradox 5.9. Is it possible for the expat manager to become more cosmopolitan and more idiosyncratic simultaneously?

Visitors to the host culture inevitably become more cosmopolitan simply because of the exposure to the many new stimuli and experiences. Paradox 5.8 reflects this change, as the expat tends to shed some noncore values but strengthens core values. Even cultural practices not related directly to values, such as preferences in food, tend to change. One expat in Thailand initially could not eat the delicious but hot Thai food yet came to love it over time. On his return to the United States, he complained frequently about the dullness of the U.S. cuisine and constantly sought out exotic restaurants that he had studiously avoided before departure.

Expats also become more accepting of the norms and values of the host culture. They begin to understand that a "yes" may mean "no" or "maybe" in different situations, and they act accordingly. While they may have been demanding and impatient in their home cultures, they become less so, not only because such practices are unsuccessful in the host culture but because of the expats' newfound acceptance of such values as "we work to live" rather than "we live to work."

Simultaneously, however, expats begin to become more idiosyncratic, taking into account the local beliefs but putting together their own value systems and their own "take" on the world. They adapt and integrate values and practices from other cultures to create a more authentic self. Frequently they change their perspective from making immediate judgments and evaluations to taking a more thoughtful approach consistent with host-culture values. In all, 48.6% of the expats talked about this paradox of contrasting cosmopolitan and idiosyncratic orientations in their interviews and described it as the most significant paradox.

Paradox 5.10. How can the expat manager simultaneously think well of the host culture and avoid being taken advantage of?

Our final two expat paradoxes fall into the category of cautious optimism. We tend to think well of the host culture if we become culturally involved at work and outside work, as the Oslands demonstrated. Positive regard for the host-country nationals is a key aspect of intercultural effectiveness. However, the typical person does not want to be taken advantage of, regardless of the culture involved. A common experience among visitors is being outrageously overcharged by taxicab drivers, which also happens in the home culture. However, many people from the United States and similar cultures tend to be accustomed to fixed and fair prices and do not like to bargain, even with taxicab drivers. Over time the U.S. expats learn that they can save a good amount of money doing so, as they are frequently charged 5–10 times what is expected in the host culture. The act of bargaining indicates to the representatives of the host culture that you are indeed becoming knowledgeable about the local culture, which increases their respect for you.

However, bargaining with a taxicab driver is a minor concern compared with the demand for a major bribe. This is the most common issue confronting expat managers when dealing with host-culture nationals (see Robertson, 2002). One senior executive of a U.S. company seeking to operate in Russia after the acceptance of capitalism after 1990 reported that at the initial formal dinner with top government officials, several of them openly and blatantly solicited major bribes. U.S. managers are required by law to adhere to strict guidelines in the area of small gifts, which are allowed, and major bribes, which are not. The acceptance of major bribes has led to lengthy jail sentences for some U.S. expats. They frequently develop alternative approaches to avoid such activities while keeping in the good graces of the host culture. The issue of bribes is irksome to many expats, as they must compete for business with European and Asian multinationals, who are legally free to offer major bribes, thus putting U.S. companies at a perceived disadvantage. As many as 54.6% focused on this issue in their interviews.

Paradox 5.11. How can the expat manager be simultaneously at home anywhere in the world and fit comfortably nowhere?

A common experience among expats is the feeling of being at home anywhere in the world yet not being completely comfortable anywhere. Also, as indicated previously, some expats grow so comfortable in the host culture that they remain as permanent residents for the rest of their lives, even though they are never completely accepted in the host culture. Furthermore, some expats become uneasy when they return to their home cultures periodically and calm down only when they come back to the host culture, even when the fit is not perfect.

Other expats move about the world every few years, sometimes changing not only geographic locations but also their employers. These cosmopolitan expats tend to become extremely knowledgeable and worldly wise. They reach a point at which returning to the home culture permanently is not preferable to the style of life to which they have become accustomed. Some of them continue to move about the world constantly or every few years for their entire careers.

Global firms tend to require 5–10 years' experience outside of the home culture for those competing for senior and top management positions. The globalized world has become borderless in many ways, and firms are representative not only of their own home cultures but also of the global culture in which they operate. It may happen, however, that the expat will feel at home anywhere but fit in nowhere, and this can be problematic for those seeking a greater sense of stability and community. Of the expats surveyed, 45.7% discussed this issue during their interviews.

Expats probably experience additional paradoxes, but the Oslands have made a major contribution to the study of this issue. They have also provided us with a classification system with four independent categories or dimensions into which these nine paradoxes fall. In doing so, the Oslands have enlarged our understanding of the dynamics of the visitor's life in a host culture.

Understanding Cross-Cultural Interactions via Cultural Sensemaking

As our discussion suggests, it is very helpful to understand the ethical system of the host culture and the paradoxes that the visitor is likely to experience. When the visitor possesses a model through which these and related phenomena can be assessed, the entire process of crossing cultures is enriched significantly. Joyce Osland and Allan Bird (2000; see also Bird & Osland, 2006) have developed a three-stage model for understanding cross-cultural interactions, particularly communications, that helps facilitate the process of crossing cultures. This model is based on the work of Karl Weick (1995) and has three stages: framing the situation, making attributions, and selecting a script.

Humans tend to frame, or structure, situations in many ways. For example, a conservative politician who argues for tax relief is suggesting that decreasing taxes will stimulate the economy, as purportedly those with higher incomes will be more motivated to invest in the economy. This is a far cry from left-leaning activists seeking the imposition of new taxes on the rich to help the poor; their rhetoric would not include the concept of tax relief but would stress responsibility to others in society, particularly the poor and the disadvantaged. Similarly, patients are more accepting of the necessity of a major operation if the doctor says "the success rate is 70%" rather than "the failure rate, including death, is 30%."

Given the constant and incessant need to make sense of the many stimuli and experiences to which we are exposed, humans tend to employ cognitive structures or schemas to interpret them, and these structures in turn elicit behavioral responses or scripts. When someone frames the situation correctly and employs appropriate schemas that have worked in the past, there is no problem. However, when the stimuli and experiences are unfamiliar, as happens in cross-cultural interactions, it is more difficult to employ time-tested schemas. It should be realized, of course, that the same problem can occur within one culture, as humans are prone to make errors.

The second stage of the model involves making attributions about the stimuli and behaviors but withholding judgment; the focus is on the particular people involved as evaluated in terms of their social identities and histories. To make such attributions, the individual should analyze the profile of a nation's culture in terms of such dimensions as individualism, power distance, and so forth; identify whether the other party is using a particular communication style, such as high context and indirect; and engage in sophisticated stereotyping by examining the cultural metaphors that serve as a shortcut for understanding a culture's values and practices (see Gannon, 2004). Finally, the individual should select a script that seems appropriate for the situation, modifying it as soon as new information becomes available.

As this discussion suggests, Bird and Osland (2006) believe that cross-cultural sensemaking is normally much more difficult than monocultural sensemaking. They also argue for sequencing, that is, framing the situation and making attributions before selecting a script and making a decision.

Similarly, Gannon (2004) has developed a four-stage model of cross-cultural understanding that complements the Osland and Bird model. In the first stage, the visitor must identify the degree to which process, or getting to know the other party personally, must be emphasized before goals and specific business items can be discussed. During this stage it is useful to identify the degree to which emotions and feelings can be expressed openly. During the second stage, the four generic types of culture provide the platform for framing the situation. Then in the third stage it is helpful to employ the various dimensions of national cultures that Hofstede and others have identified. Cultural metaphors are employed in the fourth stage to obtain a rich understanding of the host culture.

There are related models and approaches that a lack of space precludes us from examining (see, for example, Gesteland, 1999). Quite possibly and even probably, the visitor will temporarily forget about a specific model when actually interacting in the host culture. It is not necessary to know every detail of each model, but accepting their utility helps us have a detached and objective perspective for analyzing cross-cultural dynamics. Further, our brief discussion suggests some commonalities in such models. First, it is very useful to understand some cross-cultural concepts, such as the ones described in this book, before analysis and mistakes created by ignorance occur. Sequencing is also explicit in such models, and the visitor should defer evaluative judgments until a sufficient amount of independent data is available. In sum, suffice it to say that the use of such models should help enhance the cross-cultural interactions, the communications that take place, and the probability of success. Without them, the visitor must frame understanding in terms of schemas that may work well in the home culture but are of questionable value in the host culture.

Reentry Into the Home Culture

While some visitors and expats never return to the home culture, most of them do. Most of them come back as changed people, having become more cosmopolitan. They uniformly report that their experiences have been very positive in terms of attitudinal changes, improved work skills, and increased knowledge. Through the cross-cultural process they have given up some values that they once accepted completely and have simultaneously strengthened their core values. Most are eager to talk about their experiences, the people they have met at work and elsewhere, and new ideas their firms should consider implementing. It frequently comes as a surprise that others are not enthusiastic about these experiences (presumably because the others cannot identify with the expats' experiences and possibly because they view the expatriate experience as a boondoggle).

More seriously, expats sometimes return to a position of lower or changed authority, as they probably had to give up their positions in the home office in exchange for the assignment abroad. They can experience a sense of frustration if their superiors greet their newfound ideas critically and unfavorably. In extreme cases the expat will leave the firm because of a growing sense of dissatisfaction. Studies during the 1970s suggested that 9 of 10 expats performed less effectively after reentry than before the departure to the host culture. Today, because of better preparation and cross-cultural education, this figure is now only about 3 out of 10. Still, even this lower figure suggests that the expat experience is less than ideal in terms of some specific consequences, at least in some instances.

And it is not only the expat who may suffer. The spouse and children tend to go through a similar process of cultural reacclimatization. This, in turn, can have a negative effect on the expat, both at home and at work.

Gradually, however, the former expat adjusts to the environment in most instances, both at home and at work. Expats on reentry suffer from a reverse culture shock that parallels the stages of culture shock described in the opening paragraphs of this chapter, although typically with less severity because of their familiarity with the home culture. In the long run, if the individual continues to be flexible and open, it is highly probable that the expat experience will prove very beneficial. This is especially true in global firms that are demanding 5–10 years' international experience of applicants for senior-level positions. Still, while the advantages clearly outweigh the disadvantages, the expat experience does have its downside, even when reentering the home culture.

Takeaways

1. Visitors should expect to experience both culture shock in the host culture and reverse culture shock on reentry to the home culture.

2. Ethical standards are by definition based on culture or the sense of a community, whether it is a firm, a volunteer organization, or a generic culture. Such standards reflect the values and practices of the four generic types of cultures and can be universal or relative to the situation.

3. Donaldson's *ethical algorithm* is a technique that managers can employ to solve specific ethical dilemmas when completing business activities in host cultures (see pp. 102–103).

4. Ethical standards differ from legal standards and even moral standards. What is perceived as immoral in one culture, such as cannibalism and bribery, may be seen as moral in another culture. Similarly laws can be at variance with ethical standards and perceived as unfair or irrelevant by a community or culture.

5. Expats confront many paradoxes when working in the host culture, including feeling powerless and powerful, giving up some values and strengthening core values, and being at home everywhere but fitting in nowhere.

6. Awareness of such paradoxes is related to several measures of cultural involvement, both at work and away from it. As such, experiencing paradoxes is a very positive experience leading to increased insight and maturation. That is, being involved in the host culture helps broaden the perspective and understanding of the expat.

7. Understanding a host culture is most effectively completed in stages and requires the suspension of judgment until the expat has a sufficient amount of data to frame the situation correctly and act accordingly.

Discussion Questions

1. Since ethical standards are an expression of a specific culture's expectations, is it possible to have ethical standards that apply to all cultures around the globe? Why or why not?

2. Describe some examples, from either your personal experience or other sources, of relative or particularistic ethical standards. Can there be conflicting ethical standards within one culture? Why or why not?

3. Define and differentiate ethical standards, moral standards, and legal standards. Is it possible for these three types of standards to be completely separate from one another? Why or why not?

4. This chapter describes two models for understanding cultures when we cross them. What are three commonalities or conclusions that can be derived from these models?

5. Does crossing cultures involve only cross-cultural communication? Why or why not?

6. What is culture shock? Does reverse culture shock operate in the same fashion as culture shock? Why or why not? Who seems to suffer the most from culture shock, the expat or the spouse? Why?

7. How does the distinction between universal and relative ethical standards relate to the four types of generic cultures? Which of the types reflect the use of relative standards and universal standards? Please explain.

8. What is the difference between a small bribe and a major bribe? Is this distinction important? Why or why not?

Exercises

1. Each member of the class should visit the Web site of a major company, where the firm's codes of ethical conduct are normally outlined. In small groups of five persons each, discuss the ethical standards of five companies. Points to consider are (a) whether the behavior of these companies follows their codes of ethics and, if not, why not; and (b) the commonalities and differences in the five codes. One person from each group should report the results to the class, followed by questions and discussion.

2. Each person in the class should interview a manager from the United States who has either worked abroad as an expat or been intensely involved in cross-cultural business activities in one or more nations. Using the cultural metaphors in Gannon (2004) and other sources, the interviewer should construct a series of questions asking for comparisons between doing business in

the United States and doing business in a country where the manager has worked. It is particularly useful for the interviewer to read the chapter on "American Football" from Gannon (2004) and the chapter on the chosen nation to hone a number of in-depth questions that will facilitate such comparisons. Also helpful is the critical incident methodology, that is, asking the interviewee to think of a time, and then to describe it orally, when a major problem resulted directly from the differing perspectives of U.S. executives and their counterparts in the chosen nation. Each interviewer should write a five-page, double-spaced paper describing the interview, after which there can be a general class discussion.

Answers to the Two-Item Survey

For the first item, the answers are a, community sharing; b, market pricing; c, authority ranking; and d, equality matching. For the second item, the answers are a, community sharing; b, equality matching; c, market pricing; and d, authority ranking.

6

Cross-Cultural Negotiations

Negotiation may be the most difficult, challenging, engaging, complex, and fascinating activity that an individual faces in life. All of us, whether we like or dislike negotiating with other parties, are constantly involved in this activity. Ideally, negotiation encompasses a thorough grounding in and understanding of its underlying theory, best practices, and dynamics. When negotiations involve two or more cultures rather than only one, both complexity and fascination take a quantum leap.

We begin this chapter with a discussion of some fundamentals leading to success in negotiations, not only within one culture but across cultures. Next, we present an actual, extended case study of a cross-cultural negotiation undertaken by a U.S. high-tech firm seeking to enter the Chinese market around 1997. At the end of the case study are several questions that will be answered throughout the remainder of the chapter as we discuss various paradoxes. In the third section of the chapter, the focus is on negotiating metaphors that individuals from different cultures bring to the negotiation table, with special emphasis on chess and the Chinese board game of Go. Then in the final section we address several interrelated issues that bear on negotiations and that differ significantly across cultures, namely, attitudes toward time, the major types of face, and yin and yang, or the yin-yang dynamic.

Fundamentals and Best Practices

I have been involved in countless cross-cultural negotiations over the years and have taught a negotiation class to managers, undergraduate students, and MBA students during the same time. There is a well-developed research literature in this area, and I will touch on some of the major findings. However, my emphasis will be on the following: the most difficult topics to teach and to understand, best practices, and the manner in which the dynamics of negotiations play out in the real world. As an introduction to negotiations, I invite you to assume the role of the buyer in the following negotiation (see Table 6.1). However, please do not read the role of the seller (Table 6.2) until you have thought about and prepared fully for the negotiation in terms of the information presented and your negotiating strategy. If you are working in pairs, two individuals (one as buyer and one as seller) can go through the negotiation before reading further.

Table 6.1   The Buyer

You are visiting a foreign country and would like to buy a rug as a present for your spouse.

You are currently in a store that sells rugs, pillow cases, and other articles of housewares, and you have found a very good rug that would look very nice in the living room. You have seen similar rugs in this area of the country. Friends tell you that you can buy rugs here for 600 units. This particular rug seems to be of much better quality and is a very particular shade of green that you haven't found elsewhere and that your spouse would really like. You have fallen in love with it.

You have only 1,000 units left in your wallet, and it has to last the rest of your journey. You leave for home the day after tomorrow.

Table 6.2   The Seller

You are the owner of a store in a country of your choice (one that you are familiar with). You sell rugs, pillow cases, and other articles of housewares. You notice on this particular day that a foreign visitor is interested in a particular rug.

Many other stores sell similar rugs for about 700 units. This rug seems to be of much better quality and is a very particular shade of green. This rug cost you 750 units. You normally sell it for 1,000 to 1,200 units.

This store is your sole source of income.

There are many possibilities besides price that you can use to make a deal. *Feel free to use your creativity and imagination.*

This simple exercise is very engaging, and both managerial trainees and students invest a great amount of energy and thought in the process. After 15–20 minutes, I typically ask each pair to describe the first and closing offers of both buyer and seller. I also ask whether final agreement has been reached (yes or no), and I place this information on a whiteboard for all to see. Typically only half the groups achieve a final agreement, and frequently one party is much less satisfied with the agreement than the other party is. Also, the first and final offers are often very far apart, and sometimes the opening offers are so ridiculously far apart that both parties are offended, making a final agreement nearly impossible to achieve. Most important, many individuals negotiate only over price, while other individuals become creative; for example:

- The seller will include two complimentary pillows.
- The buyer will agree to give the seller the names, phone numbers, and e-mail addresses of friends and associates who will probably be interested in high-quality rugs, and the seller may also use the buyer's name as a reference when calling these people.
- The buyer will pay some of the bill in cash and the remainder with a credit card.

This exercise dramatically illustrates the two major types of bargaining, distributive and integrative. *Distributive bargaining* assumes that there is only one pie, which must be divided in some way, and those negotiating only over price exemplify the dynamics of such bargaining. However, *integrative bargaining* assumes that the pie can be expanded and that the needs, constraints, and desires of one of the parties are not necessarily the needs, constraints, and desires of the other. This is a key issue that is often overlooked; that is, it is preferable to make no assumptions whatsoever about what is in the mind of the other person and to probe gently but constantly to find out.

Herb Cohen has authored a classic book, *You Can Negotiate Anything* (1980), that rests on this key issue of information. According to Cohen, there are three elements in any negotiation: time, information, and power. The more information the negotiator possesses, the more power he or she gains in the negotiation process. For instance, frequently in cross-cultural negotiations that take place outside the United States and last at least one week, the other party will innocently inquire when you plan to return home to the United States. The proper answer is that you have an open ticket. If you identify the exact time and day, the other party may well delay serious negotiations and wine and dine you until the very last minute, knowing that you would definitely like to return with some form of an agreement for your superiors after an extended stay of a week or more. Needless to say, the other party has the most power in this situation.

However, obtaining information requires time, sometimes a great amount of it, and the negotiator must be willing to commit a good amount of time to the negotiation process if success is to be attained. Cohen provides numerous examples, one of which involved his purchasing a new refrigerator at Sears. He devoted approximately 2 hours to talking with the salesperson to establish a psychological relationship and obtain information. Initially the salesperson indicated that the cost was out of Cohen's reach. Eventually Cohen convinced him to sell the refrigerator at a much lower price that left the salesperson with little if any sales commission. Still, the salesperson was happy that Cohen promised to do business with him again and to send his friends and acquaintances to him. Also, Cohen pointed out, the salesperson didn't have any other customers at the time, so the negotiation allowed him to demonstrate his expertise, pass the time of day, and at least show effort on his part to his superiors.

The basic objective in negotiations is to obtain as much as possible while leaving the other party satisfied and happy. To accomplish this objective, the negotiator should take into account his or her own needs, constraints, and desires and the needs, constraints, and desires of the other party. Brett (2001) confirmed this pattern of success in her study of negotiators from the United States, Israel, Hong Kong, and Germany in a series of controlled experiments conducted at Northwestern University. Each group negotiated with each of the other groups sequentially. The Israeli negotiators won more and left the other party happier than did any of the other groups. Israelis have a reputation for being tough negotiators, but Brett's study enlarged this negotiating profile to indicate that they also are concerned about leaving the other party satisfied. As she points out, U.S. negotiators frequently leave much more on the table because they fail to emphasize fundamentals and best practices. She characterized the Israelis as pragmatic individualists, the Japanese as indirect strategists, and the Germans as cooperative pragmatists. Her descriptions of the U.S. negotiators imply that they are also pragmatic individualists.

Ronald Burke's classic study (1979) of integrative and distributive bargaining among managers relates directly to our discussion. He asked a few hundred managers to provide extended examples of times they resolved a problem satisfactorily and then to provide examples of times they resolved a problem unsatisfactorily. When problems were resolved satisfactorily, the *genuinely integrative style* was employed by 58.5% of the managers; that is, the needs, preferences, and desires of both parties received *full* consideration, and the pie was viewed as expansive. When final resolutions were unsatisfactory, 79.2% of the incidents were typified by a *forceful* or *tough* or *hard* style that totally disregarded the other party's needs, preferences, and desires. Of course, this hard style is distributive in nature, as it assumes that the pie is fixed. Sometimes other approaches, such as compromise, worked. However, even compromising is problematic, as the needs and desires of both parties are achieved only partially. Genuinely integrative bargaining had the highest probability of success by a very wide margin.

However, you are likely to ask, when *tough bargainers* interested in only their own needs negotiate with *soft bargainers* interested primarily in pleasing the other party or at least compromising on their opposing positions, don't the tough bargainers prevail? Indeed they do, in large part because of the relentless pressure and intensity associated with such driven people. Roger Fisher and his associates at the Harvard Negotiations Project have developed a useful integrative model for dealing with all types of bargainers, including hard bargainers (Fisher, Ury, & Patton, 1991). This model consists of four parts or principles:

- Separate the *people* from the problem. It is essential to disregard personality quirks, such as emotional outbursts, and to try to reach an agreement satisfactory to both parties (which naturally leads to the second principle).
- Focus on *interests* of both parties, not their positions. Fisher, Ury, and Patton (1991) illustrated this principle with a situation in a library that began with a fixed-pie assumption but that a librarian developed into an integrative situation. In various forms all of us have experienced this situation, which can easily degenerate into name-calling and pure power plays. One visitor to a local library was reading in a small room. He had a very bad cold. A second visitor entered the room and immediately opened the window fully. When the first party shut the window, the second party objected, saying it was too warm, and opened the window a second time. Soon the battle escalated and they began shouting and threatening each other. The librarian entered and asked for an explanation. She then closed the window and opened another one in a room across the hallway, satisfying both parties.
- Invent *options*, or complex solutions, for mutual gains by means of brainstorming, taking time out to analyze whether additional options exist, and so on.
- Use *objective criteria* and, if possible, establish them before the negotiations begin. For example, when a job search committee begins its work, it is helpful to identify the "must" criteria that any candidate must meet before the committee will consider a candidate's "desirable" criteria. The must criteria winnow the list to a few candidates, at which point the committee uses the desirable criteria to evaluate them. When objective criteria are not available, the decision process can be sequenced. For example, the nations involved in selling fishing rights to multinational corporations in their territorial waters under the Law of the Sea Treaty were seemingly at a great disadvantage, as the corporations had much more capital to expend on researching the desirability of various seabeds. To even out this situation, each nation demanded that each corporation

identify two seabeds it desired, and then the nations awarded each corporation one of its requested seabeds. Hence, to avoid ending up with an inferior seabed, the corporations would each provide two excellent choices, minimizing the amount of research each nation had to perform.

Fisher, Ury, and Patton also recommend that negotiators have a *best alternative to a negotiated settlement* (BATNA) in mind. That is, at what point are negotiators willing to walk away from a negotiation because they decided prior to the negotiation that an attractive alternative outside of the process exists? If, for instance, a person turns down a job offer because the current job has many desirable features, even though there may be problems, the current job is the BATNA. Cellich and Jain (2004) argue that the BATNA should be flexible and that the negotiator should alter it as new information becomes available. However, the negotiator should exercise extreme caution when changing a BATNA, as the negotiation process is typically intense, and it is easy to make a mistake. Having a good idea about what is minimally expected places the individual in a better negotiating position.

There are several key rules or best practices for negotiating. Before reading the list directly below, you are invited to think about your own rules or best practices and share them with at least one other class member or a small discussion group, after which a member from each group can summarize the discussion for the class.

- Listen more than you talk, as listening helps provide information and power.
- In general, do not become emotional, and use an emotional outburst only when you are employing it as a negotiating tactic, such as walking out of the room when you know the other side will beg you to come back.
- In general, don't agree to a settlement immediately. Take a break, or at least think about the agreement silently for several minutes before agreeing. Having a *trip wire*, such as saying that you need to consult with your spouse before accepting a job offer, gives you room to think and maneuver, whereas accepting an offer on the spot may leave the person or candidate with subsequent feelings that he or she had overlooked some issues or could have done better with additional thought and action.
- Many people assume that the other side will not accept a high offer and so they never make it. Be reasonable, but make initial high offers, or initial high counteroffers if an offer has already been made.
- If you face a hard or difficult bargainer, openly bring up this issue and indicate that your position is the desirability of satisfying both parties, not just one party. If the hard bargainer persists in using this style, you can indicate that it is not possible for you to negotiate under such conditions.
- Do your homework, be prepared, and take notes periodically during the negotiations, as you tend to forget what has been said throughout the process.

- Periodically summarize, identifying the key points of agreement and the key points requiring additional negotiation.
- If the negotiation proves difficult, focus on a settlement range and not a specific point within it, and indicate that you are willing to bargain within this range as long as the other party is agreeable to the concept of mutually satisfying and creative solutions. Avoid the statement "This is my bottom line" unless you really mean it, as this is a very strong signal that the negotiations are nearing finality. It is also a forceful statement that the other party may interpret as a sign of inflexibility and hostility.
- When bargaining cross-culturally, be sensitive to cross-cultural issues, such as the need to save face, defined below.
- Remember that all negotiations go through stages and that in the early stages the focus should be more on processes and getting to know the other party than on outcomes, especially when the other party comes from a high-context culture. The negotiator can shorten the time devoted to each stage, but it is important to establish trust, which takes time and effort and getting the other party to feel comfortable, even in a onetime negotiation such as buying a car. Try to establish a psychological relationship and do everything possible to enhance the feeling of trust.
- Don't finalize a deal unless you are satisfied both logically and emotionally.
- Try to convince the other side that you are at your bottom line, even though you want to avoid the term itself and may need to invoke your BATNA.
- Use simple language to avoid misunderstandings.
- Don't overestimate your ability to "read" body language. For example, while there is a stereotype that a "shifty-eyed" person is a habitual liar when negotiating, the research does not support it. Similarly, whether a person smiles or does not smile frequently may have nothing to do with the negotiations and their eventual outcome.

Weiss (1994) has provided some additional suggestions for negotiating cross-culturally. If you have low familiarity with your counterpart's culture, take advantage of one or more of the following techniques: Employ an agent or adviser, involve a mediator, induce the counterpart to follow your script, or adapt to the counterpart's script. If you have only moderate familiarity with the counterpart's culture, try to coordinate the adjustment of both parties and embrace the counterpart's script or ways of responding. If you have high familiarity with the counterpart's culture, improvise an approach or create a "symphony" (a creative solution that is very appealing to both sides).

Case Study: Entering the Chinese Market

Similar to all or most defense-related firms, the Generator Company (not the actual name of the company) employed small groups of global client-focused representatives (GCRs) in various regions of the world. This midsize company (sales of $700 million per year) had grown rapidly in recent years, in large part because of the technical superiority of its products. For several years Generator's Asian-based GCRs had been analyzing the China market, as many of its direct competitors (from the United States and elsewhere) had signed contracts with various Chinese government agencies. If Generator did not enter this huge market in the near future, there was a danger that it would become a very late mover. It could easily be shut out of the market, perhaps permanently, as many of the contracts extended over long periods and were renewable subject to fulfillment of current contractual obligations.

The typical mode of entry that Generator employed was exporting, that is, manufacturing its sophisticated products in the United States. For many of its sophisticated products it also provided ongoing technical support and updating of equipment.

There was, however, an immediate financing problem: Generator's managers were surprised to discover that this very large project needed to be supported through Japanese financing, as stipulated by Chinese law. (Please note that this requirement changed after this case ended.) The Japanese financed projects in terms of phases, or tranches, rather than guaranteeing the financing of the entire project, and they had terminated projects at various stages in the past. This method of financing was too risky for Generator. Also, the GCR team needed to become very familiar with the services of the Export-Import Bank, which was the other possible source of financing, and to do so very quickly.

Fortunately Generator employed a Chinese citizen who had studied in the United States and had worked in its U.S. offices for several years. He was able to establish personal relationships with the Chinese negotiating team. Trust was critical. Generator's products were clearly superior, but the company's reputation in China was unknown. As the Chinese negotiators indicated, they would need to put their personal reputations on the line if they agreed to sign with Generator; they would also have to persuade several levels of the Chinese bureaucracy that Generator was clearly the superior choice.

But even Generator's Chinese GCR was not prepared for the very slow pace of the negotiations, which extended for 2 years. During this period Generator's competitors were very active, and it was not unusual for Generator's team to negotiate for several hours while its competitors waited in the anteroom, and vice versa. Intense periods of negotiation—and periods of waiting for them to occur—sometimes extended more than 20 hours at a time. At one point Generator's negotiation team lived for 45 days in the hotel where the negotiations were taking place. They knew that if they went on even a very short holiday, their competitors would immediately replace them at the bargaining table.

Generator's managers at headquarters in the United States were becoming impatient with the pace of the negotiations. They instructed the GCR team to get the issues on the table and negotiate a profitable deal as quickly as possible. To that end, headquarters sent a small group of managers led by the senior company lawyer, who had never been outside the United States. This team was taken aback by the technical but sometimes trivial questions that the Chinese asked. For example, what type of paint would be used on the equipment, and how long was it guaranteed to last? The Chinese had studied the project in depth, and their technical specialists were the ones asking these questions. The Chinese team consisted of 20 people, while Generator's team had only 5 members. Generator's negotiating team did not have any technical specialists present at this time.

Moreover, some members of the Generator team did not respond well to the slow pace, which included frequent banquets at which large amounts of alcoholic beverages were consumed. A few members of the Generator team politely consumed drinks at times but turned them down at others. Some Generator managers did not drink at all. The Generator managers were also turned off by the Chinese tendency to nod their heads in agreement, especially when subsequent events indicated that they did so only to be polite. Time did not seem important to the Chinese. The headquarters managers wanted to return to the United States as quickly as possible.

An additional complication was that the contract was written in Chinese and translated into English by a Chinese translator, as Chinese law requires in such negotiations. Apparently this contract was boilerplate and had not been altered in years.

Please answer the following questions:

1. Comparing sunk and opportunity costs, should Generator terminate this negotiation as early as possible and seek other opportunities with the realization that it might be excluded from the Chinese market permanently? *Sunk costs* are those that have already accumulated and cannot be retrieved, while *opportunity costs* are those that focus on only the future when evaluating various alternatives.

2. If the answer is yes, when should it terminate the negotiations?

3. How can Generator's negotiating team reestablish its technical credibility?

4. How should Generator address the issue of the actual writing of the contract?

5. What can the Generator negotiating team do to neutralize the effect of the law that only Japanese financing must be used?

6. How can Generator's GCRs convince headquarters that the negotiations cannot be completed rapidly?

7. Generator's headquarters representatives on the team, such as the company's lawyer, did not have much international experience. How problematic would this prove to be?

8. This case study contains no information on the International Traffic in Arms Regulations and the Arms Export Control Act. If possible, please describe one to three major situations or problems that an American defense-related company might experience in any of these areas.

As indicated above, the answers to these questions are provided in the remainder of the chapter.

Negotiating Metaphors

At this point I invite you to provide your own personal metaphors for negotiating. (A metaphor means using the characteristics of one phenomenon to describe another phenomenon, such as employing the characteristics of American football to describe the United States and the business activities taking place within it.) After identifying your metaphor, please continue reading.

As expected, the range of metaphors managers provide is wide. Many of them, even among experienced managers, indicate an active dislike of negotiating, for example, an endless maze from which there is little if any chance of escape or success; jumping from a high diving board and being unpleasantly surprised by the cold water; a day at the beach, that is, everything looks fine but then the person gets sunburned and the sand is unpleasant and dirty, which necessitates a bath and perhaps even seeing a doctor if a deep sunburn produces shivering; facing a bad rush hour; a crab, that is, the desire to go into a hole to escape the situation; and housetraining a dog. Many of the metaphors stress distributive bargaining, and they include poker, or trying to outguess other players by watching their body movements and using feints and gambits; football, or destroying the other side through a deft combination of sophisticated plays and sheer power; chess; a school yard fist fight; a boxing match; a tennis match; and the "warrior yoga posture." A minority of metaphors fit into the integrative style; these include a dance such as the tango or waltz, requiring the cooperation of both parties; dueling banjos, whose combined sound can be beautiful only if the two parties work together; and a glass of chocolate combining two elements (milk and chocolate) to create a new product successfully.

Paradox 6.1. Is chess more influential than the Chinese board game of Go for strategy and negotiation?

There is an extensive literature that has compared the Western penchant for chess as a metaphor for the highly interrelated topics of strategy and negotiation and the Eastern preference for Go as the metaphor (see McNeilly, 1996). Chris Nielsen (2005) reviewed this literature in the context of the manner in which Western and Asian multinationals are entering and conquering emerging markets. Directly below we employ her logic and that of many others arguing in a similar manner.

Chess is a game of war, the object of which is to maneuver the opponent's king into a fatal position. At the end of the game there is one clear winner, but both opponents typically suffer serious losses, as exemplified by the few remaining pieces on the board. Go may be the most intellectually stimulating board game in the world, even surpassing chess. Opponents begin with an empty board and take turns placing their pieces on the points of intersecting lines. While players' objective in chess is to "kill" the opponent or competition, their objective in Go is to occupy as much space on the board as possible, rendering the opponent helpless.

Nielsen and others have argued that the Western bias for immediate and all-out victory exemplified by chess has led to the loss of many markets for American firms, which must be sensitive to quarterly returns on their stock prices so that analysts will recommend the stock to investors. These firms must constantly win and expand to satisfy analysts and investors, regardless of trade-offs, such as not investing in new technology in order to emphasize the sales of existing products. Chess reflects this intense focus on winning quickly at all costs.

Nielsen described in detail the markets that Japanese, Chinese, Korean, Indian, and Thai firms have captured in several industries, leaving their Western rivals in a distant second place. Most of these Asian multinational firms have not worried about short-term profits and have endured months and even years of losses to establish a strong market position, which is consistent with the Go philosophy of positioning, or rendering opponents helpless. Relatedly, Williamson (1997) has profiled the rules in Asia's "competitive game," four of which directly reflect the Go metaphor:

- Be first into the market.
- Control critical elements in the supply chain.
- Organize the company like a network of PCs.
- Build walled cities, or barriers to entry.

Eastern firms that rely on the Go metaphor frequently best Western firms employing the chess metaphor. In Chapter 3 we described the sad case of the once proud General Motors. Roger Smith, its CEO from 1981 to 1990, responded in a seemingly incredible manner to Carol Loomis (1993), a highly regarded *Fortune* writer who asked him what went wrong at GM during this time: "I don't know. It's a mysterious thing" (p. 41). Her most recent article is aptly titled "The Tragedy of General Motors" (Loomis, 2006). When we employ the metaphors of chess and Go to analyze why Toyota and other Asian firms have done so well, it no longer seems so mysterious. Smith and General Motors focused primarily on winning totally, as chess dictates, but they were blind to the sophisticated moves made by Toyota and other Asian firms stressing Go.

In this section we have emphasized both business strategy and negotiations, which overlap significantly but not entirely. Our second paradox focuses exclusively on negotiations.

> ## Paradox 6.2. Why do veteran international negotiators from one national culture frequently complain that their counterparts from a dissimilar national culture are simultaneously very sincere and very deceptive?

Tony Fang (1999), a native and resident of China for many years who is now a professor at the University of Stockholm, has authored a very insightful book on Chinese negotiating tactics that provides an answer to this paradox (for a similar analysis of Japan, see Johnson & Selsky, 2005). While he emphasizes only Western and Chinese negotiators, his analysis could be extended to cultural groups similar to the Chinese. He identifies three reasons for this paradox of sincerity and deception among Chinese negotiators:

1. The long history of China, going back 5,000 years, during which there were periods of instability and a resulting feeling that the market is highly risky and dangerous. From this perspective the marketplace is similar to a battle or war requiring sophisticated moves.

2. Sun Tzu's book, *The Art of War*, which Fang argues should be retitled *The Art of Peace*. The very first principle in this famous book is to avoid war if at all possible, as both sides suffer a significant loss of human life and resources. Rather, Sun Tzu, who was a general in real life, recommends that the negotiator or strategist weaken the opponent by such tactics as dividing and conquering, going into useful alliances but subordinating new partners when they are in a weakened position and no longer useful or powerful, and so on.

3. The turbulent history of China since the turn of the 20th century, including the Mao period, which many older Chinese lived through.

Of course, Chinese and Eastern negotiators are frequently not particularly happy with Western negotiators. They complain that Western negotiators do not respect them, want to get down to business too quickly, and try to win everything without leaving anything on the table. Our discussion of Go implies that the winner does not want to humiliate the loser, as the loser may become vengeful and, if given an opportunity, will retaliate fiercely.

There are other negotiating metaphors, and they tend to vary by nation. For example, the manner in which Spanish businesspeople negotiate may be compared to the adroit moves of the bullfighter. It is not uncommon for Spanish executives to make fun of their U.S. counterparts in private; at least one Spanish executive has been known to entertain his associates by shouting "el Toro," using an imaginary red cape and deftly pulling it aside to signify that a U.S. negotiator, ostensibly embracing chess, has been stymied. For additional metaphors that help to structure negotiations in different nations, see Gannon (2004) and Gelfand and McCusker (2002).

Paradox 6.3. When negotiating, is it best to make the opening offer or respond to it?

One of the best practices of negotiating described previously is that it is best to make the opening offer and make it high; if the other party has preempted the process by making the opening offer, the recommendation is to respond with an initially high counteroffer (see Cellich & Jain, 2004). However, this advice must be balanced against the need for trust in the negotiation, and frequently an insufficient amount of time is devoted to establishing such trust.

People from low-context cultures such as those found in the United States and Germany approach negotiations differently than people from high-context cultures such as those found in China and Thailand (Adair & Brett, 2005). A low-context negotiator usually devotes only a limited amount of time to getting to know the other party and then makes an initially high but seemingly reasonable offer about which he or she is willing to be flexible and is not averse to decreasing, sometimes several times. Conversely, members of high-context cultures devote much more time to getting to know the other party and identifying their needs, preferences, and desires. The opening offer comes after thoroughly understanding the other party's perspective. This approach is consistent with the game of Go and Sun Tzu's rules of engagement.

However, it is also accompanied by a great amount of haggling and probing. The initial offer, when finally made, is the result of these activities.

As suggested, many Western negotiators dislike haggling and are not willing to invest as much energy into getting to know the other party, which may account for the negative metaphors that some of them propose for negotiations. While the best practice is to make an initial high offer or counteroffer, there is a danger that the Western negotiator will not devote a sufficient amount of time to the process preceding it. Some Chinese firms operating in the global arena, such as the computer maker Lenovo, have introduced cross-cultural training courses designed to get the Chinese managers to talk more openly, both in-house and in negotiations with Westerners. The focus is on getting the message across efficiently while making the other side more comfortable and trusting. However, this is happening in only a small number of instances thus far ("Face Value," 2007).

In the Generator case study, top management in the United States was demanding that its negotiating team reach an agreement quickly. However, this demand was balanced by the desire to have an early-mover advantage in the Chinese market. Finally, the company sent its top lawyer to join the negotiating team in China. He was an extroverted person who had never been to Asia, and he was so concerned about the food that he packed one suitcase with American food he knew he could eat, such as bread and peanut butter. He acclimated quickly, however, and began to enjoy the new experiences, even to the extent of eating food sold from carts on the streets. Very quickly he realized that the team had to be enlarged considerably to include technical specialists who could talk knowledgeably about specifics with their Chinese counterparts. The Chinese team at that point had 20 members, each with specific tasks (including two members who merely observed behavior and advised the Chinese team on possible negotiating approaches), and the U.S. team had only 5 members.

Generator's top management quickly agreed to the request to send technical specialists to China, which proved to be crucial. The critiques of Generator's technology and its supposed limitations subsided, and the U.S. team realized that a breakthrough had occurred when the technical specialists from both sides began to work alongside one another at a whiteboard and jointly solved some of the technical difficulties.

The banquets and toasts continued after work hours, but now they became more informal than before the arrival of the lawyer and the technical specialists. There was now more overlap in interests and functional specialties. In particular, the culturally inexperienced lawyer proved to be a major asset, if not the major asset, for the U.S. team. He became very interested in learning about the Chinese culture and its cuisine, and it was his attempt to learn the Chinese language that brought a sense of closeness and informality as he struggled to pronounce words and was aided by the enthusiastic Chinese in attendance.

During these banquets the U.S. team members began to ask questions that had perplexed them culturally. Their major question was whether it is necessary for team members to drink at the banquets every night. Surprisingly, the Chinese answered that it was not even necessary to drink at all; they would assume that a nondrinker was either in Alcoholics Anonymous or had some health problems that would be exacerbated by drinking. Rather, the Chinese were looking for consistency: If a person drank at the first banquet but sporadically thereafter, the Chinese became distrustful because the behavior seemed calculated and unpredictable.

But there were other problems to overcome. For the U.S. team, the boilerplate Chinese contract was simply unacceptable; the Chinese team was able to persuade the government to accept a newly worded contract that was rendered in both English and Chinese to avoid misunderstandings. However, the biggest hurdle was the legal stipulation that the contract had to be financed through a Japanese bank. The leading government representative indicated that he could persuade the government to change the law, but he was personally jeopardizing his own position in the event that the project was unsuccessful. He also pointed out that if Generator did not meet or surpass expectations, it would most probably not receive any additional contracts. The law was changed and the contract was signed. As expected, the U.S. team made a special effort to ensure the successful completion of the project. This effort was due in large part to the high degree of trust that had developed between the two parties.

The dynamics of this case study suggest that any best practice, such as the admonition to make an initially high offer, should be adjusted to the realities of negotiations in a specific context. Eventually both sides were satisfied, but opening with a high offer before trust was established would have been counterproductive. There were simply too many difficulties and complexities that needed to be addressed. Working together and creating a "symphony" proved to be the best approach in this instance.

In regard to the issue of whether to terminate negotiations early, the consensus both on the team and among senior managers was that it was inadvisable to do so. Learning about the Chinese market and becoming respected in this nation were of paramount concern, given the size of the market and potential for high profit margins extending over several years if not decades. Still, it was not until 2001 that U.S. firms operating in China reported an average of more profits than losses. So the decision was risky but seemingly inevitable, given the bias for making it in terms of opportunity costs rather than sunk costs.

Finally, multinational firms must follow strict laws in international business, and this is particularly true for U.S. multinationals. As indicated earlier, bribery is of major concern, but other regulations and laws are also critical. There have been instances in which U.S. executives have carelessly provided legally restricted information during briefings and discussions when abroad. One executive lost his computer containing such information. These executives have been penalized by their companies—such as by an extended leave from work without pay—and sometimes by the U.S. government, which can even prosecute an executive for supposed infringements. Thus, the Generator case study involves more complications than our brief description highlights.

Time, Face, and the Yin-Yang Dynamic

In the final section of the chapter we examine three interrelated topics: time, face, and the yin-yang dynamic. While the three concepts are decidedly relevant to Asia, they apply to any high-context culture that stresses a high degree of socialization whereby individuals know what is expected and do not need to articulate their feelings explicitly.

> **Paradox 6.4. How can time be considered as three circles (past, present, and future) as well as only one circle?**

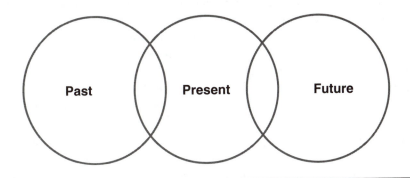

Figure 6.1   Past, Present, Future

You are invited to complete a short exercise (Cottle, 1968; Trompenaars & Hampden-Turner, 1998). I have tailored the exercise to the following instructions and discussion points:

> Think of the past, present, and future as being the shape of circles. Please draw three circles on a sheet of paper representing the past, the present, and the future. Arrange these three circles in any way that best shows how you feel about the relationship of the past, present, and future. You may use different sizes of circles. When you have finished, label each circle to show which is the past, which one the present, and which one the future.

It is very insightful to share your drawing with at least one other person who has also completed the exercise. In class the instructor can ask several individuals if they will explain their drawings, which tend to be very creative and thoughtful. The instructor can hold up each drawing for all to see, describe it, and then ask the person who drew it to explain it. There are typically many creative drawings and vivid and thoughtful explanations of them. A good final question is, among the world's major religions, whose followers would most likely draw only one circle? Keep reading to find the answer.

Let us now consider the implications of a linear-based perspective on time (past, present, and future as sequential and either separate or overlapping) and a nonlinear perspective (only one circle) in the area of negotiations. Nonlinear orientations to time tend to be dominant in large parts of Asia, Africa, and Latin America, presumably because these cultures tend to be high context. When the other party in the negotiation views time as only one circle, negotiations can be long, frustrating, and drawn out. There is little if any attempt to move the negotiation process along quickly, since one party's worldview does not slice it up into small and identifiable pieces of time.

Also, many parties adhering to the concept of one circle believe that they can ask their negotiation counterparts for additional concessions and benefits, even though the formal contract is signed. Sometimes, right before the contract is signed, one party will question the validity of some points of agreement reached early in the negotiation process. Thus the process can not only seem endless but may in fact be so. If the negotiator from the culture viewing time as one circle has a son or daughter applying for a prized admission to an elite U.S. university, the negotiator may well expect that the request to help the applicant will be honored or at least facilitated actively through letters of support. U.S. negotiators, on the other hand, are likely to view the situation very differently, given their linear perspective on time. Work and nonwork activities tend to be clearly separate in the low-context culture of the United States. Hence such a request may well be beyond what U.S. negotiators would consider reasonable.

Further, different cultures vary in their preferred orientation to time. Past-oriented cultures idealize their ancestors and achievements of the past. Present-focused cultures are typically concerned with present survival and subsistence. Future-thinking cultures are those whose members believe they can influence the future through their achievements. Trompenaars and Hampden-Turner (1998) made an important study highlighting cultural orientations toward time. He asked 15,000 managers from various nations to complete the time exercise described above and discovered that people tend to make the largest circle for the time period that their own national culture emphasizes.

He also noted whether the circles overlapped and the manner in which managers conceptualized the relationship between the past, present, and future. This national study on time orientation revealed that countries such as Germany and the United States were primarily present and future oriented. Conversely, France was much more focused on the past. Today there is controversy in France about French schools' overemphasizing past French achievements, thus diverting attention from the present and the future.

Let us now return to our discussion of the major religions of the world and the emphasis on time as only one circle. Buddhism represents a world religion with this emphasis, as the goal of life is to achieve *Nirvana,* loosely translated as a state of blissfulness. When the Buddha was asked to describe this state, he likened it to the evanescent smoke coming from an extinguished fire. From his perspective there is no past, present, or future, but only one circle of time. *Karma,* the Buddhist emphasis on a person's current state as being predetermined by past actions, is associated with the concept of the soul's essence being encased in different life forms and conditions. Even the Buddha himself supposedly went through several hundred reincarnations before achieving *Nirvana.* All these concepts relate directly to time conceptualized as only one circle.

Buddhism was an outgrowth of and reaction to Hinduism, particularly its emphasis on anthropomorphic gods and the offerings made to them at the temples. Hinduism, which evolved over many centuries and contains some seemingly contradictory ideas, included the concepts of *karma* and reincarnation, as well as the emphasis on a single circle, as part of its thought structure. Taoism, the nature-focused religion of China that counterbalances Confucianism's emphasis on earthly existence, also employs the concept of a single circle. Hence it is reasonable to argue that a large part of the world's population views time as only one circle. And, as indicated previously, large parts of Latin America and Africa adhere to a nonlinear conception of time, which is closer to the concept of a single circle than to the concept that the past, present, and future are linearly related. The implications of the acceptance, frequently unconscious in nature, of the single-circle or nonlinear orientation can be critical in many areas, including not only negotiations but also a culture's worldview and face, our final two topics. (For clear, insightful, and relatively short discussions of world religions, see Smith, 1991.) For example, while Western negotiators sequentially break up the negotiation process into discrete elements with a beginning, middle, and end, single-circle advocates believe that they can reopen the negotiation process even after seeming agreement has been reached. Sometimes this reopening occurs after days, weeks, months, and even years have been devoted to the process. Needless to say, Western negotiators tend to be frustrated in such situations.

Paradox 6.5. Is the yin-yang dynamic exclusively Asian?

It is frequently asserted that yin and yang are uniquely and exclusively Asian concepts, and more specifically Chinese concepts, that frame a distinctive worldview affecting all aspects of life, including ethics and negotiations (Chen, 2001; Fang, 2003, 2006). The underlying concept, central to Taoist and nature-focused thinking, is summarized effectively by Ji, Nisbett, and Su (2001):

> The idea of change and transformation between two opposite states is the main theme of the *I Ching* . . . or *Book of Changes*. The book not only discusses change in one direction (from young to old or from small to large), but also discusses changes from one extreme to another extreme. For example, when a moon is full, it starts to wane; when a moon is new, it starts to wax. This is the relationship between *yin* and *yang*: When *yin* reaches its extreme, it becomes *yang*; when *yang* reaches its extreme, it becomes *yin*. The pure *yin* is hidden in *yang*, and the pure *yang* is hidden in *yin*. . . . Therefore, *yin* and *yang* are dependent on each other, and transformations between the two occur when one of them becomes extreme. (p. 450)

A person who accepts the concept of the *yin-yang* dynamic tends to see the world in tones of gray rather than as a stark choice between black and white. Supposedly this orientation has contributed to the relativistic perspective of ethics that the Chinese tend to favor, as our discussion of ethics in the previous chapter implies. While this outcome seems logical, does it necessarily preclude individuals raised in Western cultures from seeing shades of gray in ethics and the negotiation process? No definitive answer can be given, but arguably Westerners can perceive the gray in situations, even though Asians may possess a superior talent for doing so.

Perhaps the best advice is to emphasize the best practices of negotiations. While worldviews do differ, in a globalizing world negotiators are becoming more and more familiar with one another's cultures. Frequently Asians prefer the Western penchant for linear negotiations. As some of them have noted to Westerners, the constant haggling associated with a yin-yang dynamic leads to a slowdown in the negotiation process. In many instances one party becomes frustrated and withdraws from the negotiation process entirely. Even without this outcome, valuable time is lost that, in a globalizing world, may well put both sides at a disadvantage as competitors take the market away from them.

Paradox 6.6. Is there only one type of face?

Another unique Chinese concept is face, which many Western cultures equate with honor. There is a chivalric tradition in the West in which honor is a key, if not the key, value. There is some overlap between the concept of honor and face, but there are clear differences that affect all types of behavior, including negotiations.

Face is the unwritten set of rules by which negotiators and individuals cooperate with one another to avoid unduly damaging one another's prestige, self-respect, and honor (Bonavia, 1989). Literally, losing face means just that: the loss of the eyes, ears, mouth, chin, forehead, and finally the entire face. No one wants to be in such a position, and the Western concept of honor is reflected in the Chinese concept of *saving face*. But the Chinese concept also includes *giving face*. Today's opponent may be an effective ally someday when the winning party needs help, and there is no use creating an undying enemy who may return to the field of battle. The game of Go, time as only one circle, and the yin-yang dynamic encompass this perspective. In Go, the losing party, even though powerless, still has control over a small area of the board. If time is indeed a single circle, one never knows what the future may bring, so it is best to both save and give face. And defining a person as only an enemy and not as a potential ally can be very harmful.

Ting-Toomey (1988), on the basis of different types of face emphasized in various parts of Asia, describes three types of face found in cross-cultural negotiations: *self-face*, referring to personal or moral integrity; *other-face*, referring to the face a person shows in negotiations; and *mutual-face*, referring to saving and giving face. At any given moment in cross-cultural negotiations, one type of face, particularly saving face or protecting one's honor, may be more important than other types. It is in this sense that there is only one type of face, especially to Westerners who are accustomed to thinking about the concept in this way.

Frequently sports are apt metaphors for describing national cultures. For example, U.S. football is reflected in business practices emphasizing power, teamwork, sophisticated moves, and many rules and regulations (see Gannon, 2004). Typically people from the United States have difficulty accepting a tie in a game, given their bias for a clear winner. However, the Japanese—who were significantly influenced by Chinese thought and practices—are much more comfortable with such an outcome. This is not to argue against the fundamental goal of bargaining, that is, obtaining as much as possible while leaving the other party satisfied. It is the manner of the negotiating process that is of concern. As we have seen previously, Israeli negotiators win more than negotiators from other cultures, but they also excel at satisfying the needs, desires, and constraints of the other party. It is with this sense of genuinely integrative bargaining—which includes the single-circle concept, the types of face, and the yin-yang dynamic—that we conclude our exploration of negotiation.

Takeaways

1. To win as much as possible in a negotiation and to leave the other party satisfied, it is important to follow best practices and to employ a genuinely integrative negotiating style.

2. While a compromising style of negotiating may be necessary in some instances, it tends to leave both parties dissatisfied. Only the genuinely integrative style is designed to avoid such dissatisfaction.

3. The key variables of time and information determine the amount of power that a negotiator has in any situation. To obtain as much information as possible, it is critical to probe constantly but gently and to guard against making assumptions and attributions as to what is occurring in the other party's mind.

4. A negotiator's metaphor of the bargaining process reflects the manner in which he or she approaches any negotiation.

5. While preserving one's honor or guarding against the loss of face is important, it is also critical to give face so that everyone's reputation and livelihood remain intact after the bargaining process has been completed.

6. Time conceptualized as only one circle increases the complexity of an individual's mind-set and any negotiating process in which the individual is involved.

7. While the concepts of yin and yang are distinctively Chinese in origin, non-Chinese negotiators follow a similar pattern when they see a vast amount of gray in the bargaining process rather than only a stark choice between white and black.

Discussion Questions

1. Differentiate distributive from integrative bargaining, and integrative bargaining from genuinely integrative bargaining.

2. The objective of a negotiation is to win as much as possible while leaving the other party satisfied. Why is it important to leave the other party satisfied?

3. Why is compromise a problematic way to approach bargaining?

4. Discuss the importance of and relationships between time, information, and power in negotiations.

5. How does a tough bargainer influence the dynamics of negotiations, and how can you deal with such a style?

6. Why do some negotiators have such a negative view of bargaining? How do metaphors of negotiation help us to understand and move beyond such a view?

7. Compare the metaphors of Go and chess as they apply to negotiations.

8. Why should the advice about making an initially high offer be counterbalanced by other considerations? Identify three such considerations.

9. What is face, and how many types of face can you identify and describe?

10. How can time be viewed as only one circle encompassing the past, present, and future? What world religions advocate such a view? What are three major implications of such a view?

11. Does the yin-yang perspective and dynamic necessarily lead to a relativistic code of ethics? Why or why not?

CASE STUDY

Generator and Its Asian Partners

To expand and operate successfully in Asia, Generator has had to work with Asian partners, in large part because regulations and laws in many Asian nations such as China and Thailand put strict limits on the manner in which companies can operate communication services. Without a partner, Generator would not be able to operate in many of these nations, if any at all.

Generator provides turnkey data link systems and technology to these partners, which are mostly government or government-related organizations. Initially Generator, consciously or unconsciously, tended to treat its partners as junior or inferior partners rather than as equals. It essentially viewed such international activities as an extension of its domestic activities. For example, Generator advertised and called projects in such partnerships "Generator Systems." This did not sit well with its partners, who actually own, operate, and manage the systems.

Gradually Generator managers realized that their goals were different from those of their Asian partners, although there was overlap. Specifically, each Asian partner was concerned exclusively with setting up a system for its nation and enhancing domestic communication capabilities. Each partner wanted recognition for its work and partnership within its national boundaries, but Generator's practices worked against this outcome. Even when making a change in products, prices, and services, Generator did so unilaterally. Asian partners did not appreciate such unilateral changes, as they had to respond to them and initiate many changes in prices and technology, among others, which affected many subsystems and people.

QUESTION: How can Generator solve these problems? The answers are provided at the end of Chapter 7, p.

PART III

The Broader Context

In Part II the focus was on the micro level of analysis, involving such behavioral issues as communicating across cultures and cross-cultural negotiations. There is, however, a broader context within which such behavioral dynamics occur. Understanding this broader context is critical for a well-rounded appreciation of the relationships between paradoxical thinking, culture, and globalization.

We begin our treatment of this broader context in Chapter 7, with an extensive discussion of the overlapping but separate topics of multiethnicity, religion, geography, and immigration. In Chapter 8 the focus is on economic development. This chapter provides some background necessary for understanding the topic, followed by a series of paradoxes emphasizing the manner in which culture and economic development are linked. We employ the same approach in Chapter 9, providing background on globalization and then a series of paradoxes concerning this topic and culture. In the final chapter, we address business firms that operate globally or seek to do so. There are three interrelated sections: (1) strategies for entering and operating in the global marketplace; (2) unique or distinctive features found within such traditional business functions as advertising, logistics, and accounting when a company operates in the global marketplace; and (3) international human resource management.

7

Multiethnicity, Religion, Geography, and Immigration

O ne fundamental issue is rarely if ever addressed by those who employ large-scale surveys to measure national cultures and their bipolar dimensions such as individualism-collectivism and power distance. Specifically, advocates of such surveys rarely if ever mention the fact that less than 10% of the 220 nations in the world are monocultural. Thus, collating the answers of various citizens within one national culture without regard to their ethnic, religious, and even geographical identities may be fallacious if and when such identities trump national culture. There is even the possibility that the summed data supposedly representing each national culture may be a statistical artifact rather than an expression of a reality, at least in some instances.

Several years ago I was giving a faculty seminar at the Universiti Kebangsaan Malaysia, which has a mixture of Muslim, Chinese, and Indian faculty and students. The topic was cultural metaphors. Each such metaphor represents a major activity, phenomenon, or institution that members of a specific national culture consider important and with which they identify emotionally or cognitively or both. We had developed several such metaphors for national cultures, including the Canadian backpack and flag, the Danish Christmas luncheon, and the Singapore Hawker Centers, in order to provide a deep understanding of each national culture (Gannon, 2004). Some members of the faculty vigorously argued that the Malaysian national culture could not be portrayed in this fashion, as there were three distinct subcultures: the Chinese subculture, which is primarily Confucian, Taoist, and Buddhist in terms of values; the native Malay subculture, which is Muslim; and the Indian subculture, which is Hindu. Indeed, there were vicious attacks on the Malaysian Chinese in the late 1960s, and many of them live in closed and protected communities with their own security guards and Chinese-language schools. However, the government has made a major commitment to decrease animosity between the three groups, and they have lived in peace with one another since the late 1960s. Still, these faculty members had a legitimate point, and it could be made for many if not most of the nations in the world. In some cases a nation will be dissolved so that two or three ethnic groups can create their own separate nations fostering their own distinctive cultures, as happened in the Balkans during the late 1990s. Even when distinct ethnic groups remain within a nation, the number of nations operating as several distinct and independent regions except on a small number of matters such as declaring war and international trade, such as Spain and Belgium, has increased.

Ironically, theorists argued originally and optimistically that increased contact across religious and ethnic lines would lead to greater understanding and harmony. This optimistic view was soon replaced by the realization that increased contact could be variously associated with positive, neutral, or negative perceptions, attitudes, and behaviors. Allport (1979) argued that several factors determine whether the outcome will be favorable, including equal status and common goals of the participants, as well as social and institutional support. This perspective mirrors the paradox that culture does and does not matter, depending on the situation; the individuals from different cultures involved in the interactions; and their respective values, current events, and so forth.

This chapter examines the closely interrelated topics of multiethnicity, religion, geography, and immigration.

Multiethnicity

Two of the most important common features used to classify different ethnic groups are similar physical features and language dialects. Typically, but not always, members of a specific ethnic group practice the same religion. It is generally possible to trace the origins of each ethnic group to a specific geographic area of the world, but prolonged geographic separation of some members from other members of the same ethnic group can result in radically different cultural outcomes, as the warlike Maoris and peace-loving Moriori showed (see Chapter 5).

Further, although it is common to classify groups racially, typically in terms of skin color, the consensus among experts is that race is not a legitimate way to classify individuals and groups, particularly since there is a great amount of intermarriage across groups. In the African American community in the United States and elsewhere, skin color is a sensitive issue. This community recognizes several gradations of skin color, frequently with increasingly negative connotations associated with "acting like Whitey." However, Brazilians of all shades tend to interact in daily life more easily than their U.S. counterparts do, although those with darker pigmentation tend to suffer lower incomes. Eugene Robinson (1999), an African American journalist, attributes the difference between Brazil and the United States to the "one-drop" theory prevalent in the United States, that is, that one drop of African blood leads to a classification as black. Needless to say, classifying individuals by race is complex under the best of conditions. Still, for the purposes of a broad classification system, race may be acceptable, particularly if individuals are given the freedom to opt out of such classification if they feel they belong to two or more racial groups. To cite but one example where such classification seems to be appropriate, approximately 80% of the people in China belong to the Han ethnic group, although there are more than 400 ethnic groups in China, and all or almost all the groups can reasonably be classified as Asian.

Paradox 7.1. Do multiethnic groups impede or facilitate the formation of national cultures?

Our discussion thus far suggests that ethnic groups impede rather than facilitate the formation of national cultures. A strong case for such a perspective seems amply justified, as numerous and vicious conflicts between ethnic groups reoccur in many nations, including the United States, which periodically is convulsed by tensions and riots involving white, Anglo-Saxon Americans; Hispanic Americans; Korean Americans; African Americans; and other groups. Moreover, it is likely that such conflicts will continue and perhaps increase as the world's population expands and globalization leads to greater interactions across ethnic groups.

However, a strong case can also be made for the proposition that ethnic groups facilitate the formation of national cultures. Prosperous nations such as the United States, Canada, and Australia have benefited enormously because of the contributions made by immigrants from different ethnic groups. For example, the stellar reputation and performance of U.S. universities is in large measure due to the fact that the German Jewish professors fleeing Europe prior to World War II became professors in the United States. Still, there are various ways of conceptualizing and talking about the integration of ethnic groups into a definable national culture, such as the "melting pot" in the United States and the "mosaic" that Canadians champion. While the melting pot suggests that ethnic differences and conflicts will dissolve over time, the Canadian mosaic indicates that each group can remain separate while simultaneously creating a sense of integration at the level of the national culture.

Sometimes the proportion of different ethnic groups in a nation can prove to be a divisive issue, especially if they experience different degrees of prosperity. For example, although the Chinese constitute only about 3% of the population in Indonesia, they are on average better off than the other ethnic groups, and jealousy of the Chinese resulted in vicious attacks on them in the late 1990s. Many of the wealthiest Chinese fled the country and are still trying to gain restitution from the government because of the officially sanctioned confiscation of property and financial wealth.

Nevertheless, such conflict is not an inevitable outcome; wise decisions relative to its ethnic groups can enhance a nation's prosperity. The island nation of Singapore, for example, has a population of 4.5 million and possesses one of the world's highest population densities: 6,416 people per square kilometer. It was racked by Communist insurrections through the 1950s and 1960s and was an extremely poor nation. To complicate matters, ethnicity could have been a very divisive issue. Although the population is only 4.5 million, there are three major ethnic groups plus many smaller ones. Chinese, the largest ethnic group, constitute 76.8%; Malays, 13.9%; and Indians, 6.9%. However, the government actively promotes home ownership by providing low-interest mortgage loans so that all or most citizens now own homes. The government also encourages entrepreneurship by providing low-interest loans to small-business owners so that they can purchase their places of business. These and related policies, based on the Confucian concept of an inclusive community, have made Singapore one of the most prosperous nations in the world.

In short, ethnic conflict is not inevitable. Rather, the decisions made relative to the manner in which ethnic groups interact can be inclusive and benefit all. Still, as discussed below, ethnic conflict occurs frequently, which leads us into an exploration of our second paradox.

Paradox 7.2. Is there or will there be a clash of civilizations?

One of the most influential books to appear during the 1990s was Samuel Huntington's *The Clash of Civilizations and the Remaking of World Order* (1996). His basic thesis is very provocative: In the post–Cold War era, in which the distinctions between the West and the Communist or Eastern bloc have faded, the most important classification system is civilizational. He believes that people and groups are searching for identities, as they always have, and that this search is now being acted out at the civilizational level. Thus, Huntington shifts the unit of analysis away from the nation to each collection of nations espousing similar cultural values as expressed primarily through religion, followed by language. Huntington argued that a civilization "is defined by common objective elements, such as language, history, religions, customs, institutions, and by a subjective self-identification of people" (p. 43). He then identified nine modern civilizations: Sinic or Chinese, Japanese, Hindu, Islamic, Orthodox (in which Russia is the core state), Western, Latin American, Buddhist, and African. The GLOBE researchers have identified similar but slightly different civilizations, as have other researchers (Triandis, 2004).

Ethnicities and civilizations significantly overlap, as both emphasize similarities in religion and language. Also, members of each civilizational culture typically but not always share similar physical features. However, there are some key differences. For example, several large and non-Western ethnic groups live in Western civilization and identify primarily if not exclusively with it.

Huntington supplements his major thesis with several provocative subthemes or subtheses, namely, that the world is, in a sense, separated into two camps, a Western one and a non-Western many; that nation-states will still be important, but that they will be influenced heavily by cultural and civilizational identities; and that the conflicts that are the most dangerous involve either the nations themselves or groups within these nations that are from different civilizations. Huntington presented various types of data to prove his thesis and subtheses. For example, in early 1993, slightly less than half of the 48 ethnic conflicts in the world were between groups from different civilizations, and the barbarous war in the former Yugoslavia was civilizational: Muslim Bosnians, Roman Catholic Croats closely identified with Germany, and Orthodox Catholic Serbs closely linked with Russia.

Huntington also presented an impressive amount of evidence on a variety of issues to support his thesis and subtheses. For example, in 1490, Western societies controlled about 1.5 million square miles out of 52.5; in 1923, 25.5; and by 1993, only 12.7. Islamic societies rose from 1.8 million square miles in 1920 to more than 11 million in 1993. In 1920, Western societies ruled 48% of the world's population, but by 1993, the corresponding figure was only 13%, and it is expected to decline even further. Notably, the West's military power leading to such vast and geographically dispersed holdings was accompanied by policies of colonialism and *mercantilism*, in which each colony had to provide natural resources to its dominant home nation. Huntington's view of culture is that it follows or is critically influenced by the distribution of power. Similarly, he showed that trade expansion follows economic union among a group of nations, as happened in the European Union (EU) and in the North American Free Trade Agreement (NAFTA). Clearly Huntington's greatest emphasis was on the rising hostility of Muslim nations toward the West, although he framed the issue in terms of Western civilization versus the non-Western civilizations. The perspective is zero-sum: When the West gains, the non-Western many lose, and vice versa.

However, Niall Ferguson (2006a) points out that the overwhelming majority of conflicts since the end of the Cold War have been civil wars, not civilizational wars. Only a minority have conformed to Huntington's model of intercivilizational wars. Also, some of the most vicious activities have involved intracivilizational wars. For example, Sunnis (85%) and Shiites (15%) are the two major sects within Islam, and they have fought with one another for centuries as well as in Iraq in recent years and in the Iran-Iraq War during the 1980s. (Note: Iran is Shiite while Iraq was Sunni-led at the time of this war.) As Ferguson stated,

> To be precise: Of 30 major armed conflicts that are either still going on or have recently ended, only 10 or 11 can be regarded in any sense as being between civilizations. But 14 were essentially ethnic conflicts, the worst being the wars that continue to bedevil Central Africa. Moreover, many of these conflicts that have a religious dimension are also ethnic conflicts; in many cases, religious affiliation has more to do with the localized success of missionaries in the past than with long-standing membership of a Christian or Muslim civilization. (p. B13)

These data suggest that ethnic intracivilizational conflict is far more threatening and pernicious than intercivilizational conflict, although even Ferguson's analysis indicated that civilizational conflict was present in at least 10 of the 30 instances he cited. Hence, at this time, it seems we are facing some puzzling and paradoxical issues. The concepts of ethnicities and civilizations do overlap, but not perfectly. Also, ethnicity rather than civilization appears to explain the majority of the recent conflicts, but it may be that civilization trumps ethnicity in some instances. Such puzzles suggest that the clash of civilizations does not represent a major threat to globalization and culture but that it seems wise not to discount this possibility entirely, given the tensions that exist in our globalizing world.

Paradox 7.3. Can national cultures exist in a multiethnic and borderless world?

As indicated above, less than 10% of the world's nations are monocultural. Still, this in and of itself does not demonstrate that national cultures—as opposed to nations considered only as separate governmental entities—do not exist. Even when a nation has several ethnic groups, some of which may deliberately distance themselves from other groups through such means as schools taught only in their own languages and their own special security police forces, government policy as well as other means may be used to foster a national culture, as happened in the case of Singapore and elsewhere. Also, there is a matter of self-selection: Immigrants from different ethnic groups tend to gravitate toward nations providing not only better economic opportunities but also a feeling of comfort and familiarity.

Still, immigration is creating friction in many nations, including the United States and several nations in the EU. Many members of ethnic groups who are citizens within one nation identify culturally with another nation, even to the extent that ethnic enclaves actively discourage interactions with the other members of the nation in which they live. There are 31 major Muslim enclaves in western Europe, and other groups such as Albanians and Romanians also tend to live in separate communities within western European nations. Ethnic tensions, including terrorist activities that are religiously justified ideologically, have occurred in such nations as France, Britain, and Spain. At least some of them also involve economic grievances concerning the lack of employment possibilities and access to educational institutions.

While national borders still exist, movement of people across them has become much more frequent than even 10 years ago. It is now fashionable to talk about a borderless world and borderless business, and to some extent this is already the reality, as both short-term and long-term visits and transactions across borders have accelerated. Still, while globalization is increasing, its influence has been felt most palpably by large multinational corporations and national governments of large nations such as India and China, which have sufficient resources to cover the transaction costs generated by international businesses and projects. Smaller companies in many nations have not benefited as much from globalization as have the multinational corporations; many of the owners of these smaller companies are primarily concerned about national and local issues affecting them. A similar pattern exists among smaller and less prosperous developing nations, although less so among the larger nations, even when the larger nations are not initially prosperous.

One interesting development is the growing identification of citizens with entities that include several nations, such as the EU. Surveys consistently indicate that citizens of many European nations have increasingly identified with the EU and decreasingly with their own nations. One glaring example is Ireland, which was a poor agrarian nation until very recently; it is rapidly globalizing and developing economically. Today agriculture employs only 7% of the population. In 1950 the gross domestic product per capita was only $2,500; today it is more than $20,000. Dublin, one of the four capitals of the EU, is the most congested city in Europe. In 1937 Conrad Arensberg (1968) published an anthropological study of the Irish countryman, whose perception of the world extended only "over the nearest hill" and no farther than 200–300 miles from his home. With the advent of television, the Internet, and membership in the

EU, this perception has broadened dramatically. As one Irish clerk informed a visitor from the United States who had not been in Ireland for more than 35 years, "We're European now." Such success stories occur in large measure because of the EU policy of providing money derived through taxes among its member nations to ignite and promote economic activities in a nation that has recently joined the EU. Once each targeted nation becomes more prosperous, its citizens pay taxes to help other targeted nations in similar circumstances.

Thus the modern concept of national culture, which originated in Europe in the 15th century, may not be an appropriate construct for evaluating many phenomena and situations. We have already seen how ethnic tensions and divisions separate groups within and across national cultures, and even Huntington's case for the salience of civilization rather than the nation as the unit of analysis has been weakened considerably although not destroyed.

However, finding the concept of national cultures useful in some situations but not all of them is paradoxical. We do not have the ability to identify a priori when national culture is critical, as reactions by citizens and governments within various nations play out in the larger context of global business, borderless business, and even ethnic and civilizational conflict. Sometimes these reactions fundamentally alter the policies and laws that a specific nation will create, thus slowing down the pace of international trade and globalization. Still, using the nation as the basic unit of analysis, rather than relying on only ethnic and civilizational identifications, is clearly appropriate in many instances, as we have argued and demonstrated throughout this book.

Paradox 7.4. Should all cultural practices be equally acceptable?

One of the most contentious issues relative to ethnicity and associated concepts such as religion and immigration is whether all cultural practices are equally acceptable, as our discussion of Paradoxes 5.1 and 5.2 indicates. Some cultures forbid infanticide, others accept beheadings as legitimate punishment for major crimes, and still other cultures have outlawed capital punishment. These and many other culturally based practices represent major issues for advocates of globalization who are seeking to harmonize laws across nations.

There is no definitive answer to this paradox, as our discussion of universal and situational ethics indicates (see pp. 100–107). Still, nations are becoming increasingly sensitive about this issue, even to the extent that many national systems of justice are being updated periodically in terms of acceptable practices elsewhere. For example, the U.S. Supreme Court still upholds the validity of capital punishment, but its nine justices have recently discussed the reasons many European nations have outlawed it. It is even possible, although not probable, that capital punishment will be forbidden in the United States at some point in the not-too-distant future. Also, the advent of agencies whose authority extends beyond the geographic limits of nations, such as the International Court of Justice and the World Trade Organization, may hasten the day when the acceptance of all cultural practices is markedly if not entirely decreased. For the time being, however, because of several interrelated factors such as multiethnicity, religion, and history, it is likely that the fierce debates over what is acceptable and unacceptable across and within national cultures will continue unabated.

Religion

As Huntington suggests, religion is a major component, if not *the* major component, of civilizations. It is also a critical feature of many if not all ethnic groups. The purpose of this section is not to provide a description and comparison of the world's major religions; you can easily obtain such descriptions elsewhere. A personal favorite is Huston Smith's *The World's Religions* (1991), which devotes a single, readable chapter to each major religion. He analyzes why each major religion arose at a particular historical moment, its major ideas and thought leaders, its overlap with other religions, and its continuing importance in the modern world.

There are many perspectives on religion, one of the most influential of which was developed by Émile Durkheim in *The Elementary Forms of the Religious Life* (1916). Durkheim described various religions in terms of their values and practices within several relatively small ethnic groups in traditional societies. He adhered closely to the etymological meaning of the term *religion*, that is, that it *ties back* directly to the values that members of each group consider critical. In this sense each religion directs, encourages, and restrains behavior and practices so that they are consistent with deeply held values, even to the extent that "altruistic" suicides of virgins were voluntarily accepted to facilitate rainmaking in a drought-plagued area. It is Durkheim's sense of the term *religion* that our discussion highlights.

Paradox 7.5. Must religion be anthropomorphic?

Many surveys report that those who are actively and regularly involved in religious organizations tend to be more satisfied with life than are others. This is an expected finding, as involvement in a community is generally preferable to isolation, and religions of many different varieties encourage an admirable number of good works that enhance a person's feelings of connection to others. Also, as Smith and others have pointed out, the significant overlap between the values of the world's major religions directly leads to practices making for a better world.

Most of the major religions of the world are *anthropomorphic*; that is, they attribute humanlike features to their one God or to their gods. Typically we think of God as kind, generous, warm, charitable, sensitive, and so forth. We employ such anthropomorphic descriptions to profile what values our religious beliefs express and to obtain a sense of religious comfort and connectivity. However, other anthropomorphic descriptions of God or gods tend to be either neutral or negative, and they include such descriptions as fair, avenging, and the final distributor of justice.

As Huston Smith pointed out, however, two of the world's seven major religions—Confucianism and Buddhism—do not include a concept of an anthropomorphic God or gods. Some authors believe that because of this exclusion, neither of these two religions is a genuine religion. Confucianism focuses primarily on the current life and the manner in which individuals can enhance community values helpful to all through adherence to a hierarchy of five relationships beginning with the emperor and extending into family relations; even the concept of an afterlife is much less developed in Confucian thought than in other major religions such as Catholicism and Protestantism (Gannon, 2004). Buddhism focuses on attaining Nirvana, a blissful state that is attained only after one has proved oneself to be completely virtuous. However, this state is radically different from the Christian concept of heaven or paradise; the Buddha himself describes it vaguely as the smoke that is left and floats away when a fire is extinguished.

There are decided advantages associated with an anthropomorphic conception of God or gods. These include a sense of peace derived from the belief that a higher power is looking out for humanity, a sense of oneness and identification with the higher power who possesses humanlike attributes, a sense of justice, and a sense of community or shared values. Still, the acceptance of an anthropomorphic perspective can be used to structure and justify controversial actions, including the aggressive use of force by one ethnic group against another. Buddhism, in particular, shies away from such usage, and it is very difficult if not impossible to find historical instances of warlike actions being framed and justified in terms of Buddhist values and beliefs. In fact, the term *Buddhist Christian* has been coined to identify those Christians who espouse meditation and peace as the pathways to a well-lived and virtuous life.

The issue of using religious imagery derived from an anthropomorphic conception of God or gods to justify warlike actions is a major issue in a rapidly modernizing world. Several groups and governments representing different major religions have employed such imagery, and frequently there is an automatic and negative response, also enveloped in similar imagery.

Thus a vicious cycle may well be created that inhibits dialog between nations and groups from different religious traditions.

It also appears that some national cultures link religion and basic values more closely than do other national cultures. *The Economist* ("Living With a Superpower," 2003) has evaluated national cultures in terms of the World Values Survey and the Pew Global Survey; while many European nations are proud of their churches, they have clearly separated religion from national government and the legal systems within each nation. These nations have become secular, with religion only periodically serving as a facilitator for strengthening cultural values and practices. But the United States is distinctive in that it is a developed nation that adheres closely to traditional religious values, as the pronouncements of its various political leaders confirm. The danger with such framing of issues, as opposed to the secular treatment that European nations and some Asian nations manifest, is that religious imagery couched in anthropomorphic language has a tendency to become ideological. *Ideology* consists of a well-developed and interrelated set of value-based ideas justifying various courses of action that its advocates tend to espouse with few if any exceptions. As such, there is a tendency to employ religious imagery to justify controversial actions that either disregard or minimize the viewpoints of assumed adversaries.

Still, because humans tend to rely on verbal imagery to communicate their sense of religions, it seems that many if not most religions will continue to be anthropomorphic. Obtaining a sense of comfort from such anthropomorphic formulations is not necessarily inappropriate. What is problematic is that this imagery may result in an inflexible ideology that is difficult if not impossible to change. This issue is confronting the world more and more frequently, particularly as many groups espousing one particular religion and way of life immigrate to other nations. It is hoped that melting pots and mosaics as envisioned by the United States and Canada will become the norm, even though many signs suggest that other, less positive outcomes may prevail.

Paradox 7.6. Does a religion necessarily require dogmas and creeds?

Almost all religions promote specific dogmas and creeds. A *dogma* represents a doctrine or body of doctrines concerning faith or morals that is formally stated and authoritatively proclaimed; a *creed* is a fundamental belief or set of fundamental beliefs that a specific religion represents. As might be expected, there is a significant overlap among some of the dogmas and beliefs that various religions champion. However, there are also some areas in which there is no overlap. It is in the nonoverlapping areas that the related issues of dogmas and beliefs can potentially be very divisive. At the very least, religions espousing specific dogmas and beliefs tend to be associated with exclusionary systems, or systems that shut out people who are not persuaded of the dogmas' supposed efficacy.

As our discussion of Samuel Huntington's work suggests, the most glaring example of religious incompatibility is Islam and Christianity, or at least certain articulations of competing dogmas and beliefs within them. In fact, the Prophet Muhammad viewed both Judaism and Christianity as important but incomplete, as they represent religions of the *book*, or Bible. From his perspective Islam is the maturation and pinnacle of religion. Islam historically has been much more tolerant of Christianity and Judaism than these religions have been of Islam. Followers of Islam have even gone so far as to provide a safe haven for conquered Jews and Christians rather than enslaving or killing them. Today's Muslim terrorism and strident opposition to the West occur primarily among small radical groups in Islam. Still, there are vast dogmatic and creedal differences among these three major religions.

One major religion, the Baha'i faith, deviates from this pattern. It promotes the unity of all people. As the Baha'i Web site states, "So far, humanity has tried everything except unity. Race, nation, sect, or class has come first." The Baha'i faith does possess a belief in one God or Supernatural Being who has created the universe. However, Baha'is believe that all religions are one in the sense that the world's great religions are part of a single unfolding divine plan. Members of the faith study the teachings of the world's major religions, as they believe that all of them offer insight and help to humankind.

In addition, there is at least one example of a Protestant-affiliated religion, Unitarian-Universalism, that deliberately avoids dogmas and creeds. It is also a religion noted for its active and disproportionate involvement in trying to make the world a better place for all. Rather than espousing dogmas and beliefs, this small denomination of approximately 250,000 members articulates a set of seven *inclusive* principles:

1. The inherent worth and dignity of every person

2. Justice, equity, and compassion in human relations

3. Acceptance of one another and encouragement to spiritual growth in local congregations

4. A free and responsible search for truth and meaning

5. The right of conscience and the use of the democratic process within local congregations and in society at large

6. The goal of world community with peace, liberty, and justice for all

7. Respect for the interdependent web of all existence of which we are a part

Each member of a congregation can structure a unique set of dogmas and beliefs if so desired, as long as they are consistent with the seven principles. Members represent a wide variety of religious faiths, which they may no longer practice, although some members also maintain membership in traditional religious congregations. They have been attracted to Unitarian-Universalism because of its principles and the manner in which it actively promotes a religion encouraging the inclusion of anyone. Some members also adhere to particular creeds and dogmas associated with traditional religions, but all members accept the seven principles as foundational.

Religious identification and conviction are individual matters, and people should be allowed to accept dogmas and creeds as long as they do not harm others. Unitarian-Universalism represents an ideal; some even argue that it is not a religion because it does not promote any specific dogmas or creeds. In a world that is searching for cross-cultural understanding, the model pursued by Unitarian-Universalism offers an approach that is inclusive rather than exclusive. As such, it may be a bellwether that can serve to enhance not only cross-cultural but also religious understanding. Its principles and the manner in which they evolve through intensive community discussion deserve our serious attention, given the conflicts in our globalizing world that are justified in terms of religious dogmas and beliefs.

Notably, leaders from major religions, including Protestantism, Catholicism, Judaism, Buddhism, and Islam, are now coming together periodically to work cooperatively on various issues, and they are open to discussions fostering integration of beliefs and practices. For example, the Dalai Lama, the spiritual leader of Tibetan Buddhism, who ordinarily schedules meetings 7 years in advance, recently met with Muslim religious leaders and stated,

> Some people have an impression that Islam is militant. . . . I think that is totally wrong. Islam is one of the world's great religions and it carries, basically, a message of love and compassion. (Sahagun, 2006)

Geography

An influential definition of culture is that it "is a shared meaning system, found among those who speak a particular language dialect, during a specific historic period, and in a definable geographic region" (Triandis, 2002, p. 16). This definition places a great emphasis on geography in the explanation of culture. Jared Diamond's acclaimed book, *Guns, Germs, and Steel: The Fates of Human Societies* (1997), persuasively argues that some national cultures became dominant simply because they spread east to west rather than north to south; it was easier for these dominant national cultures to learn from one another because there were fewer impediments to geographic movement, such as impassable mountains and waterways. Because these dominant cultures developed steel and guns first, they were at a decided advantage in terms of conquest, and the germs they imported to the new territories in America and elsewhere weakened the native populations, making them even more compliant. Given the importance of geography for culture, we explore two paradoxes in this area.

Paradox 7.7. Do geographic maps reflect cultural beliefs?

In a popular cross-cultural exercise, individuals draw a geographic map of the world without looking at one before doing so. I invite you to draw such a map before reading further, specifying the geographic size and location of major areas and nations in the world, including the United States. The drawing should take no more than 3 minutes.

Frequently U.S. citizens place the United States in a very large area in the center of their maps. When drawn to scale, however, the United States takes up a relatively small part of the map, and it is not in the central position. Experts argue that this misperception occurs for several reasons, including the fact that U.S. citizens are not well schooled in geography and, until recently, did not travel to other nations frequently. Another possibility is *ethnocentrism*: Since the United States is frequently identified as the world's most prosperous and powerful nation, its citizens may downgrade all other nations relative to it, even geographically.

Whatever the explanation, this American tendency follows a centuries-old pattern. China, once identified as the strongest and wealthiest nation in the world, referred to itself as the Middle Kingdom precisely because it considered itself to be in the center of the world. Its mapmakers drew its world maps to reflect this perception. Similarly, the first European maps placed Europe squarely in the center of the map, signifying that Europe was the center and heart of the world. Today world maps are drawn to scale, and the mapmakers avoid the errors of these earlier maps. Still, many of us tend to think of the United States as the center of the world even though facts suggest otherwise, at least in terms of geography and population.

Paradox 7.8. Has the "death of distance" nullified the importance of geography?

Globalization and borderless business depend on minimizing the importance of geographic distance. The greater the distance, the more expensive it is to transport goods and products. However, such costs are rapidly decreasing in the modern world, as the logistic and transportation systems have become more efficient. Approximately 45% of all global trade is intraorganizational, such as Toyota's making parts in Japan and having them assembled in the United States. Also, modern communication technologies integrating phones, audio, video, and the Internet have quickly gained a significant following throughout the world, thus decreasing the importance of geographic distance.

Thomas Friedman (2005) has taken the argument even further. For him, the world is flat, making it possible to do all or most major activities in any part of the world. He points to many examples, including the call centers in India, the outsourcing of professional work such as law and software development to other nations, and the virtual teams composed of representatives from many nations that businesses throughout the world are emphasizing.

Still, the inclusion of culture in the equation complicates the analysis proposed by Friedman. There are cultural impediments to borderless business and globalization, and they include the terrorist attacks on developed nations, the continuing conflict over the West's belief in free speech and resistance to it among some ethnic and religious groups, and the various definitions of what is legally and ethically acceptable in various parts of the world. Further, there are limitations associated with globalization and the presumed death of distance. The McKinsey Global Institute points out that 750,000 American service jobs, out of a total of 140 million jobs, have been sent offshore but that the probability is low that this trend will continue over the next 30 years because of such practical difficulties as language differences, management resistance, and computer incompatibilities (Samuelson, 2005; but see Paradox 9.10 for the opposing argument). Also, new jobs and opportunities have been created in the United States because of the nation's participation in the global economy.

In addition, borderless business depends on an uninterrupted supply chain that facilitates the movements of goods and services across nations. This supply chain, however, has suffered some severe but temporary disruptions brought about by terrorist activities, regional wars, and the breakdown of communication systems. The events of September 11, 2001, resulted in both a new awareness of national security and the loss of billions of dollars in a wide swath of industries extending from airlines to insurance. Such disruptions occur periodically, and they suggest that distance is still important, particularly when culture is considered.

Immigration

Immigration is a controversial issue, and perhaps the most controversial and emotional issue, confronting both the advocates and the opponents of globalization. Legal immigration to another nation, either for a specified time or permanently, is significantly correlated with globalization and is rising dramatically. However, illegal immigration exhibits the same pattern. This section focuses on three paradoxes directly related to immigration's relationship to globalization, but first we will look at some of the experiences of representative nations in the area of immigration to enrich our understanding of the complex relationship between immigration and globalization.

In the United States, immigrants were warmly welcomed for decades after the formation of the nation in 1776. The land was vast and workers were needed to build the railroads, industries, and towns. However, citizens displayed open hostility toward each new immigrant group, and it was not unusual for newspapers and magazines to publish derogatory articles and prejudicial photos, sometimes depicting the immigrants as animals.

This bias extended into the workplace. For example, there were signs in places of employment indicating that "no Irish need apply" when they began to arrive after the famine of 1845–1849. Owners of plantations in the South hired the Irish to perform dangerous and dirty work that the slaves were too valuable to do. Similarly, opposition to Chinese immigrants, who had been welcomed earlier to assist in the building of the nation, resulted in the Chinese Exclusion Act of 1882.

During the 18th century and in the early years of the 19th century, many cities teemed with immigrants living in squalid conditions. These immigrants competed with citizens for low-end and unskilled jobs. A nativist group of citizens attempted to restrict immigration, particularly after 1914, the year a peak of 1.2 million immigrants sought admission. The nativists successfully spearheaded the effort to operate a national origins system, beginning in 1921, and this system was made even more restrictive in 1924. The limit was 180,000 immigrants per year and the system favored those coming from Anglo-Saxon nations. Changes in the immigration laws since that time have tightened the criteria for admission but have provided entry to those displaced by war, famine, and political persecution.

Today the United States has 34 million immigrants, 12 million of whom are illegal. Although 6 million of the illegal immigrants are from Mexico and 2.5 million from other Latin American nations, there are significant numbers from Europe, Canada, Africa, and Asia (Berestein, 2006). The immigrant issue is particularly explosive in the Western states, and illegal immigrants make incredible efforts to enter the nation through them. Trucks carrying immigrants can even drive through underground tunnels complete with lighting. Some local communities along the border have seen the rise of armed "minutemen," who have taken the initiative of patrolling the borders in their areas. Arguments against immigration mirror those made by the nativists and include the following:

- Uneducated and untrained immigrants overwhelm the resources of the towns and cities in which they reside.
- Illegal immigrants have far higher rates of unemployment than citizens do and compete directly with legal lower-skilled workers for scarce jobs, thus depressing wages.
- No nation has a limitless capacity to absorb such workers and their families effectively. (However, even though the illegal immigrant population in the United States is at an all-time high, immigrants constituted 14.7% of the population in 1900 but only 12.1% in 2005.)

Western European nations also face immigration issues. With the formation of the EU, workers, including illegal ones, can cross borders easily. In particular, the issue of Muslim immigrants to the EU is very sensitive, as a small number of them oppose Western-style capitalism, sometimes violently. The estimated percentage of Muslims in the EU population is 4%, with nations ranging widely. France has the largest contingent at 8–10%; for comparison, the United States' percentage is only 1%. Because of religious and linguistic differences and prejudice against them, Muslims have experienced difficulty integrating into the European nations. Still, intermarriage is occurring; 25% of young Muslim Frenchwomen are married to non-Muslim men.

Australia, originally settled by undesirables from Great Britain, has become the most immigrant-influenced nation in the world. About 24% of its 18.5 million people were born in another nation, and about an equal percentage of citizens come from families in which at least one parent was born elsewhere. Australia now includes 165 nationalities. Similar to what happened in the United States, a "White-Australia" immigration policy prevailed from 1901 until 1973. Since that time Asian immigration has risen significantly, and the nation's international trade is now oriented not only to Great Britain and the West but also to Asia, a change in policy that has benefited the economy significantly.

Frequently the European colonial powers employed immigrants to work in their colonies. Malaysia serves as a representative example. The British imported the Chinese to work in the tin mines and the Indians to work as laborers on the rubber plantations or as clerks in the postal service. This divide-and-conquer policy separating the three major groups—Chinese, Indians, and Malays (who were mostly fishermen)—still influences this nation. Each of the three groups tends to live in a separate area and there is some tension among ethnic groups.

Perhaps the most interesting immigrants are those representing the reverse pattern in the Philippines. This nation, whose economy has declined dramatically since the 1970s, actively supports an overseas temporary immigration policy; 9 million Filipinos, more than 1 out of 10 in this nation of 88 million, work abroad. They toil in every nation except North Korea and sent home $10.7 billion in 2005 to help their families, an amount equal to about 12% of the Philippine gross national product. As these figures suggest, reverse immigration has become critical for the economy.

There are, then, various forms of immigration, and we have sketched only a few of them. In general, the search for employment and good jobs fuels a good amount of immigration, but there are other reasons, including the desire to escape an autocratic and repressive government.

Paradox 7.9. Will the issue of immigration derail globalization?

There are many signs that immigration may derail the movement to globalize. Various developed nations have experienced several well-publicized demonstrations against continued immigration. Some European nations have drastically tightened up their requirements for citizenship, in response to the rapid rise of immigrants entering their nations. The reality is that there are both positive and negative features associated with immigration, and it is next to impossible to make a final informed judgment as to whether it will impede and even derail globalization or facilitate and hasten its advancement. The argument put forth by Bill Owens (2006), the governor of Colorado, concerning the illegal immigration overwhelming many of that state's communities, mirrors the paradox of simultaneous derailment and facilitation, and it can be generalized to the entire debate:

> Our citizens are divided almost equally between those who see immigration as a threat to our economy and culture, and those who see immigration as part of our history and a necessary component of a healthy economy. The solution is elusive because both sides are right—and in Washington both sides have to win for such a divisive issue to be resolved. (p. A15)

An initial step in evaluating whether immigration will derail or facilitate globalization is to identify its negative and positive features. You are invited to describe these features and your personal views about immigration before reading further.

On the positive side, immigration provides a mechanism through which new ideas and practices cross national borders. Latin American immigrants to the United States, for example, sometimes return permanently to their home nations, bringing with them new perspectives on how business should be conducted and life improved. If highly educated immigrants do not return to their home nations, they contribute significantly to the economic prosperity of their host nations. Immigration also exposes people to another nation's culture and helps enlarge their perspectives. In addition, unskilled immigrants from developing nations who are seeking a better life frequently take jobs that citizens in the developed nations do not want. They also contribute to the economy through the money they spend and the taxes that many of them pay. More-educated and skilled immigrants many times establish companies in their adopted nations that facilitate national economic growth. There is even a hidden but critical reverse economic benefit, as many of the immigrants forward a large part of the wages they earn to their families residing in their home nations, as has happened in the Philippines. In Mexico, billions of dollars flow in this manner, and such aid now surpasses all government aid. In El Salvador, remittances are the key source of income.

There are, however, some negatives associated with immigration. Some immigrant groups seem to resist integration into their adopted nations' cultures for a variety of reasons. As indicated previously, there are now 31 Muslim communities as well as additional non-Muslim communities in western Europe that have not fully integrated into their adopted national cultures; in some instances radical elements within these minority communities are openly and sometimes violently opposed to the majority national culture. Such immigrant groups differ linguistically and religiously from the cultures of their adopted nations. History also plays a critical role in these immigrants' negative feelings about their adopted nations, as many of them come from nations that were once colonies of Western nations such as Great Britain and France. It is important to note that these immigrant groups also tend to possess lower levels of education and to experience significantly higher rates of unemployment than their counterparts in the host country do, although there are exceptions. For example, entrepreneurs born in India were leaders in the Internet revolution of the 1990s.

As noted above, one of the major justifications offered by opponents to immigration is that immigrants, who tend to be poor and unskilled, overwhelm the available resources of the towns and cities in which they reside, including educational and health systems and government subsidies designed to help the poor. Relatedly, immigrants compete directly for jobs that other unskilled and poorly educated workers desire, particularly in the short run. And, as suggested by Governor Owens's statement, much of the opposition is based on the cultural premise that immigrants cannot or will not choose to be integrated into the majority culture in terms of values, language, and so forth. Whatever the reasons provided, the fierce opposition to immigration paradoxically suggests that immigration has the potential to impede or even derail globalization and simultaneously to facilitate and hasten its advancement. Echoing the importance of this paradox, Martin Wolf (2004) has pointed out that restraining immigration, especially immigration of unskilled workers with few if any resources, is the one feature of globalization that distinguishes it from events in the period 1870–1914. Approximately 10% of the world's population permanently immigrated during

1870–1914, most probably the largest permanent migration in history (Goldin & Rweinert, 2006, p. 14). Developed nations want to preserve their economic advantages, which involves protecting their value-added goods and services. Hence these nations are creating mechanisms for restraining migration that their citizens see as threatening. We can expect that the movement to restrain immigration will continue in the developed nations, as our next paradox suggests.

Paradox 7.10. Can restricting immigration facilitate and promote it?

Robert Samuelson (2005, 2006), a respected economic journalist, has formulated this paradox. He emphasizes the fact, noted above, that there are an estimated 34 million immigrants in the United States, 12 million of whom are illegal. These immigrants, whether legal or illegal, are typically poorly educated and unskilled, at least during their early years in the nation, and they compete for scarce unskilled jobs also sought by native-born workers. In general, immigrant workers compare very unfavorably to the native-born population in terms of skill levels, educational attainments, and rates of employment. Hence such workers increase the magnitude of the underclass in the United States and in other nations and make it easier for employers to hire unskilled workers, whether immigrant or native born, at substandard wages. Citing research by George Borjas and Lawrence Katz, Harvard labor market economists, Samuelson points out that skill levels explain most of the wage gap between lower-paid immigrants and higher-paid native-born workers. Samuelson assumes that no nation has an unlimited capacity to absorb immigrants, especially when its native-born workers suffer because of such a policy, the unabated growth of the underclass, and the increased possibility of social unrest.

Notably, economic studies summarized by *The Economist* ("Economics Focus," 2006, p. 76) indicate that immigration, in the long run, has had only a small negative effect on the pay of America's least skilled. Even this effect is disputed. Thus, while immigration causes short-run disruptions in the labor market, they seem to disappear in the long run, although specific groups, such as poorly-educated and unskilled African American males, suffer disproportionately both in the short run and in the long run.

Although Samuelson focuses primarily on economic explanations, his paradox is apt and related to the previous paradox. There are both positive and negative features of immigration, and logically welcoming all immigrants without an equitable and effective program in place is very problematic, particularly as proponents and opponents of immigration begin to take extreme positions, as is happening both in the United States and elsewhere.

A reasonable starting point might be a focus on principles and standards that both proponents and opponents could accept in the debate, such as that the size of the underclass should not increase, that employers would be required to follow the laws, that such laws would be strictly enforced, and so on. At this point I invite you to identify other principles and standards that might be relevant for resolving the paradox that Samuelson has posed.

Paradox 7.11. Is immigration compatible with an equality-matching culture?

Throughout this book we have highlighted the four generic national cultures, one of which is the equality-matching, or egalitarian, culture, in which there is a high degree of individualism and a low degree of power distance. Only a small number of nations fit into this category, and they include Canada, Australia, the Netherlands, and the Scandinavian nations. Ironically, some of the most explosive encounters between Islam and Christianity have occurred in these nations. In 2005 in the Netherlands, a Muslim group killed Theo van Gogh, a well-known filmmaker, for directing a film that portrays Islam as hostile to women; this group has also threatened to kill a Somali-Dutch feminist, Hirsan Ali, who served in Parliament and was van Gogh's collaborator. In 2006 a concerted worldwide Islamic protest took place, directed against a Danish newspaper that had published 12 cartoons depicting the Prophet Muhammad very unfavorably. Riots in some Islamic nations, such as Pakistan and Indonesia, resulted in deaths and injuries to many participants and attacks on Danish embassies.

There is no doubt that these cartoons were offensive, and the major news outlets in the United States did not reprint them. However, the incident generated a vigorous debate about freedom of expression, one of the cornerstones of Western democracy, and the ability of Islam to adapt to it. It is ironic that the recent outbursts have occurred in Holland and Denmark, both of which have equality-matching cultures that attempt to treat everyone equitably. Both of these nations on a per capita basis have contributed much more than other developed nations have to helping developing Islamic regions. As an aside, the Islamic press shows similarly offensive cartoons about Christians, but they view the matter differently when their culture and religion are the focus of such cartoons. Islamic culture tends to be much more authority-ranking, and suppression of individual expression typically is higher than in market-pricing and equality-matching cultures. Other nations, including the United States, have experienced protests, but thus far not on the scale that these equality-matching cultures have faced.

Thus the paradox is that some Muslim immigrants want to live in these equality matching cultures, but in an authority-ranking fashion that may result in the suppression of free speech. Whether such immigration is compatible with market-pricing and equality-matching cultures is still an open question.

Takeaways

1. Favorable contact between cultures results when participants are of equal status and pursue common goals that are supported socially and institutionally.

2. Because of these reasons ethnic cultures have the potential both to facilitate and to inhibit or derail globalization.

3. Ethnic and civilizational cultures overlap, and the available evidence suggests that ethnic conflict is more prevalent than civilizational conflict.

4. National cultures are important, but economic unions such as the EU and NAFTA are increasing in significance and sometimes trump them.

5. What is legally and ethically acceptable in one nation may be unacceptable in other nations, but there is a significant movement to harmonize cultural practices across nations in such areas as the death penalty and financial and accounting practices.

6. While religions are generally related to positive outcomes, a danger of anthropomorphic religions is that they can become associated with fixed ideologies that justify controversial courses of action.

7. Some religions do not possess creeds and dogmas, although they articulate principles leading to the inclusion of all.

8. While the "death of distance" achieved through modern communication and transportation systems is increasing, geography and distance are still important and pose formidable barriers to the spread of globalization and borderless business.

9. There are both positive and negative features associated with immigration, and it seems necessary to control it and rationalize the immigration process in order to promote a system acceptable to citizens.

10. Authority-ranking cultures are associated with the restriction of free speech and, as such, are opposed to both equality-matching and market-pricing cultures on some issues, such as the depiction of religious leaders in the news and other media.

Discussion Questions

1. Differentiate the following concepts: race, ethnicity, national culture, and civilizational culture. Are they related? Why or why not?

2. What are the conditions under which ethnic cultures have the potential for facilitating and impeding globalization and borderless business?

3. Identify and rank the degree of importance that you attach to the following concepts: race, ethnicity, national culture, and civilizational culture. Why do you feel this way?

4. Do you feel that we should be "ethically neutral" when it comes to such cultural practices as the death penalty and female circumcision? Why or why not?

5. How are the larger economic unions such as the EU, the World Trade Organization, NAFTA, and the International Court of Justice influencing this issue of ethical neutrality?

6. Do you feel that all religions should possess creeds and dogmas? Why? How do creeds and dogmas relate to the inclusion of others who do not share these creeds and dogmas?

7. Have modern communication and transportation systems nullified the importance of geographic distance? Why or why not?

8. Does the conflict, stated frequently in religious terms, between authority-ranking cultures and both market-pricing and equality-matching cultures have the potential of derailing globalization? If yes, how can this conflict be minimized? If no, why not?

Exercises

1. In groups of five, develop an interview schedule or protocol containing both open-ended and closed questions focusing on the issues examined in this chapter: multiethnicity, religion, geography, and immigration. For example, "How do you feel about immigration?" followed by a question asking the interviewee to rate a specific issue on a 5-point scale. Members of some groups should interview recent immigrants, while other groups should interview long-term citizens. Preferably, the interviewees should be involved in business. Each group should analyze and tabulate its results, and a representative from each group should meet with representatives from the other groups. These two large sets of groups should each produce a summary report and present it in class, followed by questions and discussion.

2. Each small group of five should analyze one of the major religions treated by Huston Smith (1991). Using Smith and other sources, each group should develop a few PowerPoint slides to present to the class covering the era in which each religion originated and why; the religion's major concepts, creeds, and dogmas; its foundational leaders; its influence in the world today; and its similarities and differences with other major religions.

3. Class members should complete research on the incident involving the Danish newspaper's depiction of Islam in 12 cartoons. Each member should then write a three-page paper on the issue, focusing on the following questions:

   • Is the issue broader than just "the suppression of free speech versus democracy," and why?

   • Has Christianity been subjected to similar treatment at the hands of cartoonists and others in various Western and non-Western nations? If yes, please describe the incidents.

   • Should the major news outlets in the United States and elsewhere suppress these cartoons, and why? What criteria would you use to justify your answer?

Answer to What Happened: Generator and Its Asian Partners

GENERATOR managers in Asia addressed the problem initially by sensitizing GENERATOR HQ about the criticality of the issues involved. Asian partners wanted to be treated as equals, and GENERATOR HQ had to recognize that they owned the final products and could terminate future contracts if they were displeased. Thus, if GENERATOR HQ wanted to upgrade its products and technology, it first had to convince its Asian partners of the wisdom of this move and tailor the products to partner goals and requests rather than making the move unilaterally. In this way GENERATOR began to see international activities as different from purely domestic activities.

In addition, about three years ago GENERATOR started to refer to "GENERATOR ASIAN PARTNERS" whenever possible rather than to "GENERATOR SYSTEMS." Also, GENERATOR helped to create the Annual Asian Customer Meeting co-hosted by its Asian partners. This Meeting provides visibility to GENERATOR'S Asian partners in the industry.

In sum, partnerships and alliances are relatively new concepts in Asia. GENERATOR needs to demonstrate that a partnership is a two-way street.

Final Question: Can you think of other ways that GENERATOR could create such a partnership?

8

Economic
Development and Culture

Economic development is critical, not only for a specific nation but for all nations that are influencing and influenced by globalization. What happens in one nation affects other nations. It seems infeasible to champion a policy of "Fortress America" or its equivalent in any nation, given the growing and complex interdependencies among nations. The topics of economic development and globalization are separate but overlapping, and without economic development globalization is impossible.

Economic development involves a large number of complex issues about which there is a good amount of debate and controversy. However, as the chapter's title indicates, our focus will be only on some key issues in economic development that relate directly to culture. Still, it is important to have some understanding of the many complex issues about which there is debate and controversy in this field. Hence the first section of the chapter provides some background on these issues, debates, and controversies. The remainder of the chapter examines paradoxes relating economic development and culture. For purposes of discussion, the two sets of paradoxes fall into two categories: (1) trade, democracy, and open and free markets and (2) culture and change.

Background

David Ricardo constructed his famous and influential theory of international trade and development during the early years of the 19th Century.

169

Since that time this theory has provided the framework and justification for facilitating trade among nations and for globalization. Ricardo argued that three major factors lead to economic development within a nation, namely, land, labor, and capital; Joseph Schumpeter (1942), subsequently added entrepreneurship as a fourth component, arguing that it is the creative decisions and actions of entrepreneurs that lead to economic development and growth. (Schumpeter employed the term *creative destruction* to profile what happens in a capitalistic system, assuming there is a level playing field; as we will see, this assumption is questionable.) From Ricardo's vantage point, each nation must examine the comparative advantages it possesses because of its geographic location and resources, the skill sets and educational levels of its workers, and the amount of capital it can employ to develop an import-export strategy. For an example, Ricardo pointed out that the English had a natural advantage in the production of wool, while Spain emphasized wine growing, and these nations exchanged wool and wine, to the ultimate benefit and enrichment of both.

This theory of the comparative advantages of nations has been questioned increasingly in recent years. For instance, 40 of the world's largest multinational firms now employ, on average, 55% of their workforce outside the countries in which they are legally incorporated and earn 59% of their revenues outside the home nation ("Decoupled," 2006). When such multinationals become unhappy with the rules and tax policies governing them in their home nations, they can establish their home bases in nations more sympathetic to their points of view. During the past 2 years the earnings per share of major listed, or publicly traded, German companies have increased by more than 100%, 50% in France, and 35% in the United States. However, such large firms have been reluctant to hire additional employees or increase wages significantly. American wage earners have received about a 3% increase, on average, in recent years, even while earnings per share have risen rapidly.

Before Ricardo, the dominant theory of economic development was mercantilism supported by colonialism. *Mercantilism* argues that the strict regulation of the entire economy can significantly increase the wealth of a nation, primarily through the accumulation of bullion, a favorable balance of trade, the development of manufacturing and agriculture, and the establishment of foreign trading monopolies. In terms of colonization, mercantilism dictated that subjugated colonies should send a disproportionate share of their wealth and products to the home nation. Ancient Rome successfully employed the strategy of colonization for hundreds of years, and some writers refer to the 1,000-year period of Roman supremacy as the First Era of Globalization. Mercantilism supported by colonization is zero-sum, with only the home nation benefiting or, at the very least, benefiting disproportionately. Ricardo's theory, by contrast, is non-zero-sum, as all nations benefit and increase their wealth significantly. Still, as stated above, the theory is now in question.

Ricardo's perspective leads naturally to models of economic development that stress the stages through which an economy must proceed as it moves from a developing to a developed status (see, for example, Rostow, 1971). Such models generally reflect a biological bias: Each nation passes through early stages of development, followed by explosive growth, maturity, and decline, similar to what happens to human beings. However, decline is not inevitable and can be nullified, perhaps indefinitely, through wise decision making. Also, the time required to move from one to another stage has decreased dramatically. Nations such as Malaysia and Singapore were extremely poor in the 1950s but have improved dramatically since then. More recently, nations such as China and India seem to be moving through these stages very quickly. Both nations simultaneously possess sectors that require only unskilled labor and sectors that demand high levels of education and skills. For example, although the software industry in India contributes only about 1% to gross national product, it is advancing very rapidly. Some of the best software programmers in the world reside in India, particularly in the Bangalore area.

One of the most complex issues in this area of economic development is identifying the specific factors leading to economic growth. Frequently a theory will focus on only one or a few related factors, and these include the following:

- Abundant natural resources
- A hospitable climate
- A favorable geographical position, such as the intersection or center of a major trade route
- An entrepreneurial spirit and culture based on religious ideas, for example, Max Weber's famous argument that the *Protestant ethic* was one of the critical factors leading to the rise of capitalism (Weber, 1930) or, more specifically, that hard work and worldly success are external manifestations of religious people who thereby increase their chances of entering heaven (see box below)
- Trustworthy institutions such as impartial courts of law, a well-regulated banking system, and an equitable tax system in which citizens have confidence
- The clustering of related and supporting industries in a particular nation, such as the small textile and high-fashion firms in and around Milan, Italy

The Fusion of Religion and Worldly Success

I say you ought to be rich; you have no right to be poor. . . . I must say that you ought to spend some time getting rich. You and I know that there are some things more valuable than money; of course, we do. Ah, yes. . . . Well does the man know who has suffered that there are some things sweeter and holier and more sacred than gold. Nevertheless, the man of common sense also knows that there is not any one of those things that is not greatly enhanced by the use of money. Money is power; money has powers; and for a man to say, "I do not want money," is to say "I do not wish to do any good to my fellowmen." It is absurd thus to talk. It is absurd to disconnect them. This is a wonderfully great life, and you ought to spend your time getting money, because of the power there is in money.

Greatness consists not in holding some office; greatness really consists in doing some great deed with little means, in the accomplishment of vast purposes from the private ranks of life; this is true greatness.

SOURCE: From the "Acres of Diamonds" speech given at least 6,000 times by the Reverend Russell H. Conwell, the first president of Temple University. In Burr, 1917, pp. 414–415.

However, as soon as one writer identifies a particular factor, another writer proposes an equally plausible but different explanation. For example, in 1935 Amitore Fanfani (1984) argued persuasively that it was not the Protestant ethic but the Catholic ethic, found in Catholic-dominated nations such as France and Italy, that provided the framework for economic development during the Renaissance. Similarly, although the argument has been made that nations with harsh and cold climates suffer because of it, the examples of Finland and Norway do not accord with that thesis. Other successful nations, such as Japan (the world's second leading economy, after the United States), lack significant natural resources, while many nations possessing them in abundance have not progressed economically. Given the discrepancies, it seems logical to argue that a nation must possess a necessary and sufficient number of characteristics to become successful, but that the exact mix of these characteristics and the manner in which they are combined can vary. We will address this topic in more depth when we analyze the paradoxes relating culture to economic development, particularly the relationship between culture and institutions.

One of the most contentious issues among trade economists today is whether a nation's policy of promoting export-driven trade leads to a zero-sum situation in which its trading partners are at a serious disadvantage and suffer significantly, particularly in the long run. Several nations—such as

Japan and South Korea—have advanced economically since the end of World War II at least in large part because of such a trade policy. However, their populations, while large, are comparatively small (Japan's is 118 million and South Korea's 47 million) when compared with India (1 billion) and China (1.3 billion) out of a world population of 6.5 billion. Currently this issue is of great interest, since India and China are moving quickly through the stages of economic development.

It is important to note that capitalism takes many forms. When we speak of free-market capitalism, we are assuming that there is a level playing field. However, mercantilism and colonialism espoused a form of capitalism that was on a less-than-level playing field. Similarly, it is questionable whether export-driven capitalism occurs on a level playing field. There is, to use Schumpeter's famous term, *creative destruction*, but it comes from one nation's pursuing goals that restrict the operations of a free market.

Another concern is that to expand, China, India, and other developing nations require a disproportionately large amount of natural resources such as iron and oil, thus dramatically increasing the prices worldwide. A related concern is that China's and India's economies are export driven and, in the process of developing, are destroying not only unskilled but also highly skilled jobs in developed nations. The United States is particularly sensitive, as its citizens have been purchasing low-priced imports while the budget deficit has reached a historic level due partially to the imbalance between imports and exports. Given the large populations in China and India, and the emergence of other developing nations, such concerns are understandable. There is even a fear that the export-driven policies of developing nations will overwhelm the ability of the world's global trading system to function effectively.

Perhaps the greatest concern among economists is that Ricardo's trade theory, which has been accepted unquestioningly for generations and has provided the rationale for globalization, is inadequate to explain what is happening today. More specifically, a well-known phenomenon termed immiseration may be undermining Ricardo's win-win perspective. Jagdish Bhagwati, a strong defender of globalization (2004), demonstrated the mathematical proof for this phenomenon in 1958. *Immiseration* essentially means that a national economy can suffer dramatically even while growing through accumulating capital or improving productivity. If a nation exports a significant amount of a particular product, additional production and export of it would depress the world's demand and price for it, even to the point that profits turn negative, thus weakening the exporting nation. His proposed solution is the diversification of a nation's products so that the nation is not overly dependent on any one of them. However, some economists have noted that immiseration seems to be affecting developed nations with a diversified product mix, such as the United States, and that the intense price and wage competition from China, India, and other developing nations is accelerating the immiserating effect. For example, while large U.S. corporations gained by moving computer chip factories abroad starting around 1990, thereby decreasing the cost of personal computers 10–30%, the overall economy appears to have suffered due to the loss of jobs and skills and the increase in the federal deficit resulting directly from the imbalance of imports and exports (Bernstein, 2004).

Along the same line of reasoning, Roger Martin (2006) pointed out that Ricardo's assumption of harnessing a nation's natural endowments to create wealth is frequently a mirage. It is easy to understand Ricardo's example of comparative advantage in terms of English wool producers and Spanish wine growers. However, in the current environment such comparative and natural advantages are difficult to identify. General Motors and other major American auto companies assumed for decades that they had a natural advantage over their Japanese competitors in the large-car and high-end part of the market. They conceded to the Japanese only that part of the market emphasizing small and inexpensive cars. However, once the Japanese had conquered the lower end of the market, they focused on the larger cars and the more affluent part of the market. Today the Japanese auto companies are fierce competitors and frequently leaders in all parts of the market.

As discussed in Chapter 2, primarily because of the economic policies followed by Mao Tse-tung and the Communist party, China was extremely poor until 1978. At that time the Chinese Communist government under the leadership of Deng Xiaoping developed an economic strategy under which it sequentially developed one economic region before providing support for the next targeted economic region. This was a direct repudiation of the collectivization that Mao espoused, although the government and its policies remained Communist. India followed the path of democracy but with a socialistic bias, emphasizing regulations and discouraging trade and entrepreneurship. Prior to 1992 a foreign entrepreneur wishing to operate in India had to wait an average of 500 days before the initial paperwork was approved, while an Indian entrepreneur waited only about 17 days. After 1992 the government significantly reduced and in some cases eliminated such impediments that were stifling economic growth, international trade, and the vigorous movement of India into the global economy. Even the longest-ruling Communist party in the world, which governs West Bengal and its major city, Kolkata (the former Calcutta), has embraced capitalism. This party actively courts multinational corporations to operate there while restraining labor unions (Chu, 2006).

Further, it may well be that the most vexing problem is the funding for economic development. The European Union (EU) addressed this problem by providing development funds to newly admitted nations; after they moved forward economically, their citizens paid taxes to underwrite the development of nations admitted at a later time. However, since 1945 approximately $1 trillion of aid has been provided to various countries by the World Bank, the International Monetary Fund, and other international agencies, frequently with little if any success. Several African nations with abundant national resources have received generous funding—approximately $568 billion over four decades—that has been largely squandered because of corruption, mismanagement, and rivalries among different peoples and religious groups.

In the 1970s, 11% of the world's poorest people lived in Africa and 76% in Asia; by 1998 the figures were dramatically reversed: 66% in Africa and 15% in Asia (Sala-i-Martin, 2002). During this time the Asian nations opened their markets significantly, but as explained above, many of them also followed the export-driven strategy that financed much of this development. Still, these Asian nations received disproportionately fewer funds from international agencies than did their African counterparts.

Today there are several ways of ranking nations, particularly in terms of their potential to develop economically as measured by a number of indicators. These include the degree of corruption as perceived by international executives who are asked to provide bribes in exchange for business opportunities, the degree of trust by citizens in institutions such as courts and police systems, and so on. The Heritage Foundation, for example, constructs a well-known yearly ranking of national economic freedom that appears in the *Wall Street Journal* and other outlets. Transparency International, in Germany, asks international managers to assess the degree of corruption they face when doing business in specific nations, such as the degree to which they must use bribes to undertake and complete business transactions, and ranks nations accordingly. Such rankings put pressure on developing nations seeking to globalize, as an unfavorable ranking can discourage multinational firms from investing in them.

William Easterly (2006), a former economist at the World Bank, has authored a blistering attack on the specific aid programs that have been tried and have failed since World War II. One illustrative example is the top-down approach of trusting governmental leaders receiving grants and loans to administer them wisely. Another example is a bottom-up approach at the village level under which each village would receive both instruction in setting up small businesses and funding to undertake village development. Easterly has made some sensible suggestions for relatively inexpensive solutions to some of the problems, including providing clean water and 12-cent doses of malaria medicines to malaria victims. Still needed is a theory and plan into which specific suggestions can be categorized, both for the purposes of prioritization and for creating systematic long-term policies.

Recently George Lodge and Craig Wilson (2006) noted that hundreds of governmental and nongovernmental organizations identify poverty reduction as their mission. Still, Lodge and Wilson's survey of the research indicates that much of the support goes directly to governments lacking either the will or the ability (or both) to reduce poverty. They suggest that multinational corporations, while they are one of the major drivers of globalization and affluence, establish a World Development Corporation capitalized by the multinationals themselves, although governmental agencies could be active participants and contribute funds. This corporation would invest in developing nations and create profits that would then be reinvested in other developing nations. However, this corporation would face formidable difficulties, including the provision of a control system that would minimize the ineffective distribution of funds and promote the reasonable probability that profits would materialize.

While the World Bank notes that nearly half the world's population exists on $2 or less per day, and one sixth gets by on less than $1 a day, there is cause for hope. Poverty has fallen from approximately two-thirds of the developing world population in 1981 to approximately half in 2001. For the extremely poor (less than $1 a day) it has decreased from approximately 40% to 20% (Goldin & Reinert, 2006, pp. 28–29). Since World War II successive rounds of international trade talks have lowered tariffs dramatically (see Chapter 1). Today 149 out of 220 nations in the world are members of the World Trade Organization (WTO), which is the final arbiter when there is a dispute between nations trading with one another. Over time, as more nations join the WTO, its power will increase, as will its ability, it is hoped, to balance the demands of all nations adroitly and allow the non-zero-sum perspective envisioned by Ricardo to become a reality. Still, the self-interest of corporations cannot be disregarded. If there is additional decoupling between such interests and the interests of individual nations, the power and efficacy of Ricardo's theory becomes highly suspect. There are issues, debates, and controversies that need to be addressed by the WTO and the nations, and additional issues will arise in the future. Still, the WTO standards and rulings provide a reasonable and equitable framework through which many if not most of the disputes can be resolved.

Trade, Democracy, and Open and Free Markets

For our purposes the concepts of trade, democracy, and open and free markets are separate but overlapping. Frequently writers employ the term *free markets* only, or they use this term interchangeably with the related term *open markets.* There are, however, subtle differences between these two terms, since *free markets* implies both a democratic and a capitalistic form of government in which the principle of equitable treatment of all is valued and citizens elect government officials. *Open markets* are not necessarily free in this sense of the term, although the government typically encourages foreign trade. China, for instance, is capitalistic in the sense that it has open markets, but its form of government is Communist. This discussion differentiates between open and free markets when appropriate.

Paradox 8.1. Are democracy and free markets antithetical to each other?

Amy Chua (2003) has put forth an intriguing paradox supported with numerous case studies linking democracy and markets. She pointed out that after the fall of the Berlin Wall in 1989 and the movement of many European nations away from Communism to capitalism, many felt unbounded enthusiasm for the belief that democracy and free and open markets would transform the world into a peaceful global community. Since that time, however, the record is mixed at best and includes the rise of militant Islam, ethnic wars, two genocides unprecedented since the Nazi Holocaust, and the continuing and perhaps increasing threat of nuclear war.

According to Chua, developing nations face a difficult situation. Members of the majority of the population in a typical developing nation tend to be ethnically related and poor. They tend to elect popular leaders who have little if any background in or understanding of business and economics. Such leaders become dependent on knowledgeable, educated, and skilled members of a minority group that controls a disproportionate share of the national wealth.

For example, before the Indonesian riots of 1998, the ethnic Muslims constituted the overwhelming majority in the population and in any election, but the government relied heavily on the Chinese, who constituted about 3% of the population. Although the Chinese were the target in the 1998 riots, in fact only a very small percentage of them benefited significantly from the Chinese-government partnership then dominating the nation. Chua found such a pattern in Russia after 1990 with the rise of the seven oligarchs, and in other nations such as Malaysia, the Philippines, and Zimbabwe. That is to say, when a nation introduces democratic elections at the early stages of economic development, a destructive cycle is unleashed: The government becomes dependent on a small number of members in a minority group, bribery and corruption frequently occur, and demagogues appear who incite envy and hatred of the minority group.

Many of these developing nations open up their markets dramatically to international trade by lowering tariffs. However, their markets are not free in the sense that members of both the market-dominant majority and the knowledgeable and well-networked minority engage in bribery and related activities in order to placate the other group and to benefit themselves, and inequalities tend to persist and even increase, sometimes significantly. Paradoxically democracy and free markets, which exist simultaneously in developed economies, are opposed to one another in many developing nations.

Unfortunately, Chua hasn't any startling and innovative policy suggestions. Still, her incisive and insightful analysis allows us to understand more clearly the process of ethnic antagonisms and violence.

Paradox 8.2. Does trust increase trade among nations? Does increased trade lead to conflict and war among nations?

As might be expected, nations seem to prefer trading partners who are similar to them culturally. For instance, Canada's largest trading partner is the United States, and Germany exports more than 50% of its products and services to other members of the EU. Such geographical closeness also decreases the transaction costs of doing business and the overall level of risk. Alan Rugman (2005) has developed a database on the world's 500 largest multinational companies that confirms this tendency. He shows that most multinationals tend to operate primarily in specific regions of the world close to their home nations. From Rugman's perspective, globalization is a myth, while regionalization is the reality, at least for these companies. We will discuss Rugman's thesis in detail in the next chapter.

More specifically, a frequently accepted assumption is that democracy is strongly associated with peace and, by implication, with increased trade among nations. Politicians regularly treat this assumption as fact and statistical correlations tend to confirm it. However, as Mark Helprin (2006) reminds us, there have been some glaring and critical exceptions. Germany, a principal architect of World War II, was a democracy prior to it, and citizens accepted the appointment of Hitler as their leader in the 1930s, even though he was appointed rather than elected. Even Japan "saw its parliamentary democracy wax and wane in the decades before World War II, losing eventually to the militarists but resurging in 1937 almost to regain control" (p. M1).

Three economists—Luigi Guiso, Paola Sapienza, and Luigi Zingales (2005)—looked at the regular surveys that Eurobarometer conducts among

EU citizens, and particularly at those questions focusing on trusting nationalities other than one's own. Germans are the most trusted, while others, such as the Italians, rank lower. However, Guiso, Sapienza, and Zingales examined more-specific data, finding, for example, that Germans trust the British more than do the French. They then attempted to predict the amount of trade between the EU nations, considered in pairs, using four major variables: cultural trust, religion, a history of war, and wide genetic differences. They found that an increase in trust of one standard deviation between any two of the nations was associated with a 30% rise in trade between them, and with an increase in bilateral foreign direct investment of as much as 75%.

However, rather than considering trade as the dependent variable, or the one we are trying to predict, it is useful to employ it as an independent or explanatory variable to ask, as trade between nations increases, does war decline and peace increase? This question is of major importance, given that the United States is increasingly involved in trade with China, India, and other developing nations with different traditions, cultures, and governmental structures. Unfortunately, the historical record is mixed. In the late 1840s, the United States and Britain were considering war against one another because of territorial disputes in the Pacific Northwest involving the lucrative fur trade in that region. Britain, then the world's superpower, chose to emphasize peace and trade over war, and the two nations developed strong bonds that persist to this day. On the other hand, Germany and Britain increased trade significantly with one another for decades prior to World War I, but during the war itself they were fierce adversaries. Similarly, Katherine Barbieri (as cited in Ip & King, 2005) has found that increased trade is associated with a higher incidence of war, presumably because nations have more to fight about. It is hoped that such organizations as the WTO and the International Court of Justice will buffer against such outcomes. Still, there are no guarantees, and nations have sometimes violated or repudiated international treaties that they have signed.

There are, then, no hard-and-fast answers to the questions posed above. Paradoxically, increased trade is sometimes related positively and sometimes negatively to trust and war, depending on the situation. Still, the positive and strong statistical relationship between trust and trade—as reported by Guiso, Sapienza, and Zingalis—would indicate a bright future for an increasingly interdependent and globalizing world, with the proviso that supra-agencies such as the WTO must possess the power to enforce rulings involving multinational corporations and nations. Over time, members of ethnic and national cultures should learn to work together more effectively with one another, leading to a non-zero-sum outcome benefiting all.

Culture and Change

Any change, including those created by economic development, can be unsettling, as it involves doing things differently. In developing nations change frequently consists of moving from a traditional way of life to a modernized version of it. However, it is easy to overestimate the degree of difficulty and the amount of resistance that economic development can engender. If the affected individuals can see the specific benefits that will flow from the change, they tend to be willing to accept it. For example, an Internet order involving the purchase of handmade scarves is transmitted to a factory in Rovieng, a small rural village in Cambodia lacking electricity and telephone service. The factory workers then produce the custom-made scarves. Solar panels power the factory's desktop computers and a satellite dish links them to the Internet (Chandrasekaran, 2001). Because of this factory, Rovieng is much more prosperous than in the past, and its workers understand the advantages that can be derived through development and linkage with the global economy. This blending of traditional and modern ways of life was made possible through funding from a U.S. aid organization.

Similarly, Shi Yongxin, the Abbot or head of the world-famous Buddhist Shaolin Temple renowned for kung fu, employs television, films, and the Web to market the Temple as a tourist attraction. He spends a good amount of time in his chauffeur-driven jeep and flies around the world networking and advertising the Temple's appeal to tourists. Although some of the Buddhist monks grumble that he has become "too modernized," they recognize the importance of his strategy if the Temple is to survive and prosper economically (Ni, 2005).

Still, there are paradoxes in the area of economic development and change. In this section we examine them.

> **Paradox 8.3. Are institutions more important than culture for explaining economic development?**

The concepts of culture and institutions are closely related but separate. Institutions such as courts of law, police systems, governmental systems, and educational systems provide the framework in which the dynamics of life occur both at work and outside it. If citizens do not feel these institutions are trustworthy, they will tend to rely on other ways of coping, particularly by involvement in groups that are designed to circumvent the legal system, the tax system, and the police system. The sovereignty of such groups becomes of paramount importance, since they tend to buffer individuals from the random actions of untrustworthy institutions. As we have seen in Chapter 2, the Mafia in Italy arose originally because of this fact. Douglas North (1981, 1990) received the Nobel Prize in economics for showing that trustworthy institutions are critical for economic development.

The work of Mancer Olson (1982) on the rise and decline of nations supports this point of view. He has demonstrated that as the number of interest groups in a nation increases, national prosperity declines. Admittedly interest groups must be allowed to exist and operate in a democracy, as they fulfill many essential functions, including the provision of a diversity of viewpoints and dissemination of information about their activities and points of view. However, such groups can become an impediment to economic growth if they divert a nation's attention from optimal solutions, even to the point that citizens begin to view institutions as untrustworthy because of the influence interest groups exert over them. In this sense such interest groups become free riders, taking critically needed resources away from important activities. For instance, in and around Washington, D.C., there are thousands of trade and professional associations and lobbyists representing specific companies whose main focus is influencing the U.S. Congress. There have been reported instances in which a congressional leader, on the floor of the Congress, has blatantly distributed checks of lobbying groups supporting the congresspersons politically. Such actions do not inspire confidence in the independence of legislators. However, as Olson's work demonstrates, the United States is far from alone when it comes to lobbyists.

Extending the work on institutions and interest groups, Hernando de Soto (2000) attempted to answer a very ambitious question, as the subtitle of his book *The Mystery of Capital* indicates: *Why Capitalism Triumphs in the West and Fails Everywhere Else.* He began with the seminal meaning of the word *capital.* In Medieval Latin the term referred to cattle, which historically have represented sources of wealth beyond the meat that can become food. De Soto pointed out that the West has ample capital but that the rest of the world lacks it in varying degrees. It is difficult if not impossible to create capital without some initial capital. To create change, it is necessary to turn "dead" capital such as illegal shantytowns into genuine or active capital. Many of the residents of shantytowns, which are frequently sited on public lands, are very creative in providing water systems, electrical systems, and so forth for their communities. However, interest groups with dominant power manipulate the legal and real estate systems in their own favor. They frequently allow the creation of such communities, only to subsequently assert property rights over them, sometimes legally and sometimes illegally. De Soto pointed out that only about 100 years ago the United States adopted equitable rules for allowing the transfer of public or unused property legally to users of it, after which prosperity increased dramatically. Other Western nations and Japan have gone through similar transformations of making dead capital active within the past few hundred years.

De Soto and others have been amassing data to show that giving title to public land or dead capital results in positive outcomes. The problem of informal occupation of vacant land in urban areas is widespread in developing nations. As a percentage of all housing, the informal occupation rates were as follows as of 1999: 51.4% in sub-Saharan Africa; 41.2% in East Asia and the Pacific; 26.4% in Latin America and the Caribbean; 25.9%, Middle East and North Africa; and 5.7%, eastern Europe and central Asia (Angel, 2000).

In the Argentinean barrio of San Francisco Solano, on the fringes of Buenos Aires, a natural experiment occurred that tests the validity of land titling as it relates to economic development. This barrio encompasses only 1 square mile. All settlers occupied the public land and none of them owned their land or homes. Through quirks in the law and some complications of ownership, 419 settlers received title while 410 did not. There was no difference in their occupational level, social status, or financial status in 1989, as might be expected. However, since that time the titled settlers have far surpassed their counterparts in a wide range of critical indicators, for example, higher quality of house improvements, higher educational performance of children, and lower teenage pregnancy rates. Even when the conservative financial institutions would not lend them money, the titled settlers improved their homes and took risks financially that their untitled counterparts avoided. Titling seemed to lead to a greater degree of self-confidence and trust in the future (Moffett, 2005).

This issue is particularly important in developing nations such as China and Russia. More than 60% of China's population resides in the countryside, but the land is owned by regional governments who have been enforcing ownership to create factories and modern cities, taking away the livelihoods of millions of farmers and causing widespread unemployment and fierce resistance. Perhaps the major challenge facing China is providing trustworthy institutions and titling so that a civil war does not materialize.

Still, the relative importance of culture and institutions is complex and problematic. If culture is more important, then the institutions that are formed should directly reflect its peculiarities and possibly even a tendency toward a bias in which members of one group receive more equitable treatment than their counterparts do. If institutions are more important than culture, it should be possible to create relatively culture-free institutions that citizens perceive as trustworthy.

Tan and Peng (1999; Peng, 2002) completed a rigorous, quasi-experimental study focused specifically on this issue of relative importance. During the

1990s they analyzed in depth three groups of entrepreneurs who had founded businesses, focusing specifically on their strategic orientations and perceptions: native Chinese working in China under Communist governmental rule and institutions; Chinese Americans; and white, Anglo-Saxon Americans. China is a Communist nation that is institutionally different from almost any other nation. Tan and Peng hypothesized that if culture were more important than institutions, the Chinese in mainland China and Chinese Americans would tend to be significantly different in attitudes and values from their Anglo-Saxon counterparts. However, they found that the similarity between the Anglo-Saxon and Chinese American samples was significant but not that significant between the two Chinese samples. They concluded by arguing that institutions are more important than culture, thus lending support to North's original conclusion.

However, North (2005) and other economists have analyzed in depth why the distinctive Chinese approach to development since 1979 has been so spectacularly successful. As discussed above, China funds one regional economic area and ensures it is able to become successful before funding another area. North pointed out the following:

> Two features stand out: 1) While the institutions China employed are different from developed nations, the incentive implications were similar; and 2) China has been confronting new problems and pragmatically attempting new solutions. (p. A14)

North argued that there are many paths to development. From his perspective it is critical to establish an institutional structure derived from a nation's distinctive cultural institutions and accompanied by proper economic incentives. Hence entrepreneurs and companies will be motivated to make major investments and assume the risk of failure. In this sense the distinction between culture and institutions becomes blurred.

However, culture and institutions are separate concepts and can be manipulated separately. For example, in the early 1900s President Ataturk, supported by the military, changed Turkey from a theocratic Muslim nation to a secular nation in a few years, even though the population was 99% Muslim. Major changes included a shift from Islamic to European codes of law, closing of religious schools and lodges, use of the Roman alphabet, and recognition of the Western calendar rather than a religious one. He even mandated that all individuals using the main bridge leading to Istanbul understand one new word per day written in the Roman alphabet, thus hastening its acceptance. Since that time Turkey has developed economically, even though the issue of religion and its relationship to the state is still very sensitive.

This discussion lends support to the theory that there are four types of generic cultures (see Chapter 2). While China has opened up its markets, it is still an authority-ranking national culture that values a top-down approach to decision making. Its Communist framework has allowed the government to develop a distinctive strategy for economic development that would probably be inappropriate in a market-pricing or equality-matching (egalitarian) culture. Still, the fact that Turkey was able to change relatively quickly does suggest that authority-ranking cultures are capable of adapting successfully and that culture-free change, at least in a relative sense, is possible.

There may be no solution to the paradox about the relative importance of culture and institutions. They are both important. In one situation culture may be more relevant than institutions, as North's analysis of China's development suggests. However, in another situation institutions may be more important than culture, as our analysis of Turkey's development indicates. They are very closely related but separate concepts, and can be treated as such.

Paradox 8.4. Do economic development and globalization lead to individualism?

Throughout, this book has placed a major emphasis on the cross-cultural dimension of individualism-collectivism. Individualism stresses the primacy of the individual, who sees himself or herself as independent from the group and makes decisions accordingly. Collectivism is the opposite, and the individual makes decisions in terms of group values rather than personal preferences. At first glance we might expect that economic development would lead to individualism. Greater affluence allows individuals to make a wider range of choices and to satisfy a larger number of desires and needs. Case studies tend to confirm this view. For example, many women in Japan and China tend to delay marriage or avoid it, since married women are expected to take on onerous family responsibilities, including taking care of the spouse's parents within one closely integrated household. Some regional governments in China are penalizing adult children financially and even threatening to jail them if they do not take care of their parents. As indicated by Paradox 2.3, both individualists and collectivists can be selfish and self-serving, depending on the frame of reference. For example, a collectivist would act selfishly if personal preferences were more important than the group norms and wishes, as seems to be happening among some Chinese adult children. Still, the case studies uniformly support a relationship between economic growth and individualism.

However, a closer analysis of the situation yields a different and more nuanced perspective. Hofstede and Bond (1988) analyzed economic growth during the period 1967–1985 using two separate sets of data: the 53-nation Hofstede study (1980) and a replication of it focusing on 22 nations on all five continents and Asian values in particular (Chinese Culture Connection, 1987). Specifically, the Chinese Culture Connection added some items that focused on Confucian values and practices to the original Hofstede survey. The Chinese Culture Connection researchers confirmed that three of the four Hofstede dimensions exist in all 22 nations, namely, individualism-collectivism, masculinity-femininity, and power distance. However, uncertainty avoidance or the acceptance of risk did not emerge as a separate dimension and was replaced by a new dimension, Confucian dynamism. It consists of emphasizing persistence, ordering relationships by status, behaving in accordance with this order, stressing thrift, and having a sense of shame. The East Asian nations, which have experienced dramatic growth since the 1960s, scored particularly high on this dimension. Confucian dynamism is related statistically to measures of economic growth from 1965 to 1985. However, across the 22 nations none of the original four Hofstede dimensions was statistically related to measures of economic growth.

Using a sophisticated cross-lagged correlational study on his national data set, Hofstede (1980) demonstrated that increased gross national product or wealth seemed to generate more individualism than collectivism. However, this longitudinal study involved a very short historical period, 1967–1971, rendering the results of questionable value unless confirmed in larger longitudinal studies.

The case studies and survey findings in combination suggest that an increase in various aspects of individualism frequently accompanies economic growth. However, if an Asian culture is able to maintain an emphasis on traditional values such as persistence and a sense of shame, prosperity should be the result. It is not necessary that values related to economic growth be identical across all cultures. Western values may overlap with the values of the Confucian dynamic but be different. What seems to matter is that a culture manifest values both delaying present gratification for future rewards and emphasizing contributions to society (see the box earlier in this chapter). While Confucius created the concept of the ideal Confucian person who contributes time and energy to family and society, other religions, such as Judaism, Catholicism, and Protestantism, put forth similar perspectives. In this sense many cultures possess the equivalent of the Confucian dynamic, and most if not all such values seem to be rooted in spirituality and religions.

Notably, a culture can stress individualism at one time and collectivism at another, depending on the situation. Surveys typically indicate that people in the United States score at or near the top on individualism. However, during World War II and after September 11, 2001, they could be portrayed as collectivistic, emphasizing group values, sometimes at the expense of individual rights. Dipak Gupta (2006) has thoughtfully summarized why such changes in orientation can occur at different times:

> The clash of civilizations, if there is one, is between the two primal motivations that make us human. Cultures based on individualism are often at odds with the forces of the collective. Our primal need to strive for personal betterment collides with the desire to belong and to do well for the group in which we claim membership. (p. B7)

Paradox 8.5. Why do citizens vote for and accept stationary bandits as political leaders?

Thus far we have focused on developing economies and why some move forward while others falter. However, developed and developing economies can regress economically. Russia today is classified as a developing economy, and several measures associated with prosperity have changed dramatically since 1990, including a much lower average life expectancy, the decline in medical care available to the general public, and the increase in corruption and crime. Until 1990, even though Russia was underdeveloped in many ways, it was considered one of the world's two superpowers.

Other nations have also experienced such regression. Japan prior to World War II was economically and militarily strong, partly because the Japanese government consciously made a decision to modernize its industries and military in the early 1900s. It sponsored a large program for Japanese students to study in Western universities so that they would be exposed to cutting-edge research and learning, which they then introduced to Japanese industry and the military. However, Japan's defeat in World War II weakened the nation dramatically; immediately afterward the average life expectancy was less than 50. Germany's experience was similar. China, because of the collectivization that Mao Tse-tung forced on the nation between 1949 and 1976, suffered a similar fate. At least 50 million Chinese died because of illness and starvation brought about by collectivization and thoughtless government policies.

There have been many attempts to explain how and why such regression occurs. Typically it involves the ascendance of a political leader, sometimes through a democratic election, who promotes and enforces programs that in retrospect seem foolhardy and even insane. Mancer Olson (2000) addressed this issue through recourse to metaphorical reasoning. He suggested that such political leaders represent two types of banditry: roving and stationary. Genghis Khan represents the epitome of a roving bandit, as he simply plundered, killed, and confiscated resources without helping the captive population in any way. However, a stationary bandit resides in the community he eventually weakens and sometimes destroys.

At times a stationary bandit becomes the major political leader in a nation because he helps the citizenry more than the existing political leaders do. Chalmers Johnson (1962) showed that Mao's rise in China was supported by the peasantry, but not because of their feelings about their inequitable treatment at the hands of the existing Chinese government. Rather, Mao and his guerrilla army helped them fight the marauding Japanese who were pillaging their villages immediately before and during World War II. In return, the peasants supported Mao in his fight against the Chinese government.

Typically, once he becomes the political leader of a nation, such a person introduces changes that provide immediate benefits to most citizens. Hitler, for example, supported the introduction of strict hours of work that included the provision of one day off for all on Sunday and the closing of grocery stores on the weekends. Workers responded very positively, since previously many of them had no recourse but to work excessively long hours if they wished to keep their positions and avoid penury.

Olson (2000) pointed out that Stalin's long tenure in Russia can be explained in a similar manner. During the 1930s Russia experienced a period of prosperity, part of which was derived from the taxation system Stalin introduced. From Olson's perspective Stalin may have been the best tax collector in history. The citizens responded favorably to the positive actions he was able to take because of the financial resources provided by the tax system.

In all these national cultures, however, the stationary bandit led the nation on a destructive course of action. There are obviously many reasons this outcome occurs. Also, Olson's work (2000) is merely the starting point for testing the validity of the concept of stationary banditry and the economic regression of nations. Still, it provides a useful perspective that allows us to explain both the ascension of political leaders in a wide variety of contexts and the reason economic regression occurs in some situations, even when such leaders initially introduce positive changes. Such leadership represents the ultimate dilemma, as stationary bandits (in governments and corporations) provide the majority with immediate benefits that are eventually neutralized because of the excesses that the leader champions.

Takeaways

1. Trade theory's explanation of economic development is controversial, especially when it comes to economic growth. For a number of reasons the phenomenon of immiseration seems to be occurring in the United States and

other developed nations that emphasize free and open markets. One of the most important reasons is the export-driven strategy that China and other developing nations have pursued.

2. One-factor theories of economic development appear problematic. Rather, a combination of factors seems related to economic development, but their exact mix varies from situation to situation.

3. While proponents of different persuasions have championed the Protestant ethic, the Catholic ethic, or Confucian dynamism, it can be argued that these perspectives overlap significantly. The key variables seem to be hard work and an emphasis on deferring present gratification for future rewards and emphasizing contributions to society.

4. At the early stages of economic development in a nation, lawfully elected leaders from the dominant ethnic group tend to work with a small number of highly skilled and well-placed individuals from a minority group who can handle the intricacies of business and trade, both within the nation and outside it. This partnership frequently unleashes ethnic hatred of the minority group in a vicious, self-reinforcing cycle.

5. Trust influences trade positively, but the influence of trade on war is problematic. There is some evidence suggesting that increased trade generates conflict and eventually war between nations.

6. Culture and institutions are closely related but separate concepts. Economic development can be achieved by creating a program of culture-free development, as happened in Turkey. Alternatively, economic development can be actualized by creating institutions that are harmonious with the culture, as seems to be happening in China.

7. Perhaps the most promising body of work on economic development is that led by Hernando de Soto, who identifies the manipulation of dead capital so that it becomes active capital as critical, especially in the area of titling land.

8. Economic regression rather than development can occur in various ways, one of which is the acceptance of stationary bandits as political leaders.

Discussion Questions

1. Describe Ricardo's theory of international trade. What is immiseration? How is Ricardo's theory related to immiseration today? Why is the decoupling of the interests of multinational firms and interests of the nations in which they are headquartered critical not only for Ricardo's theory but also for the future of developed nations?

2. Do you feel that one factor explains economic development better than other factors? Why? Identify five such factors and your preferred factor. Why do you prefer this factor?

3. Compare and contrast the Protestant ethic, the Catholic ethic, and Confucian dynamism.

4. What are some of the major issues surrounding export-driven trade and the expanding economies of China and other developing nations?

5. How do free markets differ from open markets? How are free markets related to democracy in many nations at the early stages of economic development? Please explain.

6. Why is the influence of trust on trade different from the influence of trade on peace or war? Please compare these two relationships. How great is the magnitude of the influence of trust on trade? Please explain. How great is the influence of increased trade on war? Please explain.

7. Discuss the relationship between culture and institutions. Does culture influence institutions or vice versa? Please explain.

8. Discuss the work of Hernando de Soto. Is titling of land both necessary and sufficient for successful economic development? Why or why not?

9. How does stationary banditry relate to economic regression?

Exercises

1. Divide the class into small groups of five or less. Each group should study one of the following: the International Monetary Fund, the World Bank, the International Court of Justice, the WTO, and one or more major nonprofit organizations that work in the area of economic development. Each group should present a 15-minute analysis and critique of its selected organization to the entire class.

2. Two teams should debate, in front of the class, the relative merits and problems associated with export-driven trade. Time for rebuttal should be allowed. Class discussion should then occur.

9

Globalization and Culture

D iscussions of globalization frequently involve committed advocates of it or equally committed opponents or both, and there does not appear to be a middle ground between them. Both advocates and opponents tend to realize that they are making statements about the past and predictions about the future, and they generally do so in relatively black-and-white terms. This chapter makes a major distinction between two concepts, risk and uncertainty, but only infrequently is this distinction emphasized in the usual discussions and debates about globalization. *Risk* essentially refers to the traditional testing of hypotheses: Analysts have sufficient information to make reasonable probabilistic predictions so that they can either accept or reject a specific hypothesis. *Uncertainty*, however, means that analysts do not or cannot know enough to make reasonable probabilistic predictions. At best, they can either reject or not reject a hypothesis, but they cannot accept it fully. It is for this reason that judges instruct juries to return a verdict of "guilty or not guilty" rather than "guilty or innocent" (Bernstein, 1996). Similarly, economists using sophisticated econometric models are able to predict the state of the economy 3–6 months into the future with a low risk of inaccuracy (risk) but with much less accuracy beyond that point (uncertainty).

Frank Knight, a University of Chicago economist, based his analysis on this distinction and titled his classic book accordingly: *Risk, Uncertainty, and Profit* (1921). His viewpoint was echoed by John Maynard Keynes and many others who found it very difficult if not impossible to predict probabilistically why stock markets drop dramatically at some points in time but not at other similar points; why the Great Depression in the 1930s occurred; and why the outbreak of World War I happened in 1914, especially since trade had been increasing very significantly among the opposing nations between 1870 and 1914 (see Bernstein, 1996, and Paradox 9.7). Knight (1964) put forward the following statement expressing his point of view:

> There is much question as to how far the world is intelligible at all. . . . It is only in the very special and crucial cases that anything like a mathematical study can be made. (p. 209)

In this chapter we are using the terms *risk* and *uncertainty* to highlight some issues about which we have a good amount of certainty (risk) and much less certainty (uncertainty) in terms of outcomes. The final section of the chapter continues our discussion of social and political issues that are directly linked to globalization. Again the emphasis is on paradoxes that are significantly influenced by cultural considerations.

Risk

Globalization, by its very nature, faces many risks. As indicated above, it is possible to predict with a good amount of certainty what the actual outcomes of these risks will be. We analyze three important paradoxes focusing on this issue.

Paradox 9.1. Can global economic integration occur without political and cultural integration?

John Naisbitt (1994) believes that the major paradox facing a globalizing world is that most ethnic groups desire the advantages associated with economic integration, such as the lowering of tariffs and the ability to move capital across borders quickly, but oppose becoming politically and culturally integrated. He predicted that we will live in a world of 1,000 nations divided along ethnic, linguistic, and religious lines. This seems far-fetched, especially since there are many good reasons for a nation to be relatively large, including its attractiveness to global investors. However, many large nations have split into smaller nations since the end of the Cold War in 1990; on the European continent, more than 20 new nations have come into existence since that time. Naisbitt began his book by pointing out that Andorra, a small and ethnically distinct region in the Pyrenees between France and Spain with a population of 47,000, became a sovereign nation on March 14, 1993. Similarly, because of the Balkan Wars in the 1990s, the former Yugoslavia has been divided into four nations: Serbia, Slovenia, Bosnia, and Croatia; recently Macedonia opted to become independent from

Serbia. Even nations such as Spain and Belgium now have autonomous ethnic regions that operate independently on almost all matters except for a few common matters such as defense and foreign trade. And the examples keep multiplying.

Still, the pace of economic integration continues unabated, as more nations seek to join the World Trade Organization (WTO) in order to take advantage of favorable trading policies. The European Union (EU), which includes 27 nations and 450,000,000 citizens and is currently the largest regional trading bloc in the world, continues to grow as additional nations seek admission. And the North American Free Trade Association, involving the United States, Mexico, and Canada, has proved so successful that some neighboring nations are seeking either admission or similar arrangements. Superficially, then, the answer to the paradox is that economic integration can occur without political and cultural integration.

However, there are some provisos. Some nations, such as Britain, are members of the EU but not of its currency system, preferring their own currencies over the euro. On some critical issues one negative vote in the EU parliament can stymie any action. While European citizens increasingly identify with the EU (Chapter 7), 90% of them still give their primary allegiance to their respective nations. Similarly, Mexico and the United States continue to spar over illegal immigration to the United States, and Canadians do not want to become Americanized and sometimes express very negative opinions about people in the United States, even though the United States is Canada's largest trading partner (Gannon, 2004).

Even more troubling, the Doha round of international trade discussions has been canceled, perhaps permanently, and there are now 250 bilateral and regional trade agreements, double the number a decade ago. Such trade agreements neutralize the influence of the WTO on many issues, plausibly stopping globalization in its tracks.

Still, leaders within nations tend to prefer integration into a common economic market encompassing other nations, as a cost-benefit analysis clearly favors such a relationship. Over time, it is probable but not inevitable that cultural and political integration will occur, at least to some degree. There will be an increased tendency for individuals to marry people from other national cultures, given the ability to cross borders easily and to work in different nations, as happens in the EU. At the very least, there will be increased contact across national and ethnic lines, although this can lead to negative feelings if positively reinforcing conditions are not present (see Chapter 4). Just a few years ago each European nation operated its own separate border controls and possessed its own currency, two factors that tended to emphasize the nation rather than the EU common market. Some members of the

EU, such as Poland and the former East Germany, were part of the Soviet bloc, and their citizens experienced great difficulty obtaining permission to travel outside their respective nations. All these factors contributed to a feeling of balkanization within Europe; today the opposite situation obtains.

Thus we can expect that increased economic integration will eventually result in at least some degree of cultural and perhaps political integration but that the process will not always be smooth. Still, cultures do change, especially when citizens can see the advantages associated with economic integration. Europe, for example, is far different today from the way it was 20 years ago, but the change prior to that time was much slower, in large measure because of the clear separations between nations. As economic integration accelerates, cultural and perhaps political integration should follow to some degree, especially if positively reinforcing conditions are present. Full cultural and political integration, however, is unlikely to occur.

Paradox 9.2. Is globalization a myth?

The common usage of the word *globalization* is of relatively recent vintage, beginning around 30 years ago and increasing significantly since then. However, there are wide areas of Latin America, Asia, and Africa that have been relatively untouched by globalization. Further, Alan Rugman (2005) has developed a database of the 500 largest multinational enterprises (MNEs) in the world. His analysis of the database indicated that most MNEs primarily sell their goods and services in only one part of a triad consisting of the EU, North America, and Asia-Pacific.

Of the 500 firms, 120 operate almost exclusively in their home nations; another 320 firms make at least 50% of their sales in their home region of the triad; only 25 are biregional, with more than 20% of their sales in at least two parts of the triad plus less than 50% of their sales in their home region; only 11 firms are host-region oriented, with more than 50% of their sales in a triad region other than their own; and only 9 firms are global in the sense that they have sales of 20% or more in each of the regions of the triad but less than 50% in any one region (Rugman, 2005, p. 3; there are insufficient data for the remaining 15 firms).

Rugman made a valid case that regionalization rather than globalization is occurring, and the growth of bilateral and regional trade agreements supports his thesis. However, Westley (2006) argued that Rugman employed unduly restrictive criteria to prove his thesis. For example, General Electric obtains 46% of its sales outside the United States, but since the figure is not 50%, Rugman classifies it as a nonglobal firm. Other firms, such as Wal-Mart and Dell, while obtaining approximately 75% of their sales in the United States, are moving rapidly to globalize, even when they experience failure, as happened to Wal-Mart in Korea and Germany. Investors are interested in firms whose profits constantly and dramatically grow, and only the global marketplace offers such an opportunity in many instances.

Also, the data presented in Chapter 1 suggest a pattern of increasing interdependence among national governments, business firms, nonprofit organizations, and individual citizens. This increasing interdependence is the essence of globalization. Between 1820 and 1992, world trade increased 540-fold while population rose only 5-fold (Streeten, 2001); since 1992 trade has more than doubled, with developing nations' trade expanding at more than twice the rate of the industrial nations'. Also, as indicated in the preceding chapter, nations such as China and India and other developing nations actively encourage foreign trade. China, for example, now accounts for more than 10% of all world trade and India more than 2%, and these figures will probably increase significantly. The successive rounds of global trading agreements since the end of World War II facilitate interdependence, as does the presence of integrating mechanisms such as the WTO and the World Bank, even though there has been a delay in the Doha round of international trade talks. Technological changes such as videoconferencing and the Internet have revolutionized the manner of communication among individuals from different nations. All these facts suggest that globalization is proceeding rapidly, although admittedly some major areas of the world have been largely excluded thus far.

This is not to deny the validity of Rugman's major points. Companies usually attempt to reduce both risk and the transaction costs of doing business. As distance increases, the costs of doing business rise, and generally the risk level expands. For this reason it is sensible for an MNE to take advantage of the opportunities close to home or within its own region of the triad, where it is culturally comfortable, before proceeding to the other two regions. Still, the expansion of world trade continues unabated, as does the increased movement of goods, services, capital, ideas, and individuals across national boundaries. In short, the paradox is that globalization is both a myth and a reality, and its identification as such depends on one's point of view and the data used to justify it.

Paradox 9.3. Is globalization an old or a new phenomenon?

As indicated in Chapter 8, ancient Rome practiced a form of globalization emphasizing colonization and mercantilism, both of which were subsequently employed by European nations beginning around 1500 A.D. Other writers have noted the trade that took place along the fabled Silk Road and elsewhere and have argued that globalization in various guises existed in such situations. However, most of the discussion centers around the period 1870–1914, during which international trade and increased contact among developed nations rose dramatically. International trade (exports plus imports) as a percentage of gross national product among developed nations during 1870–1914 compares very favorably to the current situation. It was within only the past few years that the current percentage became larger than that during this earlier period, and even this change is debatable (Wolf, 2004).

There are many reasons to believe that globalization as we are experiencing it is fundamentally different from its assumed predecessors. Gupta and Govindarajan (2004) pointed out that from a corporation's perspective, there are four critical elements of globalization, namely, the globalization of the corporation's capital base, corporate mind-set, supply chain, and market presence. Today corporations can easily transfer capital electronically across borders in a matter of minutes, making it possible for them to be very flexible financially and increasing their ability to respond quickly to both opportunities and threats. As Rugman stressed, most MNEs operate primarily in their regional part of the triad, but that does not mean they do not have a market presence in the other two parts, and most of them do. Also, there is an increasing tendency for MNEs to see themselves as global corporations; some of them explicitly commit to this focus in their advertising and mission statements.

In addition, 25 years ago only a small number of business schools offered majors in transportation; the term *supply chain* was not commonly used. Today supply chain courses have become a cornerstone of the business curriculum, and corporations have increased the status and power of specialists in this area because of its criticality. An excellent example is Wal-Mart, whose current CEO, Lee Scott, was largely responsible for developing its supply chain strategy. Wal-Mart created a new business model separating it from competitors by (a) building large, cavernous stores, which allowed the company to take advantage of economies of scale; (b) linking the stores together through a *reverse-saturation model*, so that the first store in a region would be within a day's drive of its distribution center, and then filling the area in between with 150–200 stores so that goods could be delivered very efficiently as conditions demanded; (c) owning their own fleet of 50,000 trucks; and (d) having their suppliers drop off their goods at each distribution center and immediately using their own trucks to transport the goods to their own stores, thus saving dramatically on inventory costs (see

Govindarajan & Gupta, 2001). In modified form Wal-Mart has employed this strategy very successfully when entering nations such as China and Mexico.

Barry Lynn (2005) points out that global corporations are particularly vulnerable in the area of global supply chains, given the scale and scope of their influence. For example, a 1999 earthquake in Taiwan disrupted the manufacturing of semiconductors in just two plants, but the impact was so widespread that electronics factories around the world were shut down temporarily. Of course, the impact of September 11, 2001, was deep and widespread, affecting many industries and government operations and creating billions of dollars of loss both in the United States and elsewhere. Similarly, the global financial system has been subject to several crises since 1990, including (a) the bond market crisis that started but was contained in the United States in the early 1990s; (b) the East Asian financial crisis of 1997–1998, which began when international investors withdrew capital quickly from Thailand and neighboring nations; and (c) the collapse of the banking system in Russia in the late 1990s. It is also possible that a triggering event such as the use of a nuclear bomb will be sufficient to derail globalization, at least for a long time. Warren Buffett views the possibility of a nuclear terrorist attack in a major U.S. city as a reality that is waiting to occur.

Relatedly, and as mentioned in earlier chapters, Thomas Friedman (2005) has authored a popular book about globalization in which he asserts that the world is "flat; that is, the playing field has become level primarily through developments such as the Internet, videoconferencing, and new and effective ways of outsourcing. Most of the serious critiques of this book have focused on the metaphor employed, offering alternative metaphors such as a "borderless" world (Pudelko, 2006), a kaleidoscopic world of competitive dynamics and comparative advantage among firms irrespective of the national locations of their competitors (Bhagwati, 2005), and a "spiky world" in which the tallest peaks—the cities and regions driving the world economy—profit handsomely, as do those firms and individuals on the middle peaks who provide services and goods for them, while most of the world languishes and suffers in the valleys (Florida, 2005). However, it is difficult to deny that the world is *flattening*, a centuries-old process but much faster now than previously (Svejenova, 2006). Moreover, Friedman offers a useful if chronologically debatable typology for putting globalization into perspective; it involves three eras: *Globalization 1.0*, starting with Columbus's discovery of America in 1492 and ending around 1800, during which nations increased trade with one another because of developments such as steam power and the industrial revolution; *Globalization 2.0*, from 1800 until 2000, during which multinational corporations became the dominant vehicle for enhancing global trade and interdependence among nations; and *Globalization 3.0*, our current situation, in which it is possible to link individuals directly and globally, for example, by (a) call centers in India handling calls from customers in the United States to their financial institutions, (b) the outsourcing of legal work to lawyers in another nation, and (c) the use of virtual global teams linked together through videoconferencing.

In short, the world is flattening, but seemingly in a new and different manner from that of previous eras and on an unprecedented scale. Globalization is both an old and a new phenomenon, and the overlap is significant. But what the world experienced in previous eras pales in comparison to what is occurring today, especially with the ascendancy of China, India, other developing nations, and the market economy.

Uncertainty

This section addresses paradoxes laced with uncertainty, particularly in terms of outcomes. The issues addressed in these paradoxes are of paramount importance, but it is difficult if not impossible to predict what the final outcomes will be. Still, becoming sensitive to these issues is critical if we want to understand globalization in its entirety.

> **Paradox 9.4. Is there a reasonable probability that a global financial collapse will occur and undermine globalization?**

As indicated above, the world has experienced several financial crises since 1990, any one of which could have created a worldwide recession and possibly a global depression similar to that of the 1930s. Admittedly knowledge of what makes economies financially sound has improved dramatically since that time, but some knowledgeable analysts have expressed fears about financial crises that without the quick and concerted efforts of key governments and corporations might tip the scale negatively. Just in the banking area, the International Monetary Fund has identified 64 banking crises between 1970 and 1999, all of which had the potential of igniting a global meltdown (Goldin & Reinert, 2006, p. 109).

As argued explicitly and implicitly throughout this book, there are additional factors that can undermine globalization, including reactions against unlimited immigration and increased friction caused by issues related directly to international trade. Also, the experiences since 1990, which are quickly forgotten after a solution has been found, suggest that there is at least a reasonable probability that a global financial crisis will take place that will undermine globalization. Companies trading globally need assurances that their capital base is safe and sound. If they observe that a crisis is imminent, they will consider retrenching to their national markets. The paradox facing all governments and companies is that they must embrace globalization if they want to continue to remain strong but must hedge their bets so that even if a global financial crisis occurs, they may be hurt seriously but not fatally.

Paradox 9.5. Does globalization encourage nationalism?

At Wuhan University in China in 2004 I taught an Executive MBA class focusing on such topics as business strategy and globalization. As a longtime advocate of globalization, I automatically assumed that these well-educated Executive MBA students, all of whom spoke English, were of a similar persuasion. However, at one point in the discussion of globalization, one of the managers, in his mid-30s, asked pointedly, "How can globalization be stopped?" My immediate response was, "Why in the world would anyone in China be opposed to globalization?" Having visited China for the first time in 1988, when it was very poor and drab, I commented on the rising prosperity that many cities and regional areas in China were experiencing as a result of globalization. However, several of the managers made negative comments to the effect that Western multinationals were (a) taking advantage of the Chinese, (b) not respecting them in negotiations, and (c) putting many of the Chinese firms out of business. (The third of these criticisms applies to many situations involving large-scale corporations and developing or formerly Communist nations. For example, in 1990 only one international bank was listed among the top 10 in the Czech Republic, but by 2001 there were 9 out of 10, primarily because of the inefficiencies and poor loans of the Czech Republic's formerly Communist banks.)

The Chinese managers' comments pinpoint some of the reasons for a resurgence of nationalism as globalization proceeds (see Ignatius, 2005). Also, almost all citizens across the world identify primarily with their ethnic and national cultures, and globalization threatens such identification. Further, while the net impact of globalization appears to be very positive (Bhagwati, 2004), there are not only winners but also losers, such as the millions of farmers in China who are being forced off public lands (see Chapter 8 and below). Some observers have pointed out that a threat to globalization, if not its major threat, is the resurgence of ethnic and national resistance. Globalization may not directly lead to an extreme version of nationalism that seeks to reverse its unfolding process. Still, there is little if any doubt that both globalization and nationalism are increasing at a comparable pace, as the creation of new nations since the end of the Cold War and the anti-immigration feelings in Europe, the United States, and elsewhere confirm. At a minimum, it is critical that nationalism be contained to some extent if globalization is to succeed. Creating winners rather than losers and demonstrating the net advantages of globalization are ways of accomplishing this objective.

Paradox 9.6. Are nations becoming simultaneously more and less powerful because of globalization?

In 1997 Jessica Matthews published a controversial and influential article, "Powershift," arguing that because of such factors as the increase in international trade and modern communications systems, trading blocs such as the WTO and the EU were weakening and even destroying national sovereignty. There is some truth to this argument. For example, although antitrust regulators in the United States approved of General Electric's offer to purchase Whirlpool in the early 2000s, their counterparts in the EU did not, thus negating the move. Similarly, a centralized body of decision makers sets one interest rate for all nations in the EU monetary system. No nation participating in this system can set its own unique interest rate.

Further, MNEs have vast economic resources and can use them to persuade and even coerce nations to give them favored treatment. There is also some evidence that governments have received lower corporate tax revenues as a result of globalization. Factories today in developing nations tend to be modularized, at least in part so that they can be quickly disassembled and moved to another nation, sometimes within one or two days. Even non-governmental organizations such as environmental and antiglobalization groups can organize their activities on a worldwide basis and pressure national governments to change their policies and practices.

However, at least some nations are still very powerful, as the actions taken by the United States in attacking Iraq in the face of worldwide resistance and unilaterally withdrawing from the Kyoto Protocol confirm. Also, France legally stopped Yahoo! from selling Nazi trinkets, and China forced Google to censor the search results it displays for Chinese citizens. Even the sovereignty of small nations can, if used adroitly, neutralize the power of MNEs. As discussed in Chapter 6, corporations were at a decided advantage when trying to obtain permission to fish in sea- and ocean beds under the control of different nations. These firms simply had much better knowledge about the superiority of some beds over others, and many nations did not have the resources to obtain comparable information. However, under the Law of the Sea, each corporation had to provide each affected nation with two choices of beds, one of which would be leased to the corporation. Needless to say, corporations were loath to put forth unfavorable choices with which they might be saddled.

Clearly, nations have become less powerful on many issues, such as corporate expansion across borders and going outside the rules of the trading blocs within which they operate. They also experience much more difficulty and criticism when acting unilaterally. Still, as our analysis indicates, nations are still powerful and arguably are becoming more powerful. As the economic power of developing nations strengthens, the larger ones, such as China and India, should become more powerful, and the smaller ones can employ mechanisms such as the Law of the Sea to move in the same direction. Thus the paradox is that nations are, and are possibly becoming, more *and* less powerful simultaneously in this era of globalization.

Paradox 9.7. Can one nation dominate the global economy and political system?

There is sometimes a fear among large numbers of people that one nation will dominate the global economy and political system. This fear has some basis in fact. At various times throughout history one nation has tended to become dominant within a large region of other nations. The fact that ancient Rome was able to employ colonization throughout the entire known world for hundreds of years is evidence of such domination, but other examples could be cited, including that of the Soviet Union before its collapse in 1990.

Many times the fear of domination by one nation is openly and negatively expressed. In 1980, Japan's economy was expanding rapidly and threatening to overtake the U.S. economy because of a variety of factors, such as increased productivity and quality of products. At that time Public Television broadcast a widely viewed and influential special: "If Japan can, why can't we?" In 1990 *Fortune* published an article that epitomized the seemingly irrational fears and anxieties felt in the United States: "Fear and Loathing of Japan" (Smith, 1990). While Japan remains the No. 2 economy in the world and is a strong ally of the United States, it has endured economic problems since 1990, including a prolonged recession. Today very few people in the United States are worried about Japan as an economic juggernaut.

Rather, China and India are the focus of attention, and there is an increasing emphasis on the proposition that the 21st century is the Asian century.

China is of particular interest, as it controls the largest army in the world and possesses nuclear capability, as does India. Analysts from the U.S. Department of Defense are concerned that China may intend to attack neighboring nations. These analysts are preparing various scenarios so that the United States and its allies will be ready to respond if appropriate (Barnes, 2006). Simultaneously, the U.S. Department of Commerce and other government agencies are actively promoting increased trade with China.

A meaningful question to ask is whether one nation can dominate other nations both politically and economically. In a world in which key scarce resources such as potable water and arable land are decreasing significantly, it is possible for one large nation to dominate the globalizing world, but it is extremely difficult. Economically, control mechanisms such as those provided by the WTO and the EU make the task difficult if not impossible. Politically, the assumed dominant nation would face problems similar to those experienced by MNEs, such as operating complex supply chains and controlling the movement of capital across borders, but in a greatly magnified form. Similar to our conclusion regarding the clash of civilizations, we end this discussion by arguing that there is some possibility of one nation dominating the world politically and economically, but it is not very probable. Still, there is a good amount of uncertainty surrounding this paradox of possibility, given scarce resources and the scenarios of nuclear and nonnuclear attacks. For this reason it appears wise to downplay the possibility but not to discard it completely.

Paradox 9.8. Is globalization doomed?

Niall Ferguson (2005; see also follow-up article, 2006b) published a controversial and influential article in *Foreign Affairs* that made the following major points:

1. Many observers and businesspeople were optimistic prior to the outbreak of World War I because of such factors as increased international trade and contact across national cultures. They were shocked both by the outbreak of the war and by its scale and scope. One major result of the war was that globalization was stopped in its tracks until the end of World War II in 1945.

2. In hindsight, five factors precipitated the outbreak of World War I, namely, imperial overstretch of national governments, great-power rivalry, an unstable alliance system, the presence of a rogue regime sponsoring terror, and the rise of a revolutionary terrorist organization hostile to capitalism.

3. These five factors are present today, and they have the potential to stymie or doom globalization.

Ferguson argues persuasively on behalf of his major points and shows how these factors are operating today. While Great Britain was the leading power in 1870 and provided much of the capital necessary for expanding international trade, the United States is the leading power today. However, the United States is suffering from a drastic imbalance of imports over exports, thus increasing the national debt significantly and restricting the range of choices it can make financially and militarily. There is also a growing rivalry involving the United States and other nations, particularly China. Arguably, the United States overreached in attacking Iraq in 2002 because of the supposed existence of nuclear and chemical capabilities, an assumption that proved false. In the subsequent process of waging war in Iraq, the U.S. national debt rose significantly. Longtime allies of the United States in Europe and elsewhere are questioning its ability to lead because of this and other decisions. And the rise of Muslim extremism is similar to the rise of Bolshevism in Russia in the early part of the 20th century. At least from Ferguson's perspective, the similarities between the two eras are alarming.

Sesit (2005) argued in a similar manner, pointing out that other commonalities between these two periods include low inflation, rising commodity prices, new regional powers with global aspirations, state-sponsored terrorism, growing great-power rivalry, and a financially overstretched dominant power. He also noted two differences: the expansion of democracy in the current era but not in the earlier one, and an increase in the number of wars in the earlier era but a decline in the current one.

Advocates of globalization today tend to downplay these similarities between the two eras and offer a much more optimistic scenario of increasing prosperity throughout the world (Bhagwati, 2004; Friedman, 2005). Gupta and Govindarajan (2004) echoed this optimism in their assertion that globalization is inevitable, although they note that a seemingly very unlikely event such as a major nuclear attack or epidemics could derail it. Still, given our distinction between risk and uncertainty, it is plausible to consider long-term predictions as uncertain in this situation. The world can change quite suddenly, as happened prior to both world wars. In short, the fact that there are many similarities is bothersome and seems to call for increased attention to such macro-level influences.

Political and Social Issues

There are many political and social issues surrounding globalization, some of which we have discussed in previous chapters. In this section we focus on three important paradoxes.

Paradox 9.9. Does globalization increase prosperity and inequality simultaneously?

One of the critical paradoxes in the area of globalization is that it is associated simultaneously with both rising prosperity and inequality. As indicated in the preceding chapter, nearly half of the world's population lives on less than $2 a day and 16% gets by on less than $1 per day. Despite these conditions, the nations actively involved in global economic activities have consistently increased their wealth per capita. The dramatic reduction of poverty in Asia from 76% in the 1970s to 15% in 1998 is significantly related to this continent's participation in the global economy (Sala-i-Martin, 2002). This positive picture is counterbalanced by the rising inequalities that nations participating in globalization are uniformly experiencing. Perhaps the most dramatic manifestation of this phenomenon is the widened gap between the average total compensation (salary plus fringe benefits) enjoyed by CEOs and that of the average worker in a corporation. Various estimates for the United States are available, some of which suggest that the gap has risen from a ratio of 40 to 1 in 1970 to a ratio of more than 200 to 1. However, this phenomenon in varying degrees of intensity is found in many developed and developing nations, including Canada, Australia, and China. Fully 20 of the 21 developed nations that are members of the Organization for Economic Cooperation and Development (OECD) have experienced rising inequality as globalization has proceeded.

Martin Wolf (2004), a former World Bank economist who is now the chief economics commentator of the *Financial Times,* has provided a strong argument suggesting that the OECD data represent only a correlation, and that factors other than globalization explain this rising inequality. Similarly, he notes that once China is dropped from the analysis, the relationship between globalization and inequality proves to be statistically insignificant in developing nations. However, China, with a population of 1.3 billion, does represent 23% of the world's population, and dropping it from the analysis would be unrealistic.

Many other observers present data justifying the direct linkage between globalization and inequality. For example, the United States' profile on this issue of rising prosperity and inequality comprises the following trends (Parker, 2005):

• In 1970 the bottom fifth of the U.S. population received 5.4% of America's total national income, and the richest fifth, 40.9%. By 1995 the bottom fifth's share of total national income had fallen to 4.4% while that of the top fifth had risen to 46.5%. In 1970 4% of the national income went to 0.1% of the top earners; by 1998 this percentage rose to 6%.

- In the 1950s 22% of the U.S. population lived in poverty, but only 12% in today's economy are below the poverty level.
- The United States' score on social mobility, when compared with other nations, ranks in the middle of the group.
- Social mobility has decreased since the 1970s, even in the middle and the upper-middle parts of the income distribution. Such changes suggest that the United States may be separating itself into two groups: the haves and the have-nots.
- A visible manifestation of this separation is the rise in gated and walled housing communities, which are also prevalent throughout the developing world, in which power distances between social classes are great. About 7 million households in the United States, or more than 6% of all U.S. households, now live in such communities, and 40% of the new housing in California incorporates this feature.

Perhaps this paradox of rising wealth and inequality does not need to be addressed. However, history suggests that the separation of a community into two groups, haves and have-nots, is problematic. Max Weber (1930) identified the rise of the middle class, with its critical skills and abilities, as essential for the emergence of capitalism. If social mobility is lessened significantly, the size of the middle class will shrink. Also, the close association between rising wealth and inequality can create unstable and uncertain conditions that could eventually undermine the positive features of globalization. It is such instability that may well be the greatest threat to globalization, and it is one that the opponents of globalization emphasize.

Paradox 9.10. Who are the winners and losers in a globalizing world?

Globalization, as emphasized above, is related to rising prosperity, even when there are widening income and wealth gaps between social groups. Thus, at a macro level, everyone is a winner, and it is this feature of globalization that proponents stress. However, there are clear losers. Millions of farmers forced off public lands in China and elsewhere typically became unemployable and impoverished (see Chapter 8). When factories in the United States close down and their operations move to low-cost nations, U.S. unemployment rises. And, as will be discussed in our next paradox, even white-collar employment in the United States has suffered because of the outsourcing of work to other nations. Bernstein (2004) has summarized the consensus that seems to be emerging among at least some trade economists:

- The emergence of a global market for white-collar workers could lower the wages of highly skilled U.S. workers for the first time and perhaps permanently.
- Assuming that the wages of both blue-collar and white-collar workers decrease, their loss would contribute to increasing power and wealth among employers and shareholders.
- If less-expensive white-collar labor decreases the prices of U.S. exports in which the nation has a comparative advantage, such as software, the overall economy could suffer, as the discussion of immiseration in Chapter 8 suggests.

Also, the rise of globalization can be related to the shrinkage of the Amazon forests, widespread deforestation, global warming, and more. In this sense all of us are losers because of globalization.

There are, then, both winners and losers in our globalizing world. Creating safety nets for losers is ethically and morally responsible. It is still uncertain who will be the winners and losers in each specific globalizing situation. Still, the emphasis should not be on only the winners, who need no assistance. The losers, at least some of whom will require a good amount of assistance, represent the appropriate group to receive such aid, possibly on an unprecedented scale. And, as our example of the Danish success linking corporate downsizings to governmental/corporate retraining efforts suggests, creative thinking about the form of such assistance is critical (see page 23).

Paradox 9.11. Is increased education the antidote for outsourcing?

By and large, people in the United States tend to be optimistic about the future and invest heavily in ensuring that success occurs. It is for this reason that education has always been a high priority, especially engineering and business degrees, all of which are directly tied to the labor market. This investment has paid off handsomely for both educational institutions and individuals. It is common for a state university to demonstrate that a dollar invested in it results in a very high rate of return for the state in which it is located, sometimes on the order of 25-fold. Students are generally satisfied with the net benefit of a college education. Typically, a comparison of salaries received by high school graduates and college graduates is heavily in favor of the college graduates, with wages of workers with bachelor's degrees averaging 75% more than those of high school graduates in 2005 (Wessel, 2006). Over the 25-year period prior to 2000, this gap widened continually.

In the past, when there was a recession or a downsizing of a particular workforce in a corporation, the pattern was for blue-collar workers to suffer much more than white-collar workers did. Thus, not only would blue-collar workers receive lower salaries, but they would also experience greater amounts of unemployment during their lifetimes. However, census data indicate that between 2000 and 2004, after-inflation earnings of college graduates fell by 5% while those of high school graduates rose slightly (Gosselin, 2006).

Some analysts attribute part of the decline in average salaries among college graduates to globalization, as white-collar work is being outsourced more and more to developing nations, in which labor costs are much lower. Other analysts argue that the U.S. economy has benefited significantly because of outsourcing in terms of several measures, such as the overall rate of employment in national economies accepting outsourcing when compared with national economies resistant to it. They also argue, with justification, that (a) the current level of outsourcing when compared to total employment is insignificant, (b) the percentage of work affected is approximately equivalent to 2 weeks of national income per year, and (c) the gains associated with the creation of new jobs outstrip any job losses.

Still, the fact that the average salary of college graduates has declined since 2000 is worrisome, as the United States' international trade has expanded since that time, particularly imports. Alan Blinder (2006), a Princeton professor and former chairperson of the U.S. Council of Economic Advisors, has argued that we have seen only the tip of the iceberg when it comes to outsourcing. Call centers in India are merely one early manifestation of the trend. As technologies for delivering products and services over various communication systems such as the Internet improve, more highly skilled work will be subject to outsourcing. Blinder estimated that 52 million jobs are in danger in the long run, but it will take two or three decades for the technological advancements to become sufficiently refined to affect all of them. Such high-skilled jobs as software engineering are most at risk.

The solution that Blinder proposed is to reorient education to emphasize tasks that cannot easily be transmitted over communication systems to other nations. Such tasks would include personal services such as nursing, general medical practitioners, and specialists in leisure-time activities sought by the general population and, in particular, by its retired members. He also believes that soft skills and creativity will become prized when compared to relatively routine work such as that performed by software engineers. Education will still matter, but the type will change significantly if institutions are to remain directly linked to the labor market.

Blinder discussed these issues within the context of three eras: the industrial revolution, the move to a service economy, and the projected transition to a personal-services economy. Education will still be an antidote to the loss of jobs created by outsourcing white-collar employment but only if institutions and individuals move to a personal-services orientation. In this sense the traditional comparison of those with only a high school degree and those with a college degree is faulty. Many high school graduates may fare better than some college graduates, as the data on average salaries between 2000 and 2004 suggest. The comparison should be between those whose jobs can be outsourced over sophisticated communication systems and those whose jobs cannot be. Thus education is still an antidote to globalization but only if it is tied to a changed labor market emphasizing personal services, soft skills, and creativity.

Barbara Bergmann (2006) has criticized Blinder's argument due to the fact that economic growth has historically occurred in the United States because of the ready acceptance of innovations and change. Blinder's approach would downgrade the importance of innovation among individuals seeking to create a secure future in the United States. The paradox is that what is good for the economy is probably detrimental to many if not most workers within it, given modern communication systems. Unfortunately the issues of outsourcing cutting-edge telecommunications systems are still at too early a stage to provide us with a definite answer.

Takeaways

1. Most discussions of globalization do not emphasize the difference between risk and uncertainty, but it is critical to do so to obtain an accurate picture of what is happening.

2. Global economic integration can occur without cultural and political integration. Still, as the degree and intensity of globalization increase, we should expect the tendency to integrate politically and culturally to strengthen as well, at least to some extent.

3. Nationalism and globalization are, in some critical ways, opposed to one another, and both are increasing. At least to some degree, nationalism must be controlled if globalization is to extend its reach and influence.

4. Globalization is both a myth and a fact of life, depending on the manner in which it is measured. This is not to deny that regionalism in terms of Alan Rugman's triad is a reality. Regionalization is just as important and arguably more important than globalization, especially for a corporation seeking to reduce its risk levels and transaction costs. However, many markets are global, and increasingly companies are expanding globally.

5. Globalization is both an old and a new phenomenon in that its scale and scope today are unprecedented.

6. Nations are, or at least have the potential to be, simultaneously less and more powerful as globalization increases. It is unlikely, but not out of the realm of possibility, that one nation will dominate all other nations politically and culturally.

7. There are many similarities between the globalizing era extending from 1870 to the start of World War I and the current era. Such similarities suggest that increased attention should be devoted to macro-level influences and variables.

8. Globalization creates not only many winners but also many losers. Also, it is associated with both increasing prosperity and increasing inequality. Safety nets such as extensive retraining seem appropriate, possibly on an unprecedented scale.

9. Education can be an antidote to the outsourcing associated with globalization, but presumably only for work that cannot be transmitted quickly over sophisticated communication systems and the Internet. More specifically, personal services such as nursing and specialized providers of leisure-time opportunities should fare better than those performing routine work such as software engineering that can be outsourced quickly, efficiently, and at lower cost.

Discussion Questions

1. What is the difference between risk and uncertainty? Why is the distinction between these two concepts relevant in a globalizing world?

2. When would you expect cultural and political integration to increase as globalization proceeds? Why? Does economic integration require that cultural and political integration occur first? Why or why not?

3. Why is the increase in nationalism a threat to globalization? Please identify three ways to control this threat.

4. Discuss and critically analyze Alan Rugman's theory that regionalization is the reality and globalization is a myth. How does he define his triad, and why is it important? Do you agree with Rugman? Why or why not?

5. Why is globalization both an old and a new phenomenon? Identify two ways in which our current era of globalization differs from that experienced from 1870 until the start of World War I.

6. Identify two winners and two losers as globalization strengthens. Why have you selected them? Are there other winners and losers you would like to highlight? If yes, why?

7. Because of globalization, nations are becoming both more and less powerful, or at least possess this potential. Indicate how and why a nation conforms to this pattern.

8. What type of education does Alan Blinder believe can serve as a guard against or antidote to outsourcing of jobs? Why does he believe that the distinction between high school and college graduates is less relevant than it was 20 years ago? Do you agree with his analysis? Why or why not?

9. As globalization increases, so too do prosperity and inequality. Is this a major problem? Why or why not? Why do you feel this way?

Exercises

1. Form small, self-selected groups: those who want to argue in favor of globalization and those who are of the opposite persuasion. Each small group should develop a list of advantages and disadvantages associated with globalization. A recorder or secretary of each group should present the group's list to the entire class on either a PowerPoint slide or overhead. Discussion should follow each presentation.

2. Two self-selected teams representing advocates and opponents of globalization, respectively, should meet separately and prepare to debate in a formal manner. Relative advantages and disadvantages should be emphasized. Each team should be allowed some time for rebuttal. Class discussion should then occur.

3. Each student should write a five-page paper outlining the relative advantages and disadvantages associated with globalization, paying particular attention to whether each point represents a threat or an opportunity. Alternatively, the assignment could involve writing a somewhat longer group paper.

10

Business Strategy, Business Functions, and International Human Resource Management

In 1996 I attended a fascinating 3-hour case presentation in the MBA program at the London Business School. Senior managers from ICI Corporation presented the case study. It elicited a great amount of animated discussion from the MBA students, who represented a cross-section of national cultures. At the time ICI, whose headquarters is in Japan, was not doing well in Europe. Its senior management decided to change the organizational structure, moving away from a *geographic-centered structure*, in which each nation in Europe was considered the prime element. The new structure emphasized the primacy of product managers to whom the geographic national managers would report, that is, a *product-based structure*. Naturally the MBA students were intrigued by the change and what it entailed, particularly for the once-dominant national managers. When geographic national management had been the prime element, the senior managers within each nation had operated independently and received compensation based almost exclusively on the sales taking place within their respective nations. The students wanted to know how compensation for these managers would now be determined. ICI presenters indicated that the corporation had introduced a more balanced compensation package, and a dominant part of it was based on a combination of total sales in Europe and total sales in adjacent nations that needed to share resources. There was still some recognition given to sales within each nation, but to a much reduced degree.

The reasoning underlying this change was the need for the senior geographic managers in each nation to cooperate effectively with one another. Previously, since compensation was related only to sales within each respective nation, their motivation to do so was minimal. When a geographic manager asked other geographic managers for badly needed experts or for the transfer of products to meet unexpected demand, other geographic managers typically turned the manager down. Now ICI senior management was instructing them to become cooperative, and the carrot for motivating them was the revised compensation system.

At this point the discussion turned to the topics of networking, knowing other adjacent geographic managers well, and fluency in language. Many of the geographic managers could converse in four to six languages. However, the U.S. and British MBA students pointed out that they were fluent in only one language. What would happen to managers like them in such a reorganization? The ICI presenters indicated that there would be a yearlong transition to the new organizational structure. This transition would involve both numerous meetings and identification of the strengths and weaknesses of all geographic managers in terms of what was expected of them in the new product-based structure. Clearly language was an issue. ICI planned to suggest strongly if not mandate that language training be part of the reeducation process. Several of the American and British students could see themselves in this situation and questioned whether they would be able to learn to speak other languages effectively and quickly; the presenters indicated that at least some fluency was important, especially in nations adjacent to one another.

At this point the MBA students wondered what would happen if a particularly successful geographic manager were not able to adapt to the new structure. What if the manager didn't want to share resources and learn additional languages? The ICI presenters attempted to soften their response, but it was to the effect that adaptation was essential. I will leave the consequences of nonadaptation to your imagination.

This chapter addresses three issues implied in the ICI case study. First, we examine some paradoxes in the areas of business strategy. ICI changed its strategy and organizational structure in Europe and, in so doing, created a good amount of uncertainty for its managers. Next, we will focus on specific business functions such as logistics and accounting that need to adapt to the global marketplace. The third issue is the strains and conflicts that inevitably occur when a company globalizes within the area of international human resource management (IHRM).

Business Strategy

Companies that enter the global marketplace can employ a variety of ways or modes of doing so, including exporting, licensing, strategic alliances, acquisitions, and the creation of a new wholly owned subsidiary or green-field venture. However, as Hitt, Ireland, and Hoskisson (2007) pointed out, each of these approaches simultaneously possesses strengths and limitations. Exporting products is typically the first way a company gingerly steps into the global marketplace. It does not entail too much risk, as the company can stop exporting at any time. However, the costs are high and the degree of control over the sale and distribution of the product is low. Licensing another company to manufacture, distribute, or sell products is also a relatively safe approach in terms of cost and risk, but profits and control are low. To give but one example, Black & Decker attempted on five separate occasions to introduce its popular DustBuster into the Japanese market through a licensing agreement with a Japanese company. In all five instances the Japanese licensee learned how to manufacture the DustBuster through reverse engineering, terminated its licensing agreement, and started to manufacture, distribute, and sell a comparable product.

Strategic alliances involving the globalizing company and existing companies within another nation or nations are quite popular, as there are shared costs, resources, and risks. However, frequently there are enormous problems in integrating two or more organizational cultures. Mazda of Japan, for instance, had a no-layoff policy until the Ford Motor Company became the dominant shareholder and mandated that layoffs should be employed in some instances. This clash of organizational cultures proved to be problematic for Mazda. Sales declined, presumably in part because of this clash. And what was once Mazda's claim to fame and profits, Mazda engineering, as its "Mazda-engineered" advertising pointed out for years, declined in importance, in part because of the mismatch between the Ford and Mazda organizational cultures.

Of course, a globalizing company can just purchase or acquire a company in another nation or nations. This allows quick access to markets. However, the drawbacks are high costs, complex and drawn-out negotiations in some instances, and the issue of merging the acquired company with domestic operations. Various estimates suggest that it requires 7–10 years to fully integrate the acquired company into the domestic operations. Cisco Systems, for example, emphasized the acquisition of companies located very close to it in the San Francisco area for several years to facilitate integration and to minimize this problem, although it has moved away from this stance recently. In recent years the percentage of cross-border acquisitions has risen; they represent approximately 45% of all acquisitions.

Finally, a company can create and construct a greenfield venture or wholly owned subsidiary. This is a complex and high-risk strategy that is often costly and time-consuming. However, the greenfield venture does provide above-average returns and maximum control in terms of building what the home office desires.

Our discussion suggests that there is no ideal way of entering the global marketplace. Hitt, Ireland, and Hoskisson (2007) have recommended three modes of entry—exporting, licensing, and strategic alliances—for early market development. At later stages firms can take advantage of acquisitions and greenfield ventures (wholly owned subsidiaries). Still, practices seem to vary widely. For instance, a study of 117 pharmaceutical firms indicated that 84.6%, or 99 firms, employed joint ventures, while the remainder established wholly owned subsidiaries (Jiang, 2005).

Also, Alan Rugman's research (2005) on the 500 largest multinational corporations indicates that they first tend to regionalize their operations and then to globalize them, whatever the mode of entry (see Chapter 9). This approach makes eminent sense, for it allows companies to expand globally without taking on too much risk in terms of setup and transaction costs. If an acquired company is in Asia, for example, it is much more difficult for a U.S. company to manage it than if it were in Canada. The average losses of U.S. firms in China exceeded average gains until 2001, a pattern that replicated their earlier entrance into the Japanese market. Such results suggest that it takes additional time, effort, and resources to operate globally rather than regionally (see Chapter 9 & Rugman, 2005).

Thus companies face a difficult paradox. No matter what the mode of entry, none is ideal. To keep growing and to increase their stock market value, many companies must operate outside their national borders. They do so in a seemingly ideal way, first regionalizing and then globalizing. And many of them, such as Dell and Wal-Mart, have globalized very quickly. Wal-Mart, for instance, sometimes with partners, first expanded to Mexico (1991) and then to Japan (1992), Brazil (1994), Canada (1994), China (1994), Argentina (1995), Indonesia (1996), Germany (1997), Korea (1999), and the United Kingdom (1999). It met unexpectedly strong competition in Korea, which was aggravated by the Korean preference for comfortable, attractive, and medium-size food stores that are located in department stores, and recently Wal-Mart sold off its Korean operations. Similarly,

Wal-Mart's entrance into European nations such as Britain and Germany has not been smooth, and it has sold off its operations in Germany. Still, from 1996 through 2000, 27% of the company's growth in sales came from its international operations. The company is now redirecting its resources so that it can expand its operations in China and, secondarily, India.

Gupta and Govindarajan (2004) provide examples of newly formed companies that have deliberately and strategically globalized since their inception. They were born global, so to speak. However, such cases are rare and usually rely exclusively or almost exclusively on the Internet as the key vehicle for expansion. At this time we do not have sufficient information to assess whether this is a cost-effective and successful strategy in most instances.

Paradox 10.2. Is there an ideal structure for the global firm?

The consensus among experts is that a corporation's structure should be consistent with its strategy. If a firm is pursuing a *multidomestic strategy*, it tends to institute a geographic-centered structure, as our discussion of ICI suggests. There are, however, problems of competition among the geographic national managers. Also, products tend to be tailored to the tastes that exist in each local market, which normally increases costs. Such geographic structures offer many advantages, including the geographic managers' sensitivity to the needs of their customers and understanding of the complex intricacies found within each nation. At times, again as exemplified by ICI, there will be a movement toward a global corporate strategy accompanied by a product-based structure, and the advantages of geographic structures decrease markedly. However, through the use of a product-based structure, headquarters is better able to integrate the operations of its units in various nations and decrease costs in such areas as production, advertising, and sales.

Today some companies are pursuing a *transnational strategy* that supposedly allows a sensitive balancing of the multidomestic and global strategies. Companies seek to obtain the advantages of both the geographic-centered and the product-based structures while minimizing the disadvantages of each. Of course, this is much harder to achieve in practice than in theory. Essentially a transnational strategy requires a *matrix* organizational structure, as there are inconsistent demands and reporting relationships when the geographic-centered and product-based structures are employed simultaneously. Such inconsistencies are the hallmark characteristics of the matrix structure. By its very nature a matrix structure is difficult to implement, given the uncertainties related to the balancing of power, reporting relationships, and focus. At least partially for this reason, the failure rate and transaction costs of companies operating in the wider global marketplace can be higher on average than those of domestic-only and regionalized firms. Still, there is frequently no choice but to pursue a transnational strategy and employ the accompanying matrix structure if the company wants to continue its growth, as the Wal-Mart expansion in China confirms. Many firms, such as Caterpillar, Federal Express, and UPS, have been very successful in their pursuit of global opportunities, and each operates in well over 100 nations.

There is, then, no ideal organizational structure for the global firm. Companies veer from one to another organizational structure as conditions warrant, just as ICI did in 1996. While the ideal is the transnational strategy with its emphasis on both the matrix structure and constant growth, the risks of failure increase, sometimes dramatically. But for a large company whose expansion is limited in the United States by the size of the market and other factors, there is no choice if it wants its stock price to increase.

Paradox 10.3. Are organizations worldwide becoming more similar?

As more organizations enter regional and global markets, a natural assumption is that they will become more similar to one another. Ideas tend to spread, and it is easy to imagine situations in which organizations would mimic one another in terms of organizational strategies and structures. Our discussion of Paradoxes 10.1 and 10.2 would support this argument. The number of choices available in the areas of strategy and structure, at least at the most general level, is limited, which should encourage companies to follow very similar approaches. Given the increased interactions across cultures, we would also expect that individuals working within such organizations would tend to manifest increasingly similar values and attitudes.

However, as Nancy Adler (2002) has pointed out, the research is inconsistent. Some of it indicates that organizational similarities are increasing, while some of it suggests just the opposite. John Child examined the existing literature in 1981 and concluded that organizations are becoming similar to one another at the macro level. That is to say, they employ similar organizational structures. At the same time, ethnic and national cultures stubbornly resist change, even when their members work with one another for years. As noted previously, 9 of every 10 citizens in the EU identify primarily with their national cultures and only secondarily with the EU. Child's review indicated that the studies suggesting similarity focused on the macro level, while those confirming dissimilarity analyzed data at the micro or individual level.

Such studies, however, may well be dated. The rate of change today is dramatic in many instances, especially in nations such as India and China, both of which have seen the rise of a consumer-oriented middle class. The former Soviet bloc nations in Europe, such as the Czech Republic and Poland, have experienced similar abrupt changes. As noted previously, in some Asian nations women are delaying marriage and sometimes avoiding it so that they can be free of collectivistic responsibilities such as taking care of their in-laws and parents. Especially in large multinational companies, we can hypothesize that we will see more convergence than divergence in future decades. Still, ethnic and national cultures will be critical. Some divergence, regardless of the amount of knowledge and interaction, is likely to persist at the micro or individual level of analysis.

Paradox 10.4. Is China a very large or a very small market?

For several years I served as director of the Center for Global Business at the Smith School of Business, University of Maryland at College Park, in which capacity I was involved in the creation of a joint EMBA program between our business school and the University for International Business and Economics in Beijing, China. This was our first international venture and we proceeded slowly and with caution. We talked to a number of native Chinese experts in business, who continually emphasized the very large size of the market for Executive MBA (EMBA) degrees in China. Initially I accepted uncritically the argument that indeed China was a very large market, given that it has a population of 1.3 billion. However, when we completed a 10-day on-site visit in Beijing, we learned that the potential market, while possibly large, was really limited to approximately 200,000 managers and not the millions we had envisioned, based on what we had been hearing. This market limitation occurred because of the high costs associated with operating a joint EMBA program involving a U.S. university and a Chinese university. Each of our Maryland faculty would need to stay in China for 2 weekends to teach just one EMBA course, and several faculty needed to travel to China each year to meet our side of the commitment. In addition, each EMBA class in China was required to complete a business tour in the United States. Only large multinationals would be able to subsidize such costs, thus severely restricting the potential EMBA market in China.

Our experience, which proved to be very positive in that the EMBA program was successfully launched, highlights some of the issues and problems that a company faces when it goes global. The market may still be relatively large but not nearly as large as optimistic and unqualified projections would suggest. In addition, there are all sorts of personnel and IHRM issues that require attention, such as developing criteria for success and measuring a program against them, selecting candidates, integrating two or more organizational cultures, gaining language fluency so that each side can understand one another, and so forth. China may be a very large or very small market depending on the product or service being offered, and it is essential to obtain reliable and valid information to ensure that assessments of size are accurate.

Again, the example of Wal-Mart's global triumphs and failures is instructive. It initially regionalized successfully, focusing on its close neighbors, Mexico and Canada. However, it has withdrawn from Korea and Germany and faces intense competition in nations such as Brazil, England, China, and Japan. Apparently Wal-Mart has decided that its best efforts should be targeted toward China, as its CEO has indicated publicly. Still, there will be major issues to confront, including intense levels of competition from Chinese firms and other global competitors such as Carrefour, government rules and regulations favoring Chinese firms, corruption, and distance from the United States and headquarters, all of which will influence a variety of factors, such as communication and logistics. Recently I spoke to a senior executive of a competitor of Wal-Mart's that operates only in the United States. He listed the factors above plus others that motivate his firm to expand as much as possible in the United States before even considering going global. He also pointed out what is well known, namely, the growing opposition to establishing Wal-Mart stores in various communities within the United States; the company has been stymied in several instances. To complicate matters, Costco has been outperforming Sam's Clubs, Wal-Mart's answer to the strategy that Costco employs. As *Business Week* stated the matter a few years ago in a lead article, Costco is the only company that Wal-Mart fears. Given the American marketplace and Wal-Mart's place in it, it is logical that this company wants to expand significantly in China, even though the level of risk is great.

Both for the Smith School of Business and Wal-Mart, then, the Chinese market can be both small and large. Risk assessment is always problematic, even for a company or business school that decides it has no alternative but to expand into China.

Business Functions

Operating globally requires that a firm alter its business practices, which affects all its basic business functions, such as accounting, finance, advertising and marketing, and logistics and supply chain management. In this section we consider paradoxes that relate directly to business functions.

Paradox 10.5. Can accounting and financial systems of companies and financial institutions be standardized throughout the world?

One of the impediments to the globalization of company operations is standardization of accounting and financial systems. Of course, companies face this issue when operating only domestically. Geico Insurance Company is organized into geographic regions, and there is always tension across the regions because of differing operating procedures, reporting requirements, and so on. Cisco addressed this issue by developing an integration team that standardized all accounting and financial procedures in newly acquired subsidiaries so that any report could be read easily by an executive, making comparisons easy. However, as noted, it is only recently that Cisco has acquired companies outside the San Francisco area, due to the difficulties in communication confronting any firm whose headquarters is geographically removed from its subsidiaries.

Still, it is possible to create standardized financial and accounting systems, as the experience of firms such as UPS (which operates in more than 200 nations) and CitiBank confirms. A more daunting problem is standardizing accounting and financial systems in the various major stock markets throughout the world. There are wide discrepancies among the reporting requirements that various nations mandate. While such harmonization has been championed by many in recent years, movement has been extremely slow, and we can expect that national governments will safeguard their sovereignty in this area. Thus globalization faces the paradox that harmonization is essential but difficult if not impossible to achieve, at least fully. There is no reason to expect that the movement to harmonize will accelerate in the near future, given the cultural and economic pressures to which each national government responds, but the issue of the integration of national stock markets may make the issue moot.

Paradox 10.6. Should global advertising and marketing be tailored to each national and ethnic culture?

Companies also face the difficult decision of whether their advertising and branding (marketing of a particular image with which global customers readily identify, such as some of the Coke advertisements) should be standardized across national and ethnic cultures. A few years ago WPP, the largest advertising firm in the world, moved away from standardization, even though it is obviously cost-effective, at least in the short run. Evidence suggests that advertisements and branding should be tailored to each national and even ethnic culture. Even the Coca-Cola Company tailors its advertisements of Coke in this manner, although some standardization exists.

A few years ago MTV entered the global marketplace by standardizing its product offerings globally. However, the company quickly but belatedly adopted the approach of its main competitor, Channel V, which not only tailored its advertising and programs to each national market but even introduced the use of local and regional talent rather than relying solely on performers from the United States. Through this strategy MTV reestablished its dominance globally.

There are, however, costs to consider, and tailoring each ad and branding effort to each national culture is very expensive. Companies are, in many instances, adopting a compromise strategy that allows some standardization and some uniqueness, in both advertising and marketing. The balance is delicate, but choosing standardization over uniqueness or vice versa carries significant risk. This is a dilemma that any company considering the global market must confront.

Paradox 10.7. Is it possible to create and operate an airplane-based metropolis (the aerotropolis) for efficient global logistics and transportation?

John Kasarda, a professor and consultant based at the Kenan-Flagler Business School of the University of North Carolina at Chapel Hill, has become a leading exponent of the *aerotropolis*, an airplane-based metropolitan area or city (see Lindsay, 2006). Kasarda argued that such aerotropoli already exist; Bangkok is an example. Kasarda also pointed out that global gross national product has increased 154% in the past 30 years, while world trade has experienced a rise of 355%. However, these increases pale in comparison with the increase in air cargo: 3,305%. About 40% of the total economic value of all goods produced in the world, barely 1% of the weight, is shipped by air.

If Kasarda's vision proves accurate, we will begin to experience an unprecedented amount of air cargo shipment that will serve as an alternative to shipping by railroads and vessels. However, there is likely to be strong resistance to the growth of such aerotropoli, since many will view them as environmentally detrimental and unsound. The unpleasantness associated with excessive noise levels from air cargo planes may also be so great that citizens will oppose their creation and expansion. Still, as Gupta and Govindarajan (2004) have reminded us, global logistics is one of the four key elements of any globalizing firm, and such firms are likely to seek expansion of the aerotropoli to foster closer global interconnectedness. The outcome of the struggle pitting advocates and opponents of aerotropoli is uncertain, but the struggle itself has created a dilemma for many groups, including national and state governments, citizens, and global firms.

IHRM

The broader context for IHRM described in the two previous sections provides the setting in which strains and conflicts must be worked out when a company goes global. This section examines several paradoxes related directly to such strains and conflicts.

Paradox 10.8. How can IHRM be both central and peripheral when going global?

Human resource management (HRM) is an essential part of any company, regardless of its size. Jobs must be advertised, applicants must be interviewed and hired, evaluation of their subsequent performance must occur, and reward systems as well as control or disciplinary systems must be put into place. All these activities involve HRM. However, very few senior vice presidents of HRM move beyond this level of responsibility, as such *staff* activities are subordinate to *line* or operations activities such as manufacturing and sales. Rarely does a board of directors select a senior vice president in HRM to become CEO.

When a company goes global, the role of IHRM increases in importance. Problems usually manifest themselves within the areas overseen by IHRM, such as integrating divergent organizational cultures, identifying and hiring citizens in the host nation who possess much-needed skills, and understanding and conforming to the labor laws in the host nation. Thus IHRM is central to going global. Unfortunately, many companies fail to recognize the importance of IHRM when doing so and treat it as a peripheral activity. Their emphasis is frequently on the financial and accounting aspects of the global ventures, particularly during the early stages of entrance. Even manufacturing and sales, both line activities in that they are directly involved in the production, distribution, and sale of the product, are accorded their proper due, which is presumed to be greater than that given to IHRM. In this way IHRM is sometimes a poor second cousin until it becomes clear that human problems within its purview are undermining all the good work in accounting, financial analysis, manufacturing, sales, and so forth. Sometimes companies stubbornly maintain a policy of IHRM "peripherality," typically to their own detriment.

Thus IHRM is both central and peripheral to the activities of many companies that are going global. Resolving this paradox is critical if the company wants to be successful.

Paradox 10.9. How should the conflict between internal pay equity and the forces of the external labor market be resolved?

Until 1976 China's Communist government emphasized the concept of the "iron rice bowl," which signified that everyone should be taken care of in a paternalistic manner and should share the rewards and even food and lodging. Workers, managers, and their families lived in company-owned dormitories and apartments. Terminating a worker was nearly impossible, and sometimes a particularly incorrigible and terminated worker waited outside a manager's apartment for days until he was reinstated. Pressure from others in the company and their families eventually motivated frustrated managers to reinstate such workers.

China today, as emphasized elsewhere in this book, is moving very rapidly to a Western-adapted model of the corporation. Pay for performance and layoffs are occurring to some extent, and job mobility in search of better opportunities is common. Still, there is conflict and strain between the traditional collectivistic focus of the Chinese and the individualistic-based compensation and rewards systems that are being introduced. The iron rice bowl, while mentioned infrequently, is still revered in some quarters by many Chinese as a symbol of what the corporation should be. Analogous feelings exist among many citizens in formerly Communist eastern and central European nations, especially as inequality has risen. In some nations, such as Russia and Poland, some segments of the population have lost both status and their sources of income because of the abolition of the Soviet bloc.

This conflict is epitomized in the tension existing between internal pay equity systems and the forces from the external labor market dictating that talent must be rewarded. In developing nations managers possessing EMBA degrees tend to be among the first to benefit from such external forces, as they are in scarce supply and can demand much higher salaries than their less-educated colleagues can. Needless to say, conflict and strain tend to result when long-serving managers receive considerably less in compensation than their younger and better-educated counterparts do. In one instance, a U.S. company acquired a Chinese company and asked its Chinese HRM manager to propose a new, performance-oriented compensation system for managers. This manager argued strenuously for the well-known Hay system, which rank orders jobs and the levels of compensation associated with them only in terms of internal organizational factors. The U.S. managers tried to explain that such a system was counterproductive and that the company would never be able to obtain badly needed managerial talent from the external labor market if only the Hay system were employed, but to little if any avail.

How can the strain and conflict between internal pay equity and the forces of the external labor market be resolved? There is no simple answer, but one factor stands out: the necessity of educating all members of the organization about the criticality of attracting key talent from the labor market into the organization. This necessitates a widening of the compensation gap between long-term and loyal managers and the newly hired managers. The message must be regularly transmitted through all forms of communication that the possibility of long-term success will prove to be evanescent unless such a policy is emphasized. Global companies that have instituted such education and communication programs report that both managers and workers are receptive to this line of argument, even when they are still unhappy. While education and communication programs do not solve all problems, they help mitigate them in an increasingly competitive global marketplace.

Paradox 10.10. Should multinational corporations impose their values when going global?

The Kyocera Corporation is one of Japan's most successful multinational companies. It operates a division producing computer equipment in the San Diego area that was highlighted in a very popular 1980 video, *The Kyocera Experiment*. This video's introductory scene focuses on a young American engineer, surrounded by American workers and his Japanese superiors. He plays a leading role in a Shinto ritual designed to purify the new facility into which the employees recently moved. Later, problems of quality control emerge, thus jeopardizing the company's contracts and sales. In classic Japanese fashion, both the American and Japanese men in positions of authority in various functional areas (and only men held these positions in 1980) meet at night at a retreat away from work. They engage in drinking and demonstrations of humor and camaraderie and then get down to the business at hand: What are the sources of the problem with quality control and sales? Several of them publicly commit to new ways of acting and promise the others that they will cooperate and attempt to succeed, no matter what the obstacles. The session ends with all the participants singing the company song.

This is a vivid but relatively benign manifestation of cultural values being employed in the workplace. However, what if a multinational corporation imposes cultural values that are not so compatible with those of employees in the host nation? Pay for performance, as indicated in Chapter 3, represents a highly individualistic way of rewarding people and is at variance with collectivistic values, such as those symbolized by the concept of the iron rice bowl. Similarly, layoffs tend to be viewed very negatively in a collectivistic culture. When U.S. companies started to operate in Taiwan, they offered higher compensation packages and better fringe benefits than their Taiwanese competitors did. They were quickly able to attract very competent job applicants. However, when a recession occurred, the U.S. companies laid off a significant portion of their workforces, even though their employees expected to retain their positions through such adverse times. When the economy improved, the American companies had difficulty attracting job applicants because of the negative reputation the companies had garnered.

It is difficult if not impossible to avoid imposing some cultural values from the home nation when operating internationally. Still, the conflict and strain between home-nation and host-nation cultural values is a very sensitive issue, especially in such areas as compensation and guaranteed employment. As we have seen in our discussion of Nissan in Chapter 3, its then CEO, Carlos Ghosn, was widely admired for his handling of such conflicts in order to save the company. However, his approach has not been widely followed in other companies. The role of IHRM in such situations is to minimize the inevitable conflicts and strains that will occur when home-culture and host-culture values require reconciliation.

Paradox 10.11. Which works best in a global firm, individual-based or group-based reward systems?

Over many decades, seemingly innumerable studies have addressed this issue, but until recently they focused primarily on domestic-only firms. Victor Vroom (1961) summarized decades of research comparing individual piece-rate versus group piece-rate systems among factory workers in the United States. The general conclusion is that, at least within the United States, individual-based reward systems lead to significantly higher productivity than do group piece-rate systems. Seemingly the popularity of pay-for-performance systems, among both managers and employees, reflects the logic of this finding. There is, however, a downside, as both managers and employees are likely to emphasize activities benefiting only themselves, and conflict and tension in groups are common because of this tendency.

As our discussion of ICI suggests, the issue is not simple. Under some circumstances it seems preferable to institute a compensation package that is primarily individually focused, while under other conditions a group-focused package encouraging cooperation works best. U.S. salespeople, for instance, tend to respond effectively to an individual-based system emphasizing units sold. However, those working in IHRM and other positions requiring cooperation may respond effectively when group-oriented packages are stressed. Such results seem to obtain across cultures. When a company globalizes, it appears advisable to examine the prevailing cultural values and to at least attempt to tailor the compensation system to it. There will rarely if ever be a perfect matching, especially as collectivistic societies change and become more individualistic and consumer oriented. Still, at least some problems and issues can be avoided by such tailoring.

Paradox 10.12. Is the role of IHRM different from that of domestic-only HRM?

Some 30 years ago HRM was known as the field of personnel, and its organizational status was uncommonly low when compared with other functional areas. Frequently a manager who was underperforming in another functional area would be transferred to personnel, sometimes heading up the operation. Thus a self-fulfilling prophecy frequently unfolded: Personnel managers were incompetent and not to be trusted, and only underperforming managers should enter this field. Admittedly this is a very broad caricature that rarely occurred in such an extreme form, but various degrees of it manifested themselves frequently.

Over time HRM developed into a specialized field requiring specialized knowledge. Senior management typically recognized its importance and began to increase its range of responsibilities. For example, HRM managers are significantly involved in the selection of the three or four internal candidates for the position of CEO in a GE tournament, out of which one of them is selected as CEO after two years. While GE is the only company sponsoring such a tournament, other companies have added other responsibilities and role requirements to their HRM positions.

Manickavasagam (2006) has suggested that IHRM represents a quantum leap in responsibilities and role expectations. In particular, he emphasized three areas demanding increased attention for IHRM when a company operates globally: enhancing competitive advantage through continuous innovation, harnessing diversity, and developing leadership capability. These three areas are also of importance in a company operating in only one nation. But the magnitude of their complexity in a global company is daunting. In some cases hundreds of thousands of organizational members are involved globally within one company; examples include GE, Wal-Mart, Unilever, and Toyota. Innovations of all types must be constantly introduced in such areas as computer technology, quality control, and automation. While IHRM is not directly responsible for all the innovations, it is frequently involved in activities resulting from them. For instance, constant retraining of the workforce in the use of new technologies is required, as is the selection of job candidates who possess the technical skills for using such technologies. Both selection and training involve IHRM.

Harnessing diversity is an issue in a domestic-only company, regardless of the national location of its headquarters. As indicated previously, less than 10% of the world's 220 nations are monocultural. When a company enters regional and global markets, diversity automatically increases. IHRM must oversee workforces that are diverse and geographically separated from one another.

A major method for harnessing such diversity is disseminating a corporate culture globally, but this is not an easy task. As indicated previously, Cisco Systems avoided going global for years. Still, it developed a distinctive approach to disseminating a corporate culture that other companies widely admired and copied. A Cisco team from headquarters would meet with the managers of an acquired company and indicate that decision making would be decentralized. However, the acquired company had to use the same procedures and forms as those employed throughout the company. The combination of decentralization and standardization allowed both Cisco senior management and the managers in the acquired company to learn quickly how to work with one another, thus avoiding a clash of cultures. To allay fears, Cisco even introduced the policy of avoiding the termination of any one senior manager in the acquired company unless both the acquired company's CEO and Cisco's CEO agreed that such a course of action was warranted. As Cisco globalizes, it is still using the approach of decentralized decision making and standardization.

The third and final area that Manickavasagam emphasized is leadership. Managing a global company is by its very nature more difficult than managing a domestic-only company. Senior executives must travel much more in global companies, and they must respond to many more demands that emanate from the crises and needs of their divisions located in different nations. Selecting global leaders and preparing them for the rigors of their new positions fall within the purview of IHRM. Unfortunately, while leadership has been a central topic in the management literature for decades, there is a paucity of research on predicting effective global leadership. How do domestic-only leaders differ from global leaders? How many years should executives spend outside their native national culture to become comfortable with the responsibilities of global leadership? Is effective global leadership really that much different from effective domestic-only leadership? These are but a few of the questions confronting IHRM.

In short, HRM in a domestic-only firm is different than IHRM in a regional or global firm. Still, there are many similarities, some of which reflect the traditional topics in the field of personnel, such as selection, training, and performance evaluation. The scale of complexity and the increased number of stakeholders seem to be two of the hallmarks of IHRM when compared with personnel and HRM. A related hallmark is the inclusion of IHRM in the strategic areas of a company, such as enhancing competitive advantage through continuous innovation. As globalization proceeds, we can expect to see the role and importance of IHRM grow in stature, although it will seemingly always face the issue of centrality versus peripherality.

Paradox 10.13. Are HRM requirements similar throughout the globalizing world?

As our discussion of Paradox 10.12 suggests, there are common role requirements for IHRM in globalizing firms that are directly tied to the three topics that Manickavasagam emphasized. In this sense similarity is the norm. Still, HRM varies dramatically by nation. In Germany, for instance, employers in firms of more than 2,000 employees must gain the consent of worker-elected work councils before they can do any of the following: appoint or dismiss employees, set working hours, require overtime, or even change the price of lunches in the employee cafeteria. Denmark offers worker benefits that are more extensive than those found in all or most European nations. France has a large and complex body of laws and regulations regarding employment. These examples should suffice to demonstrate that each nation has its own peculiarities, especially in the area of HRM.

However, we can expect to see more convergence than divergence in the area of IHRM as globalization proceeds. Multinational corporations must meet the demands of labor markets, capital markets, and product markets, no matter where they operate. The field of IHRM has become prominent at least in part because of the growing professionalism that practitioners in various nations are emphasizing. Over time, a more unified or common worldview should emerge, not only in IHRM but also in the areas of international law, accounting systems, and financial systems. In fact, there is a very strong movement in this direction already, as demonstrated by the harmonization of the accounting systems in European nations, the integration of stock markets globally, and the acceptance of universal legal norms supported by the International Court of Justice. The future is not certain, but if current trends persist, global corporations should support similar if not identical HRM policies within each national culture.

Takeaways

1. It is important to understand the direct link between strategy and organizational structure. The links are multidomestic strategy, geographic-centered structure; global strategy, product-based structure; and transnational strategy, the matrix organization.

2. There is no ideal organizational structure, and the matrix structure is particularly unstable.

3. There are various ways of entering the global marketplace. These include exporting, licensing, strategic alliances, acquisitions, and the greenfield venture or the wholly owned subsidiary. All of them possess both advantages and limitations. The first three methods seem appropriate for initial market entry, to reduce risk and uncertainty, while the last two methods appear suitable for late market entry after a firm has developed some understanding of the global marketplace.

4. Organizations throughout the globalized and globalizing world are becoming more similar to one another at the macro level of structure. However, change is slow and sometimes nonexistent at the micro level of individual behavior.

5. Careful analysis, ideally accompanied by on-site visits, helps to determine whether a potential market is either large or small.

6. IHRM should be a critical and central activity in a global firm, but frequently corporations treat it as peripheral.

7. A recommended method for solving the conflict between internal pay equity and the demands of the external labor market is full sharing of information with all.

8. It is impossible or nearly impossible for globalizing companies to avoid the conflict between home-country and host-country values, but they can minimize it.

9. The responsibilities of IHRM are similar to those of domestic-only HRM. Still, they represent a quantum leap and a very high degree of complexity.

10. IHRM requirements vary by nation. IHRM specialists must analyze them independently for each nation.

11. The dilemmas associated with the rise of aerotropoli, the standardization and harmonization of financial and accounting systems across nations and within global companies, and the standardization of global advertising and marketing (branding) will not go away. For example, opting for a reduction in costs rather than more differentiated nation-specific advertisements, and vice versa, will occur in global companies.

Discussion Questions

1. Why is the matrix structure particularly unstable? Why is this an issue for globalizing firms?

2. Discuss and evaluate Cisco Systems' method of integrating an acquired company into its organizational structure.

3. Please review the ICI case discussion at the beginning of the chapter. Do you feel that ICI senior management is unrealistic? Why or why not?

4. Did Wal-Mart's global growth pattern confirm Alan Rugman's emphasis on regionalization rather than globalization? Why or why not?

5. Many Western companies were unprofitable in China for several years. Why didn't they withdraw from the Chinese marketplace to cut their losses?

6. Please describe three ways global companies can ensure the centrality of IHRM in their operations. Why is IHRM peripheral in many instances?

7. What is the Hay system? How does it relate to the conflict between internal equity and the demands of the external labor market?

8. Are HRM requirements becoming similar globally? Why or why not? Please give two examples.

Exercise

1. Working in small teams, analyze in depth the IHRM function of one globalizing or globalized firm. Then prepare a small number of PowerPoint slides. A new team made up of a representative from each original team will integrate the slides into a class presentation, followed by discussion.

References

Adair, W., & Brett, J. (2005). The negotiation dance: Time, culture, and behavioral sequences in negotiation. *Organization Science, 16*(1), 33–51.

Adler, N. (2002). *International dimensions of organizational behavior* (4th ed.). Cincinnati, OH: South-Western College Publishing.

Agar, M. (1994). *Language shock*. New York: William Morrow.

Allik, J., & McCrae, R. (2004). Toward a geography of personality traits: Patterns of profiles across 36 cultures. *Journal of Cross-Cultural Psychology, 34*, 13–28.

Allport, G. (1979, 1958, 1954). *The nature of prejudice*. New York: Perseus Books.

Anderson, P. (2000). Explaining intercultural differences in nonverbal communication. In L. Samovar & R. Porter (Eds.), *Intercultural communication: A reader* (9th ed., pp. 258–279). Belmont, CA: Wadsworth.

Angel, S. (2000). *Housing policy matters: A global analysis*. New York: Oxford University Press.

Arensberg, C. (1968). *The Irish countryman: An anthropological study*. Prospect, IL: Waveland Press. (Original work published 1937)

Axtell, R. (1990). *Dos and taboos around the world* (2nd ed.). New York: John Wiley.

Barnard, C. (1968). *The functions of the executive*. Cambridge, MA: Harvard University Press. (Original work published 1938)

Barnes, J. (2006, May 24). Chinese threat is expanding, Pentagon says. *Los Angeles Times*, p. A20.

Berestein, L. (2006, July 10). More than just Latinos illegally call U.S. home. *San Diego Union Tribune*, pp. A1, A6.

Bergmann, B. (2006). Letter to the editor: Bad trade. *Foreign Affairs, 85*(4), 202.

Bernstein, A. (2004, Dec. 6). Shaking up trade theory. *BusinessWeek*, 116–120.

Bernstein, P. (1996). *Against the gods: The remarkable story of risk*. New York: John Wiley.

Berry, M., Carbaugh, D., & Nurmikari-Berry, M. (2004). Communicating Finnish quietude: A pedagogical process for discovering implicit cultural meanings in languages. *Language and Intercultural Communication, 4*, 261–280.

Bhagwati, J. (2004). *In defense of globalization*. New York: Oxford University Press.

Bhagwati, J. (2005, August 4). A new vocabulary for trade. *Wall Street Journal*, p. A1.

Bird, A., & Osland, J. (2006). Making sense of intercultural collaboration. *International Studies of Management and Organization, 35*(4), 115–132.

Blinder, A. (2006). Offshoring: The next industrial revolution? *Foreign Affairs, 85*(2), 113–128.

Blustein, P. (1994, Dec. 1). A spiced smoke makes Indonesian firm very hot. *Washington Post*, pp. B11, B14.

Bonavia, D. (1989). *The Chinese*. London: Penguin.

Bond, M., Wan, K., Leung, K., & Giacalone, R. (1985). How are responses to verbal insults related to cultural collectivism and power distance? *Journal of Cross-Cultural Psychology, 16*, 111–127.

Boyacigiller, N., Kleinberg, M., Phillips, M., & Sachmann, S. (2004). Conceptualizing culture. In B. Punnett & O. Shenkar (Eds.), *Handbook of international management research* (2nd ed., pp. 99–167). Ann Arbor: University of Michigan Press.

Brannen, M., Gomez, C., Peterson, M., Romani, L., Sagiv, L., & Wu, P. (2004). People in global organizations: Culture, personality, and social dynamics. In H. Lane, M. Maznevski, M. Mendenhall, & J. McNett (Eds.), *Handbook of global management: A guide to managing complexity* (pp. 26–54). Oxford, UK: Blackwell.

Brett, J. (2001). *Negotiating globally*. San Francisco: Jossey-Bass.

Brislin, R. (2000). *Understanding culture's influence on behavior* (2nd ed.). New York: Harcourt Brace.

Brockner, J., Ackerman, G., Greenberg, J., Gelfand, M., Francesco, A., Zhen, X. C., et al. (2001). Culture and procedural justice: The influence of power distance on reactions to voice. *Journal of Experimental Social Psychology, 37*, 300–315.

Brown, S. (2006, January 4). Taking note of our worlds: Local scientist says how we speak influences the music we make. *San Diego Union Tribune*, Quest section, pp. 1–4.

Burke, R. (1979). Methods of resolving superior-subordinate conflict. *Organizational Behavior and Human Performance, 5*, 396–410.

Burr, A. (1917). *Russell H. Connell and his work*. Philadelphia: Winston.

Burrough, B., & Helyar, J. (1990). *Barbarians at the gate*. New York: Harper & Row.

Cairncross, F. (2001). *The death of distance*. Boston: Harvard Business School Press.

Carroll, S., & Gannon, M. (1997). *Ethical dimensions of international management*. Thousand Oaks, CA: Sage.

Cellich, C., & Jain, S. (2004). *Global business negotiations*. Cincinnati, OH: Thompson South-Western.

Chandrasekaran, R. (2001, May 13). Cambodian village wired to the future: Satellite internet link transforming economy and culture. *Washington Post*. National News section, p. 1.

Charon, R., & Colvin, G. (1999, June 21). Why CEOs fail. *Fortune*, 44–54.

Chatman, J., & Barsade, S. (1995). Personality, organizational culture, and cooperation: Evidence from a business simulation. *Administrative Science Quarterly, 40*, 423–443.

Chen, M. (2001). *Inside Chinese business: A guide for managers worldwide*. Boston: Harvard Business School Press.

Cheng, N. (1982). *Life and death in Shanghai*. New York: Penguin Books.

Child, J. (1981). Culture, contingency and capitalism in the cross-national study of organizations. In L. Cummings & B. Staw (Eds.), *Research in organizational behavior, Vol. 3* (pp. 303–356). Greenwich, CT: JAI Press.

Chinese Culture Connection. (1987). Chinese values and the search for culture-free dimensions of culture. *Journal of Cross-Cultural Psychology, 18*(2), 143–164.

Chu, H. (2006, May 12). Communists lead Kolkata's capitalist makeover. *Los Angeles Times,* p. A33.

Chua, A. (2003). *World on fire.* New York: Doubleday.

Cohen, H. (1980). *You can negotiate anything.* New York: Lyle Stewart.

Collins, J. (2001). *Good to great.* New York: HarperCollins.

Collins, J., & Porras, J. (1994). *Built to last.* New York: HarperCollins.

Cottle, T. (1968). The location of experience: A manifest time orientation. *Acta Psychologica, 28,* 129–149.

Cramton, C. (2001). The mutual knowledge problem and its consequences for dispersed collaboration. *Organization Science, 12,* 346–371.

Cramton, C., & Hinds, P. (2004). Subgroup dynamics in internationally distributed teams: Ethnocentrism or cross-national learning? *Research in Organizational Behavior, 26,* 231–263.

Decoupled. (2006, Feb. 25). *Economist,* 75–76.

de Mooij, M. (2005). *Global marketing and advertising: Understanding cultural paradoxes* (2nd ed.). Thousand Oaks, CA: Sage.

de Soto, H. (2000). *The mystery of capital: Why capitalism triumphs in the West and fails everywhere else.* New York: Basic Books.

DeWoskin, R. (2005). *Foreign babes in Beijing: Behind the scenes of a new China.* New York: Norton.

Diamond, J. (1997). *Guns, germs and steel: The fates of human societies.* New York: Norton.

Donaldson, T. (1989). *The ethics of international business.* New York: Oxford University Press.

Donaldson, T., & Dunfee, T. (1994). Towards a unified conception of business ethics: Integrative social contracts theory. *Academy of Management Review, 19,* 252–284.

Donaldson, T., & Dunfee, T. (1999). *Ties that bind: A social contracts approach to business ethics.* Boston: Harvard Business School Press.

Dorfman, P., Hanges, P., & Brodbeck, F. (2004). Leading and cultural variation: The identification of culturally endorsed leadership profiles. In R. House, P. Hanges, M. Javidan, P. Dorfman, & V. Gupta (Eds.), *Culture, leadership, and organizations: The GLOBE study of 62 societies* (pp. 669–720). Thousand Oaks, CA: Sage.

Durkheim, E. (2001). *The elementary forms of the religious life.* Oxford, UK: Oxford University Press. (Original work published 1916)

Earley, C. (1993). East meets West meets Mideast: Further explorations of collectivistic versus individualistic work groups. *Academy of Management Journal, 36,* 685–698.

Easterly, W. (2006). *The white man's burden.* New York: Penguin Press.

Economics focus: Myths and migration. (2006, April 8). *Economist*, 76.

Eisenhardt, K. (2000). Paradox, spirals, ambivalence: The new language of change and pluralism. *Academy of Management Review, 25*(4), 703–705.

Face value: bold fusion. (2007, Feb. 17). *Economist*, 70.

Fanfani, A. (1984). *Catholicism, Protestantism, and capitalism.* Notre Dame, IN: University of Notre Dame Press.

Fang, T. (1999). *Chinese business negotiating style.* Thousand Oaks, CA: Sage.

Fang, T. (2003). A critique of Hofstede's fifth national culture dimension. *International Journal of Cross-Cultural Management, 3*(3), 347–368.

Fang, T. (2006). From onion to "ocean": Paradox and change in national cultures. *International Studies of Management and Organization, 35*(4), 71–90.

Ferguson, N. (2005). Is globalization doomed? Sinking globalization. *Foreign Affairs, 84*(2), 64–79.

Ferguson, N. (2006a, Feb. 27). The crash of civilizations. *Los Angeles Times*, p. B13.

Ferguson, N. (2006b). The next war of the world. *Foreign Affairs, 85*(5), 61–74.

Finkelstein, S. (2003). *Why smart executives fail.* New York: Penguin.

Fisher, G. (1988). *Mindsets.* Yarmouth, MA: Intercultural Press.

Fisher, R., Ury, W., & Patten, B. (1991). *Getting to yes* (Rev. ed.). New York: Penguin.

Fiske, A. (1991a). The four elementary forms of sociality: Frameworks for a unified theory of social relations. *Psychological Review, 99*, 698–723.

Fiske, A. (1991b). *Structures of social life.* New York: Free Press.

Florida, R. (2005, October). The world is spiky. *Atlantic Monthly*, 48–51.

Friedman, T. (2005). *The world is flat.* New York: Farrar, Straus & Giroux.

Gannon, M. (2001). *Working across cultures: Application and exercises.* Thousand Oaks, CA: Sage.

Gannon, M. (2004). *Understanding global cultures: Metaphorical journeys through 28 nations, clusters of nations, and continents* (3rd ed.). Thousand Oaks, CA: Sage.

Gannon, M., Gupta, A., Audia, P., & Kristof-Brown, A. (2006). Cultural metaphors as frames of reference for nations: A six-country study. *International Studies of Management and Organization, 35*(4), 37–47.

Gausden, J. (2003). *The giving and receiving of feedback in central European cultures.* Unpublished master's dissertation, University of Salford, UK.

Geertz, C. (1973). *The interpretation of culture.* New York: Basic Books.

Gelfand, M., Bhawuk, D., Nishii, L., & Bechtold, D. (2004). Individualism and collectivism. In R. House, P. Hanges, M. Javidan, P. Dorfman, & V. Gupta (Eds.), *Culture, leadership, and organizations: The GLOBE study of 62 societies* (pp. 438–512). Thousand Oaks, CA: Sage.

Gelfand, M., Higgins, M., Nishi, L., Raver, J., Dominguez, A., Murakami, F., et al. (2002). Culture and egocentric perceptions of fairness in conflict and negotiation. *Journal of Applied Psychology, 87*(5), 833–845.

Gelfand, M., & Holcombe, K. (1998). Behavioral patterns of horizontal and vertical individualism and collectivism. In T. Singelis (Ed.), *Teaching about culture, ethnicity, & diversity* (pp. 121–132). Thousand Oaks, CA: Sage.

Gelfand, M., & McCusker, C. (2002). Metaphor and the cultural construction of negotiation: A paradigm for research and practice. In M. Gannon & K. Newman (Eds.),
Handbook of cross-cultural management (pp. 292–314). Oxford, UK: Blackwell.

Georgiadou, Y., Puri, S., & Sahay, S. (2006). The rainbow metaphor: Spatial data
infrastructure organization and implementation. *International Studies of
Management and Organization, 35*(6), 48–70.

Gesteland, R. (1999). *Cross-cultural business behavior* (2nd ed.). Copenhagen, Denmark:
Copenhagen Business School Press.

Goldin, I., & Reinert, K. (2006). *Globalization for Development.* NY: Palgrave Macmillan.

Gosselin, P. (2006, March 6). That good education might not be enough: American
workers at all levels are vulnerable to outsourcing, experts say. *Los Angeles Times,*
pp. A1, A9.

Govindarajan, V., & Gupta, A. (2001). *The quest for global dominance.* San Francisco:
Jossey-Bass.

Guiso, L., Sapienza, P., & Zingales, L. (2005). *Cultural biases in economic exchange.*
Social Science Research Network, Working Paper #601.

Gullahorn, J., & Gullahorn, J. (1963). An extension of the U-curve hypothesis.
Journal of Social Sciences, 19(3), 33–47.

Gupta, A., & Govindarajan, V. (2004). *Global strategy and organization.* New York:
John Wiley.

Gupta, D. (2006, Jan. 4). When worlds collide: Individualism and collectivism are not
an easy fit. *San Diego Union Tribune,* p. B7.

Hall, E. (1959). *The silent language.* New York: Doubleday.

Hall, E. (1966). *The hidden dimension.* Garden City, NY: Doubleday.

Hall, E., & Hall, M. (1990). *Understanding cultural differences.* Yarmouth, ME:
Intercultural Press.

Harrison, L., & Huntington, S. (Eds.). (2000). *Culture matters: How values shape
human progress.* New York: Basic Books.

Haslam, N. (Ed.). (2004). *Relational models theory: A contemporary overview.* Mahwah,
NJ: Lawrence Erlbaum.

Helprin, M. (2006, Jan. 15). The myth that shapes Bush's world. *Los Angeles Times,*
pp. M1, M15.

Herskovits, M. (1948). *Man and his works.* New York: Knopf.

Hitt, M., Ireland, D., & Hoskisson, R. (2003, July 28). Intellectual property. *Business-
Week.*

Hitt, M., Ireland, D., & Hoskisson, R. (2007). *Strategic management: Competitiveness
and globalization* (7th ed.). Cincinnati, OH: Thomson South-Western.

Hofstede, G. (1980). *Culture's consequences.* Beverly Hills, CA: Sage.

Hofstede. G. (2001). *Culture's consequences* (2nd ed.). Thousand Oaks, CA: Sage.

Hofstede, G., & Bond, M. (1988). The Confucius connection: From cultural roots to
economic growth. *Organizational Dynamics, 16*(4), 4–21.

Hollinger, C. (2000). *Mai pen rai means never mind.* New York: Houghton Mifflin.

House, R., Hanges, P., Javidan, M., Dorfman, P., & Gupta, V. (2004). *Culture, leadership,
and organizations: The GLOBE study of 62 societies.* Thousand Oaks, CA: Sage.

Huntington, S. (1996). *The clash of civilizations and the remaking of world order.* New York: Touchstone, Simon & Schuster.

Ignatius, D. (2005, April 21). Nationalism in an era of globalization. *San Diego Union Tribune*, p. B8.

Inglehart, R., Basaanez, M., Diez-Medrana, J., Halman, L., & Luijkx, R. (Eds.). (2004). *Human beliefs and values: A cross-cultural sourcebook based on the 1999–2002 Value Surveys.* Mexico City: Xiglo XXI Editores.

Ip, G., & King, N. (2005, June 27). Is China's rapid economic development good for the U.S.? *Wall Street Journal*, pp. B1, B4.

Iyengar, S. (1998, August). *Rethinking the value of choice: A cultural perspective on intrinsic motivation.* Paper presented to the Culture and Psychology Conference, Stanford University, CA.

Iyengar, S., & Lepper, M. (1999). Rethinking the value of choice: A cultural perspective on intrinsic motivation. *Journal of Personality and Social Psychology*, 76, 349–366.

Jarvenpaa, S., Knoll, K., & Leidner, D. (1998). Is anybody out there? Antecedents of trust in global virtual teams. *Journal of Management Information Systems*, 14(4), 29–36.

Jarvenpaa, S., & Leidner, D. (1999). Communication and trust in global virtual teams. *Organization Science*, 10(6), 791–815.

Javidan, M., Dorfman, P., Sully de Luque, M., & House, R. (2006). In the eye of the beholder: Cross cultural lessons in leadership from Project GLOBE. *Academy of Management Perspectives*, 20(1), 67–90.

Ji, L., Nisbett, R., & Su, Y. (2001). Culture, change, and prediction. *Psychological Science*, 12(6), 450–456.

Jiang, F. (2005). Driving forces of international pharmaceutical firms' FDI into China. *Journal of Business Research*, 22(1), 21–39.

Johnson, C. (1962). *Peasant nationalism and Communist power: The emergence of revolutionary China, 1937–1945.* Palo Alto, CA: Stanford University Press.

Johnston, S., & Selsky, J. (2005). Duality and paradox: Trust and duplicity in Japanese business practice. *Organization Studies, 27*(2), 183–205.

Karau, S., & Williams, K. (1993). Social loafing: A meta-analytic view of social integration. *Journal of Personality and Social Psychology*, 65, 681–706.

Knight, F. (1964). *Uncertainty, risk, and profit.* New York: Century Press. (Original work published 1921)

Kotter, J. (1982). *The general managers.* New York: Free Press.

Kroeber, A., & Kluckhohn, F. (1952). Culture: A critical review of concepts and definitions. *Peabody Museum Papers*, 47(1), 170–210.

Lane, H., Maznevski, M., Mendenhall, M., & McNett, J. (2004). *Handbook of global management.* Oxford, UK: Blackwell.

Lau, D., & Murnighan, J. (1998). Demographic diversity and faultlines: The compositional dynamics of organizational groups. *Academy of Management Review*, 23, 325–340.

Laurent, A. (2002). INSEAD working paper. Adapted in Adler, N. (2002). *International dimensions of organizational behavior.* Cincinnati, OH: Thomson South-Western.

Layard, R. (2005). *Happiness: Lessons from a new science.* New York: Penguin.

Lewis, M. (2000). Exploring paradox: Toward a more comprehensive guide. *Academy of Management Review, 25*(4), 760–777.

Liker, J. (2004). *The Toyota way.* New York: McGraw-Hill.

Lindsay, G. (2006, July/August). Rise of the aerotropolis. *Fast Company,* 76–85.

Living with a superpower. (2003, January 4). *Economist,* 18–20.

Lodge, G., & Wilson, C. (2006). *A corporate solution to global poverty: How multinationals can help the poor and invigorate their own legitimacy.* Princeton, NJ: Princeton University Press.

Loomis, C. (1993, May 3). Dinosaurs? *Fortune,* 36–42.

Loomis, C. (2005, Feb. 27). Hewlett Packard: Why Carly's big bet is failing. *Fortune,* pp. 48–60.

Loomis, C. (2006, Feb. 20). The tragedy of General Motors. *Fortune,* 59–75.

Lou, S. (2005). *Sparrows, bedbugs, and body shadows.* Honolulu: University of Hawaii Press.

Lynn, B. (2005). *End of the line: The rise and coming fall of the global corporation.* New York: Doubleday.

Manickavasagam, J. (2006). Human resources development strategy. In C. Mann & K. Götz (Eds.), *Borderless business* (pp. 107–122). Westport, CT: Praeger.

Mann, C. (2006). Strategy in a global context. In C. Mann & K. Götz (Eds.), *Borderless business* (pp. 33–69). Westport, CT: Praeger.

Martin, R. (2006, Jan. 16). What innovation advantage? *BusinessWeek,* 102.

Maslow, A. (1970). *Motivation and personality* (2nd ed.). New York: Harper & Row.

Matthews, J. (1997). Powershift. *Foreign Affairs, 76*(1), 51–66.

McNeilly, Mark. (1996). *Sun Tzu and the art of business.* New York: Oxford University Press.

Mendenhall, M. and Oddou, G. (2000). *Readings and Cases in International Human Resource Management.* (3rd Edition). Boston: PWS-Kent.

Mendenhall, M., Kuhlman, T., Stahl, G., & Osland, J. (2002). Employee development and expatriate assignments. In M. Gannon & K. Newman (Eds.), *Handbook of cross-cultural management.* Oxford, UK: Blackwell.

Mintzberg, H. (1973). *The nature of managerial work.* New York: Harper & Row.

Moffett, M. (2005, Nov. 9). Barrio study links land ownership to a better life. *Wall Street Journal,* pp. A1, A12.

Morrison, T., Conaway, W., & Borden, G. (1995). *Kiss, bow, or shake hands: How to do business in sixty countries.*

Naisbitt, J. (1994). *Global paradox.* New York: William Morrow.

Nam, S. (1991). *Cultural and managerial attributions for group performance.* Unpublished doctoral dissertation, Lundquist College of Business, University of Oregon.

Ni, C. (2005, Dec. 4). Kung fu monks go modern. *Los Angeles Times,* pp. A1, A9.

Nielsen, C. (2005). The global chess game . . . or is it Go? Market-entry strategies for emerging markets. *Thunderbird International Business Review, 47*(4), 397–427.

North, D. (1981). *Structure and change in economic history.* New York: Norton.

North, D. (1990). *Institutions, institutional change, and economic performance.* Cambridge, MA: Harvard University Press.

North, D. (2005, April 7). The Chinese menu (for development). *Wall Street Journal,* p. A14.

Olson, M. (1971). *The logic of collective action: Public goods and the theory of groups.* Cambridge, MA: Harvard University Press.

Olson, M. (1982). *The rise and decline of nations.* New Haven, CT: Yale University Press.

Olson, M. (2000). *Power and prosperity: Outgrowing Communist and capitalist dictatorships.* New York: Basic Books.

Organ, D., Podsakoff, P., & MacKenzie, S. (2006). *Organizational citizenship behavior.* Thousand Oaks, CA: Sage.

Osland, J. (1995). *The adventure of working abroad.* San Francisco: Jossey-Bass.

Osland, J., & Bird, A. (2000). Beyond sophisticated stereotyping: Cultural sense making in context. *Academy of Management Executive, 14*(1), 65–77.

Osland, J., & Osland, A. (2006). Expatriate paradoxes and cultural involvement. *International Studies of Management and Organization, 35*(4), 91–114.

Owens, B. (2006, April 12). The huge immigrant tide—I have a plan [Letter to the editor]. *Wall Street Journal,* p. A15.

Parker, J. (2005, July 16). Degrees of separation: A survey of America. *Economist,* 1–20.

Peng, M. (2002). Cultures, institutions, and strategic choices: Toward an institutional perspective on business strategy. In M. Gannon & K. Newman (Eds.), *Handbook of cross-cultural management* (pp. 52–66). Oxford, UK: Blackwell.

Peters, T., & Waterman, R. (1982). *In search of excellence.* New York: Harper & Row.

Pfeffer, J., & Sutton, R. (2006). *Hard facts.* Boston: Harvard Business School Press.

Pierson, D. (2006, Jan. 3). Cantonese is losing its voice. *Los Angeles Times,* pp. A1, A6.

Polzer, J., Crisp, C., Jarvenpaa, S., & Kim, J. (2006). Extending the faultline model to geographically dispersed teams: How co-located subgroups can impair group functioning. *Academy of Management Journal, 49*(4), 679–692.

Pudelko, M. (2006). Some good recipes for globalization—but quite a few ingredients are missing. *Academy of Management Perspectives, 20*(2), 78–80.

Putnam, R. (1993). *Making democracy work: Civic traditions in modern Italy.* Princeton, NJ: Princeton University Press.

Quinn, R., & Cameron, K. (1988). *Paradox and transformation.* Cambridge, MA: Ballinger.

Redfield, R. (1948). Introduction. In B. Malinowski, *Magic, science, and religion.* Boston: Beacon Press.

Rhoads, C. (2006, Jan. 19). In threat to Internet's clout, some are starting alternatives. *Wall Street Journal,* pp. A1, A7.

Robertson, D. (2002). Business ethics across cultures. In M. Gannon & K. Newman (Eds.), *Handbook of cross-cultural management* (pp. 361–392). Oxford, UK: Blackwell.

Robinson, E. (1999). *Coal to cream*. New York: Free Press.

Romano, L. (2005, Dec. 26). College graduates' level of literacy is found declining. *San Diego Union Tribune*, p. A3.

Rostow, W. (1971). *The stages of economic growth* (2nd ed.). Cambridge, UK: Cambridge University Press.

Rugman, A. (2005). *The regional multinationals: MNEs and "global" strategic management*. Cambridge, UK: Cambridge University Press.

Russell, B. (1913). *Principia mathematica*. Cambridge, UK: Cambridge University Press.

Sachmann, S., & Phillips, M. (2004). Contextual influences on culture research. *International Journal of Cross-Cultural Management*, 4(3), 370–390.

Sahagun, L. (2006, April 16). Dalai Lama, Islamic groups meet. *Los Angeles Times*, pp. B1, B9.

Sala-i-Martin, X. (2002, May). *The world distribution of income estimated from individual country distributions*. National Bureau of Economic Research working paper No. 8933. Cambridge, MA.

Samuelson, R. (2005, June 8). Sabotaging the assimilation process. *San Diego Union Tribune*, p. B8.

Samuelson, R. (2006, March 8). We must make the melting pot work. *San Diego Union Tribune*, p. B8.

Schumpeter, J. (1942). *Capitalism, socialism, and democracy*. New York: Harper & Brothers.

Sesit, M. (2005, August 4). Geopolitical risk: History's constant. *Wall Street Journal*, p. C12.

Shweder, R. (2000). Moral maps, "First World" conceits, and the new evangelists. In L. Harrison & S. Huntington, *Culture matters* (pp. 158–177). New York: Basic Books.

Smith, H. (1991). *The world's religions*. San Francisco: HarperCollins.

Smith, K., & Berg, D. (1987). *Paradoxes of group life*. San Francisco: Jossey-Bass. (Paperback edition published in 1997)

Smith, K., & Berg, D. (1997). Cross-cultural groups at work. *European Journal of Management*, 15(1), 8–15.

Smith, L. (1990, Feb. 26). Fear and loathing of Japan. *Fortune*, 50–60.

Smith, P., & Bond, M. (1998). *Social psychology across cultures*. Boston: Allyn & Bacon.

Smith, P., Bond, M., & Kagitcibasi, C. (2006). *Understanding social psychology across cultures*. Thousand Oaks, CA: Sage.

Steers, R., & Sanchez-Runde, C. (2002). Culture, motivation, and work behavior. In M. Gannon & K. Newman (Eds.), *Handbook of cross-cultural management* (pp. 190–216). Oxford, UK: Blackwell.

Stein, R. (1999, Dec. 27). Science notebook. *Washington Post*, p. A11.

Stewart, E., & Bennett, M. (1991). *American cultural patterns: A cross cultural perspective* (2nd ed.). Yarmouth, ME: Intercultural Press.

Stewart, T. (1996, March 18). The nine dilemmas that leaders face. *Fortune*, 38–47.

Streeten, P. (2001). Integration, independence, and globalization. In *Finance and development* (pp. 20–45). Washington, DC: International Monetary Fund.

Sugawara, S. (1998, August 21). From debt to desperation in Japan. *Washington Post*, p. G3.

Svejenova, S. (2006). Quo vadis, Europe? *Academy of Management Perspectives*, 20(2), 82–84.

Tan, J., & Peng, M. (1999). *Culture, nation, and entrepreneurial strategic orientations: Implications for an emerging economy.* Working paper, Fisher College of Business, Ohio State University.

Ting-Toomey, S. (1988). A face negotiation theory. In Y. Kim & W. Gudykunst (Eds.), *Theory in intercultural communication* (pp. 213–235). Newbury Park, CA: Sage.

Triandis, H. (2002). Generic individualism and collectivism. In M. Gannon & K. Newman (Eds.), *Handbook of cross-cultural management* (pp. 16–46). London: Blackwell.

Triandis, H. (2004). Foreword. In R. House, P. Hanges, M. Javidan, P. Dorfman, & V. Gupta (Eds.), *Culture, leadership, and organizations: The GLOBE study of 62 societies* (pp. xv–xix.). Thousand Oaks, CA: Sage.

Triandis, H., & Gelfand, M. (1998). Convergent measurement of horizontal and vertical individualism and collectivism. *Journal of Personality & Social Psychology*, 74, 118–128.

Trompenaars, F., & Hampden-Turner, C. (1998). *Riding the waves of culture* (2nd ed.). New York: McGraw-Hill.

Vroom, V. (1961). *Work and motivation.* New York: John Wiley.

Wallace, P. (1999). *The psychology of the Internet.* Cambridge, UK: Cambridge University Press.

Weber, E., & Hsee, C. (1998). Cross-cultural differences in risk perception, but cross-cultural similarities in attitudes toward perceived risk. *Management Science*, 49(9), 1205–1217.

Weber, E., Hsee, C., & Sokolowska, J. (1998). What folklore tells us about risk and risk taking: Cross-cultural comparisons of American, German, and Chinese proverbs. *Organizational Behavior and Human Decision Processes*, 75(2), 170–186.

Weber, M. (1930). *The Protestant ethic and the spirit of capitalism* (T. Parsons, Trans.). New York: Charles Scribner's Sons.

Weick, K. (1995). *Sensemaking in organizations.* Thousand Oaks, CA: Sage.

Weiss, S. (1994, Spring). Negotiating with "Romans"—part 1. *Sloan Management Review*, 51–62.

Welch, J. (with Welch, S.). (2005). *Winning.* New York: HarperBusiness.

Wessel, D. (2006, May 18). College grad wages are sluggish, too. *Wall Street Journal*, p. A2.

Westley, D. (2006). Book review: The new multinationals: MNEs and global strategic management. *Journal of International Business Studies*, 37(3), 445–449.

Westwood, R., & Chan, A. (1995). Headship and leadership. In R. Westwood (Ed.), *Organisational behavior: Southeast Asian perspectives* (pp. 118–143). Hong Kong: Longman.

Williams, P. (2002). *The paradox of power.* New York: Warner Books.

Williamson, P. (1997). Asia's new competitive game. *Harvard Business Review, 75*(5), 55–67.

Wolf, M. (2004). *Why globalization works.* New Haven, CT: Yale University Press.

Yu, A. (1996). Ultimate life concerns, self and Chinese achievement motivation. In M. Bond (Ed.), *The handbook of Chinese psychology* (pp. 227–246). New York: Oxford University Press.

Yu, A., & Yang, K. (1994). The nature of achievement motivation in collectivist societies. In U. Kim, H. Triandis, S. Kagitcibasi, S. Choi, & G. Yoon (Eds.), *Individualism and collectivism: Theory, method, and applications* (pp. 239–250). Thousand Oaks, CA: Sage.

Index

About the Author

Martin J. Gannon (Ph.D., Columbia University) is Professor of International Management and Strategy, College of Business Administration, California State University, San Marcos. He is also Professor Emeritus, Robert H. Smith School of Business, University of Maryland at College Park. At Maryland he held several administrative positions, including the Associate Deanship for Academic Affairs and the Founding Directorship of the Center for Global Business, and received the University's International Landmark Award.

Professor Gannon has authored, coauthored, or coedited 80 articles and 16 books, including the critically acclaimed *Understanding Global Cultures: Metaphorical Journeys Through 28 Nations, Clusters of Nations, and Continents* (Sage, 3rd ed., 2004; 4th ed. in progress), *Handbook of Cross Cultural Management* (2001), *Dynamics of Competitive Strategy* (1992), *Managing Without Traditional Methods: International Innovations in Human Resource Management* (1996), and *Ethical Dimensions of International Management* (1997).

Professor Gannon has been the Senior Research Fulbright Professor at the Center for the Study of Work and Higher Education in Germany and the John F. Kennedy/Fulbright Professor at Thammasat University in Bangkok and has served as a visiting professor at several Asian and European universities. He has also been a consultant to many companies and government agencies. Professor Gannon has lived and worked in more than 25 nations for various periods as a visiting professor, consultant, and trainer.

For additional information on Professor Gannon, please visit his homepage at California State University, San Marcos: www.csusm.edu/mgannon